# COMPLETE CONDITIONING FOR SWIMMING

Dave Salo, PhD
Scott A. Riewald, PhD

Human Kinetics

**Library of Congress Cataloging-in-Publication Data**

Salo, Dave, 1958-
   Complete conditioning for swimming / Dave Salo, Scott A. Riewald.
       p. cm.
   Includes index.
   ISBN-13: 978-0-7360-7242-7 (soft)
   ISBN-10: 0-7360-7242-X (soft)
   1.  Swimming--Training.   I. Riewald, Scott A., 1970-  II.  Title.
   GV837.7.S25 2008
   797.2'1--dc22

                                                     2008004226

ISBN-10: 0-7360-7242-X
ISBN-13: 978-0-7360-7242-7

**Acquisitions Editor:** Tom Heine; **Developmental Editor:** Leigh Keylock; **Assistant Editor:** Laura Podeschi; **Copyeditor:** Jan Feeney; **Proofreader:** Coree Clark; **Indexer:** Betty Frizzéll; **Permission Managers:** Carly Breeding and Martha Gullo; **Graphic Designer:** Fred Starbird; **Graphic Artist:** Tara Welsch; **Cover Designer:** Keith Blomberg; **Photographer (cover):** Adam Pretty/Getty Images; **Photographer (interior):** Neil Bernstein, unless otherwise noted; **Photo Asset Manager:** Laura Fitch; **Visual Production Assistant:** Joyce Brumfield; **Photo Office Assistant:** Jason Allen; **Art Manager:** Kelly Hendren; **Associate Art Manager:** Alan L. Wilborn; **Illustrator:** Denise Lowry; **Printer:** United Graphics

We thank the United States Olympic Committee in Colorado Springs, Colorado, for assistance in providing the location for the photo shoot for this book.

Human Kinetics books are available at special discounts for bulk purchase. Special editions or book excerpts can also be created to specification. For details, contact the Special Sales Manager at Human Kinetics.

Printed in the United States of America          10   9   8   7

**Human Kinetics**
Web site: www.HumanKinetics.com

*United States:* Human Kinetics
P.O. Box 5076
Champaign, IL 61825-5076
800-747-4457
e-mail: humank@hkusa.com

*Canada:* Human Kinetics
475 Devonshire Road Unit 100
Windsor, ON N8Y 2L5
800-465-7301 (in Canada only)
e-mail: info@hkcanada.com

*Europe:* Human Kinetics
107 Bradford Road
Stanningley
Leeds LS28 6AT, United Kingdom
+44 (0) 113 255 5665
e-mail: hk@hkeurope.com

*Australia:* Human Kinetics
57A Price Avenue
Lower Mitcham, South Australia 5062
08 8372 0999
e-mail: info@hkaustralia.com

*New Zealand:* Human Kinetics
P.O. Box 80
Torrens Park, South Australia 5062
0800 222 062
e-mail: info@hknewzealand.com

E4277

To the memory of Mike Nishihara, the former head strength and conditioning coach for the United States Tennis Association, whom I had the privilege of working with for three years before his untimely passing in September of 2007. I learned a great deal from him in those years, information that transcended strength and conditioning to include how to get the best out of people in general. Mike, you will be missed by all those who ever had the opportunity to meet you.

*Scott Riewald*

# Contents

# DVD Contents

## Fitness Tests

Core Stability Test

Shoulder Flexibility Test

Scapular Stabilization Test

Rotator Cuff Strength Test

Vertical Jump Test

## Dynamic Warm-Ups

Caterpillar

Shoulder Internal and External
Rotation

Helicopter Lunge

Ankle Rotation

Knee Hug

Leg Cradle

## Lower-Body Foundational Strength Exercises

Squat

Lunge

Monster Walk

Ankle Dorsiflexion

Seated Hamstring Curl With
Elastic Tubing

Single-Leg Deadlift

## Upper-Body Foundational Strength Exercises

Lat Pull-Down

Core Chest Press

Reverse Fly

Seated Row

Standing Internal Rotation

Posterior Chain Exercise

## Stroke-Specific Exercises

## Freestyle and Backstroke

Lunge With Rotation

Kicking With Ankle Weights

Back Extension With Rotation

High-to-Low Chop

Russian Twist

One-Arm Medicine Ball
Throw-Down

## Butterfly and Breaststroke

Medicine Ball Leg Lift

Medicine Ball V Crunch

Bent-Over Row

Bent-Over Lateral Raise

Medicine Ball Throw to the
Ground

Sumo Squat

Chest Fly

# Core Training

## Dryland Progressions

Prone Bridge
Back Bridge
Side Bridge
Dying Bug
Bird Dog

Seated Medicine Ball Chest
   Pass
Seated Medicine Ball Toss
Leg Drop
Knees to Chest

## In-Water Progressions

Front Balance Drill

Back Balance Drill

## Single Dryland Exercise

T Exercise

## Power Exercises

90-Degree Jump Turn
Seated Medicine Ball Twist
Shoulder Pullover
Streamline Jump
Figure-Eight Medicine Ball
   Pass and Throw
Explosive Wall Chest Pass
Explosive Rotational Throw

Medicine Ball Squat With
   Chest Throw
External Rotator Catch and
   Toss
Plyometric 90/90 Ball Drop
Hang Clean
High Pull
Push Press

## Flexibility Exercises

Hip Flexor Stretch
Ankle Stretch
Spinal Twist

Hip Twist
Streamline Stretch

## Injury Prevention Exercises

## Shoulder

Shoulder Retraction With
   External Rotation
Catch Position External
   Rotation
Chest Punch

Upper-Body Step-Up
Sleeper Stretch
Towel Stretch

## Knee

Star Drill

Elastic-Band Kick

# Total Running Time . . . . . . . . . . . . . . . . . . . .80 minutes

# Acknowledgments

When we first started this book project, I thought, *This will be pretty cool and shouldn't be that difficult.* I'd been involved in ancillary ways on several book projects before, and becoming a lead author seemed to be the next step. Well, as we got into it, I found writing a book carries a number of challenges—most notably finding the time to write while also working full time and keeping up with two young children. But we eventually got there, and many thanks to Human Kinetics—Tom Heine and Leigh Keylock in particular—for keeping things on track.

I would also like to thank the United States Tennis Association—Mike Nishihara, Paul Roetert, and Todd Ellenbecker in particular—for the many discussions we had on strength and conditioning and making training match the demands of the sport. Working with those individuals and the elite athletes helped test and solidify many of my philosophies on strength and conditioning.

I'd also like to thank all of the people and organizations who supported this project, specifically Phil Page and the Thera-Band Academy. They donated many of the elastic resistance bands and other products used in the photo and DVD shoots and have a diverse product line that makes strength training possible for anyone, whether they have access to a weight room or not. I'd also like to thank Haven Barnes, Kim Matz, Jane Rynbrandt, and Branden Rakita for serving as the models in the book and on the DVD, and Bob Seebohar for his contributions to the nutrition chapter.

Finally, and most importantly, I would like to thank my family—Suzie, Maddox, and Callie—for their support and encouragement during this whole process. If not for them, I would have given up on this a number of times. Thank you, and I love you.

*Scott Riewald*

# Introduction

Welcome to *Complete Conditioning for Swimming,* a one-of-a kind book that will take you into the world of strength and conditioning and show you practical ways to use dryland and in-water strength training to improve your performance in the pool. The world of sport is changing as athletes are constantly looking for ways to gain an advantage over their competitors. Swimming is no different. Maybe you know of swimmers who have looked to new technology, such as drag-reducing full-body suits, to improve their performance. Or maybe you've seen other swimmers employ the services of a sport psychologist to try to gain a mental edge over their competitors.

It is great that swimmers can tap into all of these new advances, but sometimes they forget about the most important thing—training the body. Strength and conditioning, in particular, often gets left by the wayside. This book shows you how to bring strength training and conditioning into your swimming program and how to do it correctly to enhance performance and prevent injuries.

## IMPORTANCE OF STRENGTH AND CONDITIONING FOR SWIMMERS

If you look at the top swimmers in the world today, most, if not all, engage in some sort of strength training. The swimmers we train at USC and the Irvine Novaquatics are no different. We have developed a structured strength and conditioning program for our swimmers that complements the in-water work we do. Notice we do not just use the term *dryland training* when talking about strength training. That is because our strength and conditioning program is a combination of dryland training and in-water strength training. We do this to ensure that any strength gains that swimmers make are transferred to the water. Our strength and conditioning philosophy is based on two principles that we believe are critical in swimming today:

1. *Strength and conditioning can help prevent injuries.* If nothing else, you should perform maintenance exercises to prevent many common swimming injuries, including swimmer's shoulder.

2. *Strength and conditioning can enhance performance.* Swimming requires a balance of endurance and power—and strength training can develop both of these attributes and improve your in-water performance. If you are not engaging in some type of strength training, you are falling behind your competitors who are.

This two-pronged philosophy underlies our approach to training, and we have seen improved performance when strength and conditioning is appropriately integrated into an athlete's overall training plan.

## UNDERSTANDING THE DEMANDS OF SWIMMING

The importance of strength and conditioning becomes even clearer when you reflect on the demands of swimming. Consider the following:

• Competitive swimming events range in distance from 50 to 1,500 meters and last anywhere from 20 seconds to over 15 minutes—and that is not even including the open-water swimming events that can be as long as 25 kilometers. Consequently, swimmers will draw on various energy systems to fuel their performance depending on the length of the race. Strength training and conditioning will help you train the energy systems you need for the races you swim.

• Swimming is a full-body sport and requires the *coordinated* activation of muscles in legs, the core, and the upper body with virtually every stroke that is taken. A breakdown in any one area can have negative consequences—that is, it can result in injury and poor performance. Strength training will build core stability and develop coordination between the body segments that will reduce drag while improving propulsion.

• Even though swimming is a non-weight-bearing sport, and the legs do not take the pounding they do in other sports, the repetitive nature of the swimming stroke can lead to overuse injuries, such as swimmer's shoulder and breaststroker's knee. Strength training can address strength and flexibility imbalances and reduce the risk of injury.

• Swimming places unique demands on the core of the body that are unlike those seen in any land-based sport. Because you need to generate force and propulsion by pressing against a fluid surface, you need to be even stronger and more stable through the core than other athletes. Strength training, particularly exercises done in the water, can improve your feel for the water and improve your stroking and kicking power.

• There are very few sports in which the demands of a race differ so dramatically from those of a practice. Training sessions can last as long as four hours, and some swimmers engage in multiple practice sessions a day. Contrast that with competitions, which involve shorter periods of high-intensity activity, often separated by periods of warming up and cooling down. Making intelligent choices about warming up and cooling down, two important components of training and conditioning, will facilitate recovery and keep you primed to swim at your best all the time.

• Swimming encompasses four distinct strokes that use different muscle groups. Stroke-specific exercises will help you build the strength, power, and flexibility required in your particular events.

These are just some of the factors that make swimming unique in the world of sport. Take all of this into account, and you can quickly understand how swimming performance is dependent on so many factors.

Swimming in and of itself *will* build strength and power, but only to a point. A well-structured strength and conditioning program, one that prepares your body for the demands of the races you swim, will help you achieve those extra gains that will set you apart from your competitors in the pool.

## STRENGTH AND CONDITIONING FOR EVERYONE

This book was not designed just for elite athletes. In fact, it was designed with all swimmers in mind. Whether you are a fitness swimmer or a top-ranked age-group swimmer, a triathlete or a masters swimmer, a coach or even a swim parent, the information in this book will help you integrate strength and conditioning into your training program.

We do want to take a moment to address the needs of young swimmers. Any time the topic of strength training is mentioned in the same sentence as young swimmers, several questions related to safety typically come up. Though it should be a concern of any coach or parent, in actuality, the risk of injury associated with young swimmers engaging in a strength training program is very low. While every exercise and activity carries with it some level of injury risk, both the National Strength and Conditioning Association and the American Academy of Pediatrics have issued position papers that state that youth strength training can be safe and effective if the following conditions are in place:

• Proper technique is taught and required in *every* repetition of *every* exercise.

• A coach who is skilled in program design and exercise technique supervises *every* training session.

A well-designed strength and conditioning program can enhance performance, even for young swimmers. While young athletes will not build large muscle mass, they will see improved strength and coordination, increased bone density, improved self-image and self-confidence, and a greater potential for preventing injuries. All of these should be appealing to young swimmers. Additional guidelines on developing appropriate youth strength training programs are provided in chapter 11, Year-Round Sample Programs.

## USING THIS BOOK

Have you ever picked up a book on swimming and after reading a few pages asked yourself, "What does this mean, and how am I supposed to use this information to become a better swimmer?" *Complete Conditioning for Swimming* is a nice blend of theory and application: You get the science (in easy-to-understand language) but also receive plenty of information on how to put the science into practice.

This book has some attributes that make it especially reader friendly.

• Many examples of in-water and dryland exercises, complete with step-by-step descriptions and pictures, will improve your swimming performance. We realize swimming is a unique sport. Therefore, the exercises presented are somewhat different from what you might find in a book that is written for football players or track athletes.

• An accompanying DVD shows many of the exercises in action. A picture contains the information of a thousand words, but a video contains the information of a thousand pictures. Exercises seem to make more sense when you can see them being performed correctly. The exercises that are demonstrated on the DVD are listed on the DVD Contents on pages vi and vii and are marked with this symbol in the text: ⦿ **DVD**

• Sample training plans can be used right out of the box or used as templates so that you can design your own program. The sample plans take some of the pressure off—you won't have to design your own training regimen right away.

• This book is based on science, but it is also easy to read. We take special care to put even the most complex science into layperson's terms and use special sidebars to highlight the most important points in each chapter.

Whether you are a swimmer who swims to stay fit or one who wants to get fit to swim, you will benefit from the content in this book. We're confident that if you make strength and conditioning a part of your swim training, you will see your performance in the pool improve.

We hope you enjoy this book. Have fun and get stronger!

# Chapter 1

# Testing for Swimming Fitness

You're starting on an adventure, a journey into the world of strength and conditioning for swimming. You'll learn how strength training and conditioning drills can complement the work you do in the pool and elevate your performance. However, before you embark on this journey, you need a map—some idea of where you are, where you're going, and how you will get there. When it comes to swimming, one of the best ways to find out where you are and what you need to work on is to test yourself periodically. Luckily, there are several simple tests you can do with little or no fancy equipment to establish benchmarks that you can compare yourself to later and help you improve your performance in the pool and reduce your risk of injury. These tests include simply counting your strokes when you swim, performing test sets in the pool, and conducting orthopedic tests to evaluate strength and flexibility. Using the results of these tests, you can assess where you stand in relation to your competitors, identify strengths and weaknesses, assess improvements, and establish performance-based goals for the season.

If you are like most swimmers, you already test yourself whether you know it or not. Every time you step up on the blocks to race or watch the clock during practice, you are testing your swimming proficiency. Swimming is one of those sports, unlike football or baseball, where your performance can be measured directly against the clock—and time does not lie. But how much does a time really tell you? Sure, you can tell if you are faster than your competitors, but can a race time or a split tell you why your stroke fell apart on the third 50 of the 200 butterfly? Can it help you understand why you always seem to develop shoulder pain halfway through practice? Maybe it's a technique flaw that causes your stroke to break down in the middle of your race. Maybe you have a strength imbalance that is contributing to an injury. Or maybe you're not taking care of yourself nutritionally and that is what's causing you to fall short of achieving your performance goals. This list could go on indefinitely, but the bottom line is that time alone rarely tells the whole story about a swimmer. To better understand how some of these other factors contribute to your performance, you should undergo periodic testing. Regular testing plays a vital role in understanding your strengths and weaknesses, particularly as they relate to strength, technique, injury prevention, and swimming efficiency.

## MEASURING SWIMMING EFFICIENCY AND EFFICACY

Fast swimming is built on efficiency and efficacy. Efficiency means being able to swim fast while exerting little wasted effort and energy. Efficacy is the power to produce a result, which in this case means effectively using the forces you generate to get you down the length of the pool. Both concepts rely on the ability to generate the forces that propel the body through the water appropriately while also minimizing the resistance you experience so your body knifes through the water. The ability to do this is influenced by several factors:

- Stroke technique
- Strength, power, and flexibility
- Body position and streamlining in the water
- Level of fitness
- Body type and shape

So how can you tell your efficiency and efficacy in the water? Amazingly, there is a relatively simple test you can use: Count the number of strokes it takes you to complete each length of the pool. We'll call this your stroke count. The better you are at reducing drag and generating propulsion, the lower your stroke count will be. There is no magic number of strokes it should take a swimmer to complete a length of the pool when swimming at a given pace, and your stroke count will likely differ from that of your training partners. The key is to establish a benchmark of what you do now and set a goal of trying to improve on that number—both in practice and in races. As you become better at knifing through the water, or generating propulsion, you should find that the number of stokes it takes you to cover a set distance at a given pace should decrease. For example, you may swim 100 freestyle repeats on a 1:15 pace while taking 16 strokes per length. As you develop greater efficiency and become more effective at

Swimming technique that is efficient and effective enables you to slice through the water.

using the force to generate propulsion, you may take 15 or even 14 strokes per length while holding that same 1:15 pace.

With any test, you need to compare "apples to apples," and you need to keep some things in mind when you compare your stroke count.

• *Maintain your pace.* It is easy to lower your stroke count if you swim more slowly and really exaggerate the distance you travel with each stroke. Your goal, however, is to take fewer strokes while swimming at the same pace or an even faster pace than you swam before.

• *Maintain your stroke rate*, or how fast you turn your arms over, as you work on improving your stroke count. Again, it is easy to travel farther with each stroke when you slow everything down, but that does not necessarily mean you've improved your efficiency. At the University of Southern California, we place a lot of emphasis on swimming with specific combinations of stroke rates and speeds. Stroke rate and how to measure it in greater detail are discussed in the following sections.

One way to track your stroke count is to simply count the number of strokes you take per lap consistently during practice as well as in races. You do not have to count strokes on every lap, but if you start to see your stroke count increase over the course of a workout or a set, ask your coach what you are doing differently. It could be that your technique has changed or you have become fatigued. Also, keep a diary of your times and stroke counts from your races. Table 1.1 contains a sample diary that you can use to monitor your stroke count in races. Have a teammate count your strokes on each lap and enter the information along with your split times to see how you are progressing.

## Table 1.1   Split and Stroke Count Diary

| Event: | | Meet: | | Date: | |
|---|---|---|---|---|---|
| | Split | Stroke count | Stroke rate | Distance per stroke | Comments and notes |
| 50 meters | | | | | |
| 100 meters | | | | | |
| 150 meters | | | | | |
| 200 meters | | | | | |
| 250 meters | | | | | |
| 300 meters | | | | | |
| 350 meters | | | | | |
| 400 meters | | | | | |

## COUNTING STROKES IN PRACTICE

Swimmers are always asking me to watch their strokes and tell them how they look. "Is my stroke getting any better? Has my efficiency improved?" I ask them, "How many strokes did you take, and what was your time when you finished?" This is information swimmers can get on their own without my telling them anything. That is my basic model: Counting strokes, measuring stroke rates, and relating those to a swimming pace help swimmers focus on efficiency. The fewer strokes you take and the faster you go, the more efficient you become. I harp on my swimmers a lot about being aware of stroke count. Most swimmers do not think this way naturally; they just go through the motions and miss out on opportunities to assess their efficiency and identify ways to improve this area of their swimming.

## CALCULATING STROKE RATE AND DISTANCE PER STROKE

There is a wealth of additional information you can get from a race above and beyond split times; you just need to know where to look. Remember, time alone can tell you only so much about your performance. This information is so important that several swimming organizations, such as USA Swimming, offer a service called Race Analysis for their elite nationally and internationally ranked swimmers. These organizations use a computerized system to break races down to give information on such things as reaction time, time spent underwater off the walls, and swimming velocity. While you may not be able to have this comprehensive analysis done on your races, you can measure some variables yourself. These are stroke rate (SR) and distance per stroke cycle (DPS). SR and DPS are important because both factors directly influence how fast you swim:

Swimming speed = DPS × SR

Consider the implications of this relationship. You will improve your speed if you can do the following:

1. Increase your stroke rate while maintaining the distance you travel with each stroke.
2. Increase the distance traveled with each stroke while maintaining your stroke rate.
3. If you can increase both simultaneously, you will swim faster still.

Before going any further, let's discuss these terms a bit more.

## Stroke Rate

Stroke rate is a measure of how fast the arms "turn over" and is typically expressed in cycles per minute. For example, a freestyle swimmer with a stroke rate of 58.5 stroke cycles per minute would take that many stroke cycles every minute she swims. Keep in mind that both arms pull together in butterfly and breaststroke, so the start of one pull to the start of the next pull represents one stroke cycle. In freestyle and backstroke, both arms pull independently, and a stroke cycle is measured from the start of one arm pull to the start of the next arm pull made by the *same* arm (for example, the time from right-hand entry to the next right-hand entry). While there are many reference points you could choose to define the start and stop of a stroke cycle, the important thing is to choose one to maintain consistency in your measurements.

Stroke rate is something you can have a friend, coach, or training partner measure. There are many stopwatches now that have a stroke rate function and will compute your stroke rate for you. But even if you do not have a stopwatch that computes stroke rate, you can figure this out on your own with a normal stopwatch and by doing some simple math.

1. Have a teammate or your coach time how long it takes you to complete three stroke cycles. Start the watch at the beginning of a stroke cycle (for example, right-hand entry in freestyle) and stop the watch at the start of the fourth stroke cycle. This represents three full cycles.
2. Compute your stroke rate using the following equation:

$$SR = \frac{3}{(\text{Time, in seconds, to complete 3 stroke cycles})} \times 60$$

3. This equation will give you a measure of the number of stroke cycles you take per minute.

---

**PERFORMANCE TIP**

Elite swimmers have used Race Analysis at the Olympics and other major competitions to evaluate their race performance, identify areas to improve between trials and finals, and identify the race strategies used by their competitors.

---

## Distance per Stroke

Distance per stroke (DPS) is a measure of how far you travel with each stroke cycle you take and is typically expressed in meters traveled per cycle. Distance per stroke is directly related to how effectively you pull. Counting strokes is pretty straightforward, but how do you compute the distance you travel with each stroke? The key is to rearrange the equation to find the following:

$$DPS = \frac{\text{Swimming speed}}{\text{SR}}$$

To compute distance per stroke, you will need to know your split (to get your swimming speed) as well as your stroke rate.

1. Have your coach record your splits every 50 meters during your race or get the official splits from the meet results.
2. Compute your stroke rate using the previous equation. Have a team-mate time how long it takes you to complete three stroke cycles once every 50 meters and compute your stroke rate. It is typically best if you compute stroke rate during the second half of the 50.
3. Plug the splits and stroke rate data into the following equation.

$$DPS = \frac{50}{(\text{50-meter split time, in seconds}) \times \text{SR}} \times 60$$

4. The result of this calculation tells you how many meters you travel with each stroke cycle.

Note: There will be some small errors in the DPS measurement since a part of your 50-meter split time is not actual swimming time—some time is spent underwater pushing off the wall or setting up for the turn. These computations will likely overestimate your DPS slightly. However, if you use this method consistently, you will be able to compare swims and see how distance per stroke improves over the course of a season.

## Comparisons to Race Data of Elite Swimmers

To give you a means of comparison, a series of tables in appendix A (pages 227-230) highlight average stroke rate, distance per stroke, and velocity data of elite-level swimmers for the four strokes. The data come from the

2000 Olympic finalists and the finalists, semifinalists, and selected non-finalists from the 2000 United States Olympic Trials. Appendix B (pages 231-235) also presents the race data from the U.S. Olympic Trials broken down into 50-meter increments so you can see how these race variables change over the course of the race. Again, keep in mind that because of the way you are measuring your distance per stroke, your values may be slightly elevated compared to the numbers in the tables. You can directly compare your stroke rate data, however.

When you look at the race analysis data presented in this book, it may be tempting to think you have to swim your races in the same way as these elite athletes. While all of these data can be beneficial and help you to see where you stand in the world of swimming, the most important comparisons you can make are with yourself. You can take some general guidelines and trends from the information, but remember that every swimmer is different and no two swimmers will swim a race in exactly the same way. Even in the Olympic finals, there can be a lot of variability in the way swimmers approach a race.

Keep a log of your performances and test results (use table 1.1 as a sample log). Then compare your future swims to what you have done in the past. Are you getting better? Do you see your performance and swimming efficiency improving? If so, that is what ultimately matters most, and this type of analysis is the best marker of your success.

### PERFORMANCE TIP

Stroke rate and distance per stroke both contribute to swimming speed, and the combination of variables that is right for you depends on several factors, including your muscular makeup, body size and shape, and physiology. In general, taller, stronger swimmers swim with a stroke length–dominated stroke (that is, longer distance per stroke), whereas shorter swimmers and those with more slow-twitch muscle fibers tend to swim with higher stroke rates. Along these same lines, males tend to swim with a higher distance per stroke, whereas females swim with a higher stroke rate.

## TESTING THE KINETIC CHAIN

The body is set up in a series of links called the kinetic chain. It's easy to think of the body as a set of individual segments that do not interact or influence each other: You have your shoulders that you use to generate propulsion during your pull, your legs that help with the kick, the torso that assists with body rotation, and so on. However, all of these segments are in fact linked together, much like the links of a chain. What happens in one part of the body is influenced by what is happening in other parts of the body. When viewed this way, the force you can generate with your pull is affected by a variety of other factors:

- Leg strength and the effectiveness of the kick
- Core stability and the ability to maintain a streamlined body position
- Strength in the muscles of the upper back that stabilize the shoulder blades

In a strong kinetic chain, forces are shared among the various muscle groups throughout the body, and power can flow from one segment to another. Any weakness in the kinetic chain, whether it is because of a lack of flexibility or a strength deficit, can have far-reaching effects. When one link is weak, it places greater stresses on the other body parts and can quickly lead to injury. Why did you develop that tendinitis in your shoulder? Is it truly because you have a weak rotator cuff, or could it be because you have poor core stability or an asymmetry in your stroke that requires the injured shoulder to do more work than it should? Let's look at several tests you can use to assess your physical strengths and weaknesses along with the health of your kinetic chain. As you perform the following tests, realize that there are no swimming-specific data to compare your results to. However, the tests still have incredible value. Test yourself at the start of each season to establish a benchmark in each area and identify areas of weakness and then retest periodically to assess improvements.

## Core Stability Test  ◉ DVD

Core stability (discussed in greater detail in chapter 5) is critical for swimming performance. Insufficient strength in the core musculature, or the inability to control the force that's produced by those muscles, can lead to injury and inefficiency when swimming. The core stability test assesses the strength and control you have over those muscles. To get the best estimate of your core stability, you will need a blood pressure cuff and a teammate to assist with this exercise.

1. Lie on your back, maintaining the normal curvature of your spine.
2. Place the blood pressure cuff under the small of your back and bend the hips and knees 90 degrees.
3. "Lock down" the pelvis by contracting your abdominal and lower-back muscles. The goal is to contract these muscles so the pelvis does not move during the exercise.
4. In this position, your partner should inflate the blood pressure cuff to read a pressure of 40 mmHg.
5. Alternate straightening and lowering the right and left legs toward the floor and returning to the starting position (see figure 1.1).

6. Focus on maintaining a constant pressure of 40 mmHg in the blood pressure cuff throughout the exercise.

7. Repeat until you have performed 10 repetitions with each leg.

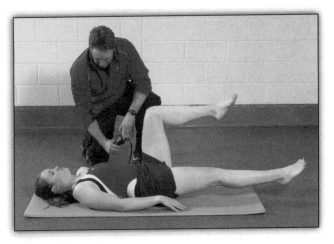

In performing this test, many athletes can do one of three things. They attempt to stabilize the pelvis in these ways:

Figure 1.1 Core stability test.

1. Pushing the lower back into the ground (flattening out the back), which causes the pressure in the blood pressure cuff to rise
2. Arching the back, which causes the pressure in the cuff to drop
3. Adequately stabilizing the pelvis (and maintaining the pressure in the blood pressure cuff) using the abdominal and lower-back muscles for the entire 10 repetitions

Ideally, swimmers should be able to achieve the third scenario, but unfortunately, most athletes fall into one of the first two categories. It is not uncommon to find athletes who are able to stabilize the pelvis and perform this test admirably for several repetitions, but they fatigue quickly. If you find you fall into either of these first two categories, you will want to perform the core strengthening exercises provided in chapter 5.

## Shoulder Flexibility Test

Swimmers commonly exhibit a reduced range of motion in the shoulder, particularly in internal rotation (see table 1.2). Internal rotation is a big component of virtually every stroke you take. Through this repetitive motion, the muscles can become quite strong but also develop tightness. Any decreased range of motion can cause the ball-and-socket joint in the

### Table 1.2 Shoulder Range of Motion in Swimmers and Nonswimmers

|  | Internal rotation | External rotation | Complete ROM |
| --- | --- | --- | --- |
| Swimmers | 50 degrees | 100 degrees | 150 degrees |
| Nonswimmers | 70 degrees | 90 degrees | 160 degrees |

shoulder to move abnormally or place undue stress on the structures in the shoulder, either of which could predispose you to injury.

To assess any deficiencies, a health care practitioner should periodically measure range of motion in the shoulders.

1. Lying on a treatment table, raise the right arm 90 degrees to the side and flex the elbow 90 degrees as well. Your fingers should point upward toward the ceiling in the starting position.

2. Without moving the upper arm, rotate the shoulder backward into external rotation as far as you can (see figure 1.2a). Hold this position while the examiner measures the amount of external rotation using a goniometer.

3. Rotate the shoulder forward into internal rotation as far as you can (see figure 1.2b). Hold this position while the examiner measures the amount of internal rotation.

4. The examiner should push lightly on the front of the shoulder throughout the test to stabilize the shoulder blade and minimize movement. Otherwise, inaccurate measurements will be recorded.

5. Compute the total range of motion (the amount of internal rotation plus the amount of external rotation).

6. Perform the test on the other shoulder as well.

Address deficits in internal rotation by performing the following stretches included in chapter 8:

Cross-arm stretch (page 158)
Sleeper stretch (pages 158-159)
Towel stretch (page 159)

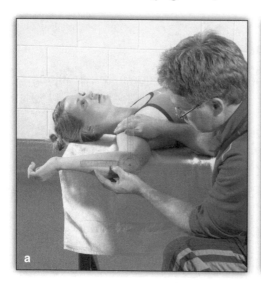 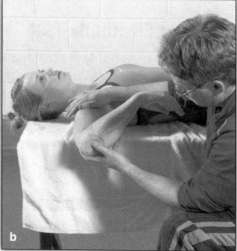

Figure 1.2 Shoulder flexibility test: *(a)* external rotation and *(b)* internal rotation.

# Scapular Stabilization Test

The scapular stabilization test evaluates the strength of the muscles that control the shoulder blades. When these muscles are weak, greater stress is placed on the muscles of the rotator cuff, and the chance of impingement increases. This test is fairly simple to perform, but it does require the assistance of a teammate, coach, or health care practitioner.

1. With your hands at your sides, hold a 1- to 2-pound (0.5 to 1 kg) weight in each hand.
2. Slowly lift the weights until they are above the head, and then slowly lower the weights back to the starting position (see figure 1.3). The arms should move in what is called the plane of the scapula—not straight out to the side, but approximately 30 degrees forward of that position.
3. The tester should watch how the shoulder blades move during this test.
4. Perform 10 repetitions of this exercise to induce some fatigue in the muscles.

Normally, the shoulder blades will stay flush with the torso and rotate upward and downward in a smooth motion as the arms are raised and lowered. When there is weakness in the scapular stabilizers, the shoulder blades will pop off the torso at some point during the movement, especially when the arms are lowered. It is not uncommon for swimmers to exhibit weakness in the scapular stabilizers. However, this weakness can often be corrected by performing some of the exercises included later in the book:

Seated row (page 50)

Shoulder blade pinch (pages 152-153)

Shoulder retraction with external rotation (page 153)

Chest punch (pages 156-157)

Upper-body step-up (page 157)

Figure 1.3　Scapular stabilization test.

## Rotator Cuff Strength Test ⊙ DVD

The four muscles of the rotator cuff (teres minor, infraspinatus, subscapularis, and supraspinatus) are responsible for generating force and stabilizing the shoulder in all of the swimming strokes. The internal rotators tend to become stronger than the external rotators in swimmers, setting up a force imbalance in the shoulder. The rotator cuff strength test examines the strength in the external rotators to determine if additional strengthening of these muscles is needed. This test is best performed by a qualified health care provider.

1. In a seated position, raise your left arm out to the side 90 degrees and flex the elbow 90 degrees as well. Your hand should point to the ceiling.
2. The examiner should gently stabilize your elbow with one hand while trying to internally rotate your shoulder by pushing on your wrist (see figure 1.4).
3. Try to maintain the initial 90–90 position; do not let the examiner rotate your shoulder.
4. Based on your strength, the examiner will score you on a scale of 0 to 5. Most swimmers will be rated a 3, 4, or 5.
   - 5 (normal strength): You are able to maintain the 90–90 position without pain when the examiner applies a maximal force.
   - 4 (good strength): You are able to maintain the 90–90 position without pain against a moderate force from the examiner. When a stronger force is applied, the shoulder will move slightly into internal rotation.
   - 3 (fair strength): You are not able to withstand any resistance applied by the examiner.
   - 2 and below (poor strength): You will not even be able to hold the arm in the 90–90 position against gravity without additional support.

A score of 5 is considered normal; anything less indicates you need to strengthen the external rotators. Perform the following exercises outlined in chapter 8.

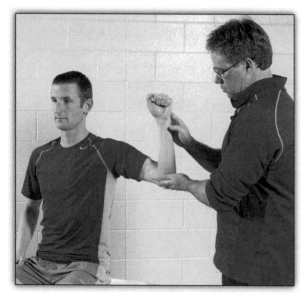

Figure 1.4    Rotator cuff strength test.

Standing external rotation (page 154)

Catch position external rotation (pages 154-155)

Full can (page 155)

Ball rotation (page 156)

# Vertical Jump Test

The vertical jump is a test of lower-body power, a combination of force and speed. Explosive lower-body power will allow you to drive off the starting blocks or off the wall after every turn. Leg strength also is the foundation of a strong kick.

You can measure vertical jump without using any special equipment.

1. Stand facing a wall and reach with both hands while keeping both feet flat on the ground. Have a partner mark the tips of your fingers using chalk. This establishes your reach height.

2. Put some chalk on the fingers of your right hand and turn sideways to the wall.

3. Jump as high as you can without taking any approach steps. Touch the wall with your hand at the peak of your jump, leaving a chalk mark (see figure 1.5).

4. Perform at least two jumps; continue until you are not able to jump any higher.

5. Measure the height of the highest mark on the wall for your jump height.

6. To calculate your vertical jump, subtract your reach height from the jump height.

There are several commercial products you could also use for measuring your vertical jump height. If you use one of these devices, you would measure your vertical jump in the following way:

Figure 1.5 Vertical jump test.

1. After adjusting the height of the vertical jump testing device, reach with both hands while keeping both feet flat on the ground. This establishes your reach height.

2. Jump as high as you can without taking any approach steps. Hit as many of the vanes on the testing device as possible.

3. Perform at least two jumps to measure your jump height. Perform additional trials as long as you are able to jump higher.

4. To calculate your vertical jump, subtract your reach height from the jump height.

To improve your lower-body power, incorporate the exercises in chapter 6 into your training regimen.

# TESTING PERFORMANCE WITH IN-WATER TESTS

You can use several test sets in the pool to assess your swimming performance. Three tests are presented in this chapter to help you monitor and improve your performance.

# 3 × 300 Test Set: Establishing Training Paces

Many swimmers want to know what pace they should use to maximize their physiological development. Ideally, you want to train at or near what is called your threshold pace—the swimming speed at which lactate production in the muscles equals the body's ability to remove it. This is the maximum pace at which you will be able to sustain a steady-state, constant-pace swim.

We use a test set of 3 × 300 with 30 to 60 seconds of rest between swims to determine an appropriate threshold pace. The 300-meter intervals are long enough for you to reach a steady state but short enough to fit into your practice time and also maintain your interest and motivation.

## Procedure

1. After a proper warm-up, select a lane to perform your swims. Ideally, you will swim by yourself.

2. From a push, perform the 3 × 300s, swimming as fast as you can while maintaining a consistent pace. Your goal is to swim all three 300s hard but at a steady pace. You do not want to sprint the first 100 and see the pace drop off considerably throughout the rest of the swim.

3. Have a teammate or a coach record your 100-meter split times on each swim. Take 30 to 60 seconds of rest between swims.

4. At the end of the set, compute an average 100-meter pace from all three swims. This should be a fairly good indicator of your threshold pace—the pace you want to train at to improve your overall conditioning.

Perform this test once a month. As you become more fit, you should find that your performance on this test improves. Consequently, you will want to adjust your training paces accordingly.

Note: We talk a great deal in this book about training at race intensity during practice. Race intensity will almost always be faster than the pace recorded in this test set, so make sure you adjust your pace appropriately when training at racing speed.

# Pulse Plots: Assessing Fitness and Recovery

Many times swimmers do not have an accurate way to measure the physiological improvements that come with training. One easy way to do this is to use pulse plots. Pulse plots establish a relationship between swimming intensity and heart rate, a relationship that provides insight into your level of fitness as well as your ability to recover from a swim. Heart rate is a good estimate of swimming intensity—the harder the swim, the faster the heart will beat—and how quickly the heart rate drops after an intense swim reflects the body's ability to recover.

Let's look at an example of this. At the start of the season, a swimmer may swim a 100-meter freestyle in 1 minute and record a heart rate of 160 beats per minute immediately after the swim. At some point later in the season, when this swimmer's fitness has improved, we would not only expect the swimmer to be able to swim the same pace at a lower heart rate, but we would also expect to see the swimmer recover more rapidly after the swim. The pulse plot takes all of this into account.

### Procedure

1. Swim a series of 8 × 100-meter swims on a 4-minute time interval. You should increase the pace (swimming intensity) on each of the first four 100s from 70 percent to 100 percent effort. Then decrease the swimming intensity from 100 percent back to 70 percent effort on each subsequent swim outlined as follows. Within each swim, try to maintain a constant pace.

   Swim 1: 70 percent effort

   Swim 2: 80 percent effort

   Swim 3: 90 percent effort

   Swim 4: 100 percent effort

   Swim 5: 100 percent effort

Swim 6: 90 percent effort

Swim 7: 80 percent effort

Swim 8: 70 percent effort

2. After each swim, find your pulse in the carotid artery on your neck and record the number of times your heart beats in 10 seconds at the following times:

   • The first 10 seconds after you finish the swim (for example, from the time 0:00 until 0:10; 0:00 represents when you touch the wall)

   • 30 seconds after you finish the swim (from 0:30 to 0:40)

   • 1 minute after you finish the swim (from 1:00 to 1:10)

   Note: You want to record the number of beats in those 10-second intervals (for example, 20 beats) and *not* your heart rate (which would be 120 beats per minute).

3. Your coach or a teammate should record the swim time and the sum heart rate (the sum of the three heart rate measurements taken after each swim).

4. After practice, create a graph showing your swimming speed and the sum of the pulses (see figure 1.6). Compute your swimming speed by dividing your finish time (in seconds) by 100.

5. You should be able to draw a straight line between the points on the graph.

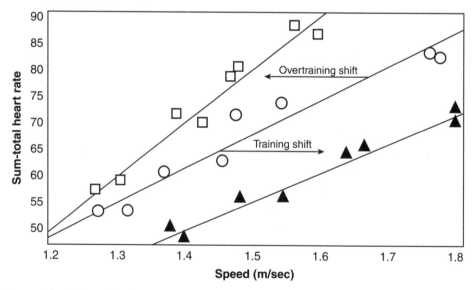

Figure 1.6   This pulse plot shows three sets of data. A shift to the right demonstrates a positive training adaptation, while a shift to the left may represent overtraining or a loss of fitness.

Adapted from D. Salo, 1993, *SprintSalo* (Pittsburgh, PA: Sports Support Syndicate), 32.

### Evaluating Your Results

The pulse plot can help you assess your training status. As your fitness and ability to recover improve, the line drawn on the graph should shift to the right. This indicates you are able to swim the same speed with a lower heart rate or your heart recovers to a resting level more quickly. If the plot happens to shift to the left, it may indicate overtraining. An overtrained swimmer will have a higher-than-expected heart rate for a given swimming pace or will not recover as quickly.

We recommend you perform this set every three to four weeks to evaluate improvements. You can also perform this set using a set of 8 × 200-meter swims on a 7:00 send-off interval. The evaluation of the data would be identical to what is described for the 8 × 100-meter test set.

## Heart Rate Recovery Test: Assessing Fitness

You can use the heart rate recovery (HRR) test to assess your health as well as your overall fitness level. A swimmer with a higher fitness level will see a considerable drop in heart rate in the first minute after intense exercise.

### Procedure

1. After a strenuous set or a fast swim, immediately find your carotid artery in your neck.
2. Use your fingers (not your thumb) to count the number of times your heart beats in a 10-second time period. Multiply this number by 6 to get your heart rate.
3. One minute after your swim, once again count the number of times your heart beats in 10 seconds. Multiply by 6 to get your recovery heart rate.
4. Subtract the recovery heart rate from the initial heart rate.

### Evaluating Your Results

- An average person will see the heart rate drop by 15 to 20 beats per minute within the first minute after exercise.
- Swimmers and elite athletes should see the heart rate decrease by at least 25 beats per minute in this same amount of time.
- Swimmers who show lower-than-normal HRR should work to improve their fitness and aerobic conditioning. These swimmers should also visit a physician for an evaluation and some appropriate exercise recommendations.

Note that some experts recommend using a heart rate of 120 beats per minute as a recovery benchmark. In this case, you should record the time it takes for your heart rate to get to 120 beats per minute after a race or a hard set. The more quickly your heart rate drops, the more fit you are. Record these times and compare them to future tests to assess the rate at which your fitness is improving.

# Chapter 2

# Warming Up and Cooling Down

The warm-up and cool-down are closely related processes. Although they may be separated by a considerable amount of time in a workout, they both deal with the same thing—preparation. The warm-up prepares the body to race and perform at a high level. The cool-down starts the recovery process and is essential for getting the body ready for the next practice or the next race. Although the warm-up and cool-down are critical components of any training or competition session, swimmers often do not do enough in these areas.

Let's draw an example from another sport—track and field. In a typical training session, sprinters may spend 30 to 40 minutes warming up the body, engaging in dynamic flexibility exercises that increase the body's temperature, and preparing the body and muscles for high-intensity performance. Then they conduct their workout—several high-intensity sprints, working on the quality of their running—followed by another 30 minutes of stretching and cool-down activities. Up to 75 percent of a 90-minute workout may be devoted to either preparing the body for the upcoming practice or helping the body to recover and get ready for the next practice or competition. Should swimming be any different?

Running and swimming have different physical demands, but the concept of preparation transcends sport. Swimmers should include a general warm-up period that lasts at least 10 minutes and, depending on the length and intensity of the training session, a 15- to 20-minute cool-down period. Often swimmers overlook these elements, but let's look at why these aspects of your training are so important to performance.

## PREPARE FOR YOUR SWIMMING LIKE AN OLYMPIAN

In my many years coaching, I've had the opportunity to work with several elite athletes as they've developed from young age-group swimmers to collegiate and national champions. I've found it interesting to watch how they've all learned the importance of a proper warm-up and especially a proper cool-down. Jason Lezak (the American record holder in the 100-meter freestyle, with a time of 48:17) is a perfect example of this. Early in his swimming career, he did not take the warm-up very seriously. Now in his 30s, Jason has become very systematic about his warm-up because he sees how it prepares his body for fast swimming. His typical routine includes a lengthy dryland warm-up in which he performs some dynamic stretching. He then goes through a swimming warm-up, which has remained the same for as long as I have coached him. Jason also spends no fewer than 30 minutes after a race to properly cool down. He is not always that diligent after a training session, so as the coach, I build some cool-down sets into his training that will at least begin the recovery process. I often tease Jason, a sprinter, that at major competitions (Olympic Games, World Championships) he is in the water longer during his cool-down after races than he is in most practices. However, he now knows this is what he needs to do in order to prepare for the next race.

# WARMING UP TO SWIM

The basic purpose of the warm-up is to increase muscle and core body temperature. It is the first thing you should do when getting ready for a practice or competition. When the body is warm, the muscles are able to function more efficiently, contracting with greater force through a greater range of motion.

A good warm-up also does many other things to get the body physically ready for high-intensity swimming:

- It primes the cardiovascular and respiratory systems, enhancing the body's ability to pump blood and deliver oxygen to working muscles.

- It develops dynamic flexibility, or flexibility with motion. The warm-up actively puts muscles and joints through their ranges of motion, enhancing flexibility and improving stroke efficiency. (Dynamic flexibility is different from static stretching, which is described in greater detail in chapter 7.)

- It gets the body's biochemistry working optimally. The body's physiological systems should be warmed up to optimal levels to support high-intensity swimming.

- It gets the mind "talking" with the muscles, improving coordination and efficiency of movement.

- It helps reduce the risk of injury. Jumping right into high-intensity swimming without warming up puts the body at an increased risk of injury ranging from muscle pulls to heart complications.

Think of the body as a car. To get the best performance from your car, you don't just jump in and race away—you want to drive slowly for several miles when you first start the engine before engaging in any hard driving. The engine functions better when it is warm; asking the car to do too much before it is properly warmed up can lead to engine damage or poor performance. The body behaves in much the same way. The warm-up provides the opportunity to ease into a workout gradually while making sure all systems are functioning at a high level before you start your high-intensity training.

## Prepractice Warm-Up

At USC and at the Irvine Novaquatics, we like to make the warm-up a designed set, and I've actually used the same warm-up routine for much of my coaching career. Doing the same warm-up every day gives the coaches 15 minutes to assess the physical and mental state of the team. I can very easily relate what I'm seeing in the water to what I've seen the swimmers do on other days and determine whether we need to alter our training strategy for the day. I can quickly make any necessary practice adjustments and tailor the workout appropriately based on the warm-up performance of the team as a whole and as individuals.

So what is the secret warm-up that has helped produce numerous Olympians and national champions? The specific warm-up that we've used with the Irvine Novaquatics and now the University of Southern California is as follows:

- 400 swim at a moderate pace
- 4 × 100 swim at a higher intensity
- 4 × 50 swim at an even higher intensity

As boring as this may seem, by doing the same warm-up day after day, the swimmers learn to prepare their bodies the same way before each practice. The swimmers use this time to conduct their own assessments of how they are feeling as they know the training intensity will increase once the warm-up is over. If you are a swimmer who also serves as your own coach, taking the time to do this assessment is especially important. Listen to your body during the warm-up and adjust your focus or training goals for the day if necessary. Here are some examples of situations you might encounter:

- You realize your power and strength are not where they should be and you should alter your practice goals to focus on maintaining technique throughout each set rather than being so concerned with hitting your goal times.

- You just don't feel quite right in the water and you realize you will have to dig deep to make it through the workout. Or it could mean you need to take additional time to warm up for this practice.
- You find that your mental focus is not there and you should therefore take the time to readjust your approach, change your expectations of what you hope to get out of the workout, or add more drills to the workout.
- Maybe you feel great, are ready to go, and are excited by really pushing your body to its limit.

## Precompetition Warm-Up

The consistency behind your warm-up should extend to competitions as well, and we use essentially the same warm-up routine at meets, with only a few modifications. Again, this all comes back to the importance of using the warm-up as part of an established routine that you *know* prepares your body to swim fast.

What follows is our typical precompetition warm-up. Upon completion of this routine, our athletes are fairly confident their bodies are ready to perform.

1. 400 swim at a moderate pace. The focus is on maintaining form, getting the heart rate up, and developing a familiarity with the competition site (details such as flag placement, 15-meter mark, lighting).
2. 4 × 100 swim increasing the intensity. Mix up the strokes during this set.
3. 4 × 50 swim, again increasing intensity to a higher level.
4. 200 to 300 kick. The swimmers focus on going fast into and out of the walls.
5. 6 × 50 drill plus build swim. Work on stroke technique the first 25 meters and then build speed during the second 25 of each swim.
6. 12 to 20 × 20-yard sprints. These are full-speed swims to rev up the engine.
7. Pace work plus dive work as needed.

Competitions also offer an additional challenge because it's not uncommon to have to warm up multiple times during a day—once at the start of the session and again before each swim. You should do your main warm-up before your first swim and then use shorter warm-ups before subsequent swims. These secondary warm-ups can be shorter, but you should still follow the same general principles—start out with some easy swimming and then use some higher-intensity swims to get your pulse up and your body warm.

Here are some general preevent warm-up guidelines:

- Finish the main warm-up at least 30 minutes before your race.
- If possible, get back in the water 10 to 15 minutes before your race.
- Use mostly moderate-intensity swimming at 50 to 65 percent effort.
- Gauge the intensity of your effort as you warm up before an event. Swim hard enough to get the body warm, but not so hard that you fatigue yourself before you step on the blocks.
- Finish the preevent warm-up as close to the start of your event as possible—ideally within 5 minutes of when your race is set to begin.

The warm-up clearly helps to prepare you physically, but it also helps to prepare you mentally for competition. Developing a consistent warm-up helps to equalize the importance you place on different competitions. While various levels of competition carry different levels of anxiety, you want to enter each race with the same level of focus and preparation. Using a consistent warm-up routine tells your body, "We've been here before and we know this is what it takes to swim fast."

## Using a Dryland Warm-Up

Everything discussed so far has centered on performing an in-water warm-up. However, when training time is limited or pool space is unavailable at a competition, coaches and swimmers may opt to use a dryland warm-up. A dryland warm-up should have two main components: a general warm-up and a dynamic warm-up.

The general warm-up should be a moderate-intensity activity that uses many of the large-muscle groups in the body to elevate body temperature. Examples of this include light jogging, riding a stationary bicycle, or jumping rope. The general warm-up should last 5 to 10 minutes or until you break a light sweat.

Dynamic warm-up exercises involve movement and are designed to improve dynamic flexibility while also keeping the body temperature elevated (sample dynamic warm-up exercises are presented in the next section). Choose exercises that target the specific muscle groups used in swimming, and perform each exercise for 15 to 30 seconds. The total dynamic warm-up should take 5 to 10 minutes to complete. You can incorporate elastic tubing in the exercises and create swimming-specific drills that enhance the entire dryland warm-up procedure.

Should static stretching be a part of the warm-up? In short, no. Static stretching is best performed at the end of a practice as part of your cooldown. Recent evidence shows that stretching before a practice or competition might actually hurt athletic performance. While the research in this area has not looked specifically at swimming, the data and conclusions drawn from other sports are just as appropriate to your performance in the pool. If you still think that you should include stretching as a part of your prepractice routine, make sure you stretch after completing the warm-up, when your muscles are warm, to get the greatest benefit. For more information on improving flexibility, see chapter 7.

## Sample Dynamic Warm-Up Exercises

Following are several exercises that warm up the joints and muscle groups important to swimmers.

# Forward and Backward Arm Circles

**Focus:** Warm up the muscles of the shoulders, upper back, and chest.

**Procedure**

1. Start by swinging your arms forward, slowly making small circles.
2. Gradually increase the speed of the motion and increase the size of the circles.
3. After 10 to 15 seconds, stop and switch directions. Again, start slowly with small circles and increase the speed and size of the movement.

# Dryland Swimming

**Focus:** Warm up the muscles of the shoulders, particularly the upper back and the rotator cuff, using a swimming-like motion.

**Procedure**

1. Attach a piece of elastic tubing (of low to moderate resistance) to a fence or other stationary object, looping one end around each hand.
2. Lean forward at the waist so the upper body is parallel to the ground.
3. Perform arm pulls that mimic the swimming strokes, taking care to maintain proper pulling technique throughout.

# Torso Rotations

**Focus:** Warm up the muscles of the trunk and torso using rotational movements.

**Procedure**

1. In a standing position, place your hands on your hips.
2. Bend to the left as far as you can and slowly rotate your body in a clockwise direction, making a big circle with your upper body by rotating to the front, then to the right, and then to the back.
3. Gradually increase the speed of the rotation.
4. After 10 to 15 seconds, switch directions, starting slowly and gradually increasing speed.

# Caterpillar

**Focus:** Warm up the muscles of the shoulders, upper back, core, hamstrings, and lower legs.

**Procedure**

1. Start in a plank position, with both hands and feet on the floor and the back flat *(a)*.
2. Slowly walk your feet forward until you feel a stretch in your hamstrings or calves *(b)*.
3. Immediately walk your hands forward back into the plank position.
4. Repeat the movement sequence for 20 to 30 seconds.

# Toe Raises

**Focus:**  Warm up the muscles of the ankle and lower leg.

**Procedure**

1. From a standing position, slowly raise yourself up onto your toes.
2. Hold this position for a count of 3 and lower the heels back to the ground.
3. As you increase strength and balance, try this exercise using one leg at a time.

# Shoulder Internal and External Rotation

**Focus:**  Warm up the muscles of the rotator cuff.

**Procedure**

1. From a standing position, hold your arms out to your sides and bend the elbows 90 degrees so the hands point to the sky (a).
2. Rotate your upper arms forward so the hands now point forward or slightly downward (b) and then back to the starting position. The range of motion will depend on your flexibility.
3. Start slowly and gradually increase the speed of the movement over the course of 15 to 20 repetitions.

## Helicopter Lunge

**Focus:** This exercise targets the entire body (arms, torso, and legs) and requires coordination, flexibility, and strength.

**Procedure**

1. From a standing position, extend your arms out to your sides so they are parallel to the ground.
2. Slowly rotate the hips and upper body from side to side so the arms move like helicopter blades.
3. After 10 to 12 repetitions, gradually start to drop into a lunge with each rotation.
4. Start slowly, and with each repetition drop a little farther into the lunge.

## Side Lunge

**Focus:** Warm up and build flexibility in the adductor muscles of the inner thigh.

**Procedure**

1. In an athletic position (knees and hips bent slightly, facing forward, weight on the balls of your feet), step sideways with the left leg.
2. Feel a stretch briefly in the inner right thigh before stepping with the right leg and returning to the athletic position.
3. After 10 to 12 repetitions like this, switch directions. Step to the right and feel the stretch in the inner part of the left thigh.

## Ankle Rotation

**Focus:** Warm up the muscles of the ankle and improve ankle mobility.

### Procedure

1. From a seated position, cross your right leg over your left leg and grab the right foot with both hands.

2. Rotate the ankle through its full range of motion, making 10 to 12 full rotations in the clockwise direction and the same number in the counterclockwise direction.

## Knee Hug

**Focus:** Warm up and build dynamic flexibility in the hamstrings and lower back. It also challenges balance and core stability.

### Procedure

1. From a standing position, lift the right knee and pull it into the chest. Simultaneously raise yourself up on the toes of your left foot.

2. Hold this position for a count of two before returning to the starting position.

3. Pull the left knee to your chest while rising up on your right foot.

4. Continue alternating right and left sides until you perform 10 to 12 repetitions on each side.

# Leg Cradle

**Focus:** Target the muscles of the groin and hip while also challenging balance and core stability.

**Procedure**

1. From a standing position, lift the right leg and grab the knee with the right hand and the ankle with the left hand.

2. Pull the ankle and lower leg toward your chest while raising yourself up on the toes of your left foot.

3. Hold this position for a count of two before returning to the starting position.

4. Pull the left ankle toward your chest while rising up on your right foot.

5. Continue alternating right and left sides until you perform 10 to 12 repetitions on each side.

# COOLING DOWN FOR RECOVERY

Coaches agree, and exercise physiologists confirm, that the cool-down is an important component of swim training. However, few coaches include enough cool-down time into their sessions. Most coaches have only a limited time for training, and the main sets typically carry a higher priority in a workout. As a result, the cool-down is typically reduced to around 100 to 200 yards of easy swimming. We do observe, however, that most of the better swimmers take the necessary time (up to 20 minutes) to cool down, especially if a training session has been exceptionally intense. While time often dictates whether a cool-down is included after training, the cool-down might be as important as the preceding training.

## PERFORMANCE TIP

While many equate the onset of fatigue with the presence of lactic acid, it is actually the associated decrease in pH that leads to fatigue. Lactic acid is actually used by the body to re-form glucose in the muscles or liver and provide more energy when sufficient oxygen becomes available.

# MAKING THE COOL-DOWN A PART OF PRACTICE

Athletes typically do not want to spend time cooling down properly after a training session. Because of this, I frequently incorporate a specific, low-intensity cool-down set as the conclusion of a training session. As an example, Larsen Jensen (2007 NCAA 500- and 1,650-yard freestyle champion), if left to his own devices, would exit the pool after training, regardless of how intense the preceding work might have been. To help make sure he cools down appropriately, I have him swim a set of 12 × 50 leaving every 1:00, for example, measuring heart rate at the end of each repeat. The goal is that Larsen will have fewer than 17 beats in 10 seconds after each 50 (representing a heart rate of 102 beats per minute). If he can achieve this, I know he is well on his way to being fully recovered for the next training session.

## Purpose of the Cool-Down

Understanding the physiological processes that occur with the cool-down may shed light on its importance. In basic terms, the cool-down brings the body back down to a normal level and begins the recovery process, setting the stage for the athlete to be able to perform at a high level in the next practice or race. During intense training or during a race, the body relies heavily on anaerobic metabolism to fuel energy needs. The anaerobic energy system is capable of supplying muscles with a great deal of energy (in the form of adenosine triphosphate, or ATP) very quickly, but the downside is that the pH within these working muscles decreases quickly as well. Going hand in hand with this change in pH is an increase in lactic acid (measured as lactate in the bloodstream). The ability of the muscles to perform work under these conditions becomes compromised, and fatigue sets in.

The process of cooling down allows the body to return to a more normal state. While impractical for most swimmers, it is possible to measure the amount of lactate produced after a practice or a race. Typically you will see lactate concentration rise over the first several minutes after exercise and then decline over the next 20 to 30 minutes to near-normal levels. The following are some points related to how lactate is produced by and cleared from the body:

- The intensity of the swimming primarily determines how high the blood lactate concentration will rise. This in turn will affect the rate at which it declines back to normal resting values. Sprinters, who have a higher concentration of fast-twitch, power-generating muscle fibers, produce a higher lactate concentration than endurance swimmers, but it also takes longer for sprinters to clear it from their bodies.

- With all else equal, a better-conditioned swimmer will see the lactate concentration rise higher and decline faster than a less-conditioned swimmer.

- Swimmers who perform a cool-down increase the rate at which the blood lactate returns to its normal resting value.
- Older swimmers typically take longer to clear the lactate and require a longer cool-down than younger swimmers. Masters swimmers, for example, will likely avoid the muscular discomfort after an exceptionally hard training session or intense competition by performing a longer cool-down.

### PERFORMANCE TIP

After a race or an intense swim, blood lactate levels can climb 10 to 20 times higher than normal resting levels.

## Guidelines for a Postrace Cool-Down

In general, a proper cool-down should consist of *at least* 15 minutes of moderately paced swimming—and cooling down even longer is usually better. In fact, information from USA Swimming suggests that the shorter the event, the longer you should cool down:

- *50- and 100-meter races:* Cool down for 25 to 30 minutes at an intensity that keeps the heart rate at approximately 120 to 130 beats per minute (20 to 21 beats in 10 seconds).
- *200- and 400-meter races:* Cool down for 20 minutes, maintaining a heart rate of 130 to 140 beats per minute (21 to 23 beats in 10 seconds).
- *Races longer than 400 meters:* Cool down for 10 to 15 minutes, maintaining a heart rate of 140 to 150 beats per minute (23 to 25 beats in 10 seconds).

This information can serve as guidelines for shaping your cool-down. Of course, all swimmers are unique, and your experience might differ from what an average swimmer experiences. If you want to know how your body responds to a cool-down, it might be valuable to work with a physiologist and conduct your own lactate clearance test. This has proven effective with many of the swimmers I've coached, including Jason Lezak, Aaron Peirsol, and Amanda Beard.

The guidelines presented here encourage an active cool-down. In general, the body removes lactate most efficiently when you "do something" in your cool-down, such as swim at 55 to 65 percent of your maximum velocity. Recovery will also occur passively even if you are not able to do *anything* after you race. While it's great to know that your body will be recovering as you drive home after practice or sit and watch TV at the end of the day, understand that passive recovery will occur much more slowly than active recovery. The rate of recovery may not be important for those swimmers who have only a few training sessions a week, but some swimmers might have as many as 11 training sessions per week when you take into account morning and afternoon training times as well as dryland and weight training. For those swimmers in particular, the active cool-down is critical.

Testing of elite-level swimmers shows that most swimmers cool down only 40 percent of what they should before they get out of the pool at a competition.

Swim meets present some potentially complicating circumstances relating to a cool-down. What if you swim multiple events a day or there is not a cool-down pool to swim in? If possible, it is important to cool down after every race if you want to swim your best the next time you step on the blocks. Even if there is only a short amount of time between swims, getting in the pool immediately after your race will help with recovery. Unlike the warm-up, where you can get by with doing less after you've gone through the main warm-up at the start of the day, the amount of time you need to spend cooling down may actually increase with each event you compete in.

If there is no cool-down pool, you should perform some type of moderate-intensity cool-down activity, such as light jogging or riding a stationary bike. Maintaining an intensity that represents 55 to 65 percent of your maximal effort should facilitate the recovery process without causing undue fatigue. Even stretching has been shown to be an acceptable form of cooling down if you do not have access to a pool or other activity. The point is that your body will recover more quickly if you perform a moderate-intensity activity rather than sit and wait for the recovery process to happen.

# Chapter 3

# Tailoring Training for Specific Strokes and Events

I an Thorpe has been quoted as saying, "I swam the race like I trained to swim it. It is not mathematical. I just let my body do it. It is a lot easier if you let your body do what it is trained for." This is a great example of what it means to engage in what's called swimming-specific training—training that is focused on doing *exactly* what is needed to prepare the body to compete. Swimming-specific training takes into account the specific events raced, muscle groups used, and intervals and times required in practice. The same approach should hold true for you and your training; it should be tailored to help you achieve your swimming goals, whether they are to maintain fitness or become the fastest in your district, your state, or even the world. Amazingly, however, when you look at the things swimmers do, it's hard to tell how their training carries over to their races. Ask yourself whether pure, endurance-based training puts you in the best position to swim your fastest 200-meter butterfly or your most powerful 100-meter freestyle. Is training only freestyle the best way to swim a fast 200 IM? Will you swim your fastest if you do not do any type of strength training? This chapter is all about how you can use strength training and physical conditioning to match your swimming-specific goals. We present some guidelines on building foundational strength and then performing stroke-specific and event-specific exercises. As you read through this chapter, think about how you can bring more specificity to your training.

# TRAINING FOR YOUR EVENT: THE ENERGY SYSTEM CONTINUUM

Competitive swimming races range in length from 50 to 1,500 meters. And when you get into triathlons and open-water swimming, the race distances become even longer—perhaps 25 kilometers or more in some open-water competitions. Traditionally, energy production has been thought of as coming from one of three specific energy systems; each system produces ATP (adenosine triphosphate)—a high-energy molecule that helps fuel muscle contractions and other physiological processes—at the appropriate times depending on the intensity and duration of the exercise. This concept would suggest that at different intensities of exercise, one system would prevail over the others. While this is generally correct, it also gives the impression that there is little interaction between the described systems. In fact, these three systems overlap to provide an energy continuum (see figure 3.1) to fuel a full range of athletic performance. Depending on the length and intensity of the race, your body will operate at a different point on the energy continuum and call on different processes to fuel your performance (see table 3.1 for more specifics on the parts of the energy continuum).

The majority of the ATP is produced by a process called glycolysis, the breakdown of glycogen and sugars stored in the body. Glycolysis occurs as part of the energy continuum and has anaerobic and aerobic components.

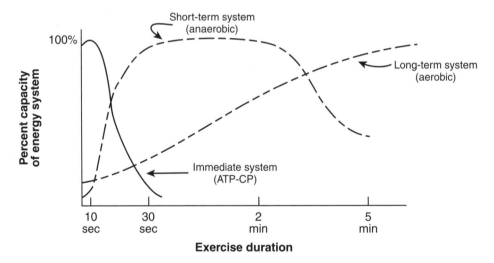

**Figure 3.1**  Three energy systems form a continuum that fuels the body for performance.

Adapted, by permission, from W.D. McArdle, F.I. Katch, and V.L. Katch, 1981, *Exercise physiology: Energy, nutrition, and human performance* (Philadelphia, PA: Lea & Febiger), 134.

## Table 3.1 Characteristics of Energy Systems

| Energy system | Characteristics |
|---|---|
| Anaerobic glycolysis | Anaerobic—does not require oxygen |
| | Fuels high-intensity swimming lasting up to 3 minutes |
| | Energy is derived by breaking down glucose molecules—1 glucose molecule produces 2 ATP |
| | Generally associated with fast-twitch (type II) muscle fibers |
| | An end product is lactic acid (lactate in the blood) |
| Aerobic glycolysis | Aerobic—requires oxygen |
| | Fuels endurance-based performances lasting longer than 3 minutes |
| | Energy is derived by breaking down glucose molecules—1 glucose molecule produces a net gain of 36 ATP |
| | Can also derive energy from breaking down fat |
| | Percentage of energy derived from fat and carbohydrate is dependent on swimming intensity—the higher the intensity, the greater reliance on glucose |
| | Generally associated with slow-twitch (type I) muscle fibers |
| ATP-CP | Anaerobic—does not require oxygen |
| | Fuels intense swimming lasting 0 to 20 seconds |
| | ATP production is limited by amount of creatine phosphate (CP) present in the muscles |
| | Generally associated with fast-twitch (type II) muscle fibers |

**Anaerobic Glycolysis (Short Term)**  The first phase of glycolysis is anaerobic, meaning that oxygen is *not* required for energy to be produced. Anaerobic glycolysis provides the majority of the energy used by working muscles during moderate-duration, high-intensity exercise (such as 100-meter and 200-meter events). While anaerobic glycolysis can produce a great deal of energy initially, muscles fatigue quickly. Additionally, a by-product of this energy system is lactic acid; this lactic acid will continue to build up as long as you continue to engage in high-intensity activity. Lactic acid has long been thought of as a waste product that comes with high-intensity exercise, but in reality it is more like a holding cell. Once the high-intensity exercise ceases, the lactic acid can be metabolized to produce additional energy. Regardless, ultimately the buildup of lactic acid, in conjunction with a change in intramuscular pH, contributes to fatigue and impairs a muscle's ability to contract forcefully during prolonged high-intensity swimming. One of the important outcomes of including high-intensity training in your training plan is that the body becomes better able to adapt to the pH changes that occur. As a result, the body can be trained to tolerate higher-intensity training loads for longer periods while also enhancing recovery.

**Aerobic Glycolysis (Long Term)**   In the presence of oxygen, the glycolysis continues and additional ATP is produced from each molecule of glucose. Aerobic glycolysis is generally associated with longer, lower-intensity exercise (events 400 meters and longer). While this process generates large amounts of ATP, it is slower and insufficient to support the energy needs of high-intensity exercise. However, in theory, as long as oxygen is available and the exercise intensity is low enough, you should be able to exercise indefinitely. Aerobic glycolysis is also essential for recovery after an intense period of exercise or a race.

**ATP-CP (Immediate)**   In addition to aerobic and anaerobic glycolysis, ATP can be generated from the immediate breakdown of a substance called creatine phosphate (CP). This is known as the ATP-CP pathway. A limited quantity of CP is stored in the muscles and is readily available to fuel muscle contraction. This process is usually associated with the initial few seconds of high-intensity muscular work (such as the 50-meter freestyle).

While we think of these energy systems as contributing to energy production at various points along a time line, the reality is that at every level of intensity, ATP production occurs both anaerobically and aerobically. A swimmer does not suddenly shift from one energy system to another, and in fact uses each of the three in every event, even in the shortest and longest events. Consider the *approximate* contributions for several events:

- In the shortest swimming event, the 50-meter sprint, the contributions for each of the systems are estimated to be ATP-CP, 65 percent; anaerobic glycolysis, 30 percent; and aerobic glycolysis, 5 percent.
- For a 200-meter event, the contributions are roughly ATP-CP, 10 percent; anaerobic glycolysis, 50 percent; and aerobic glycolysis, 40 percent.
- In a 1,500-meter swim, the breakdown is approximately ATP-CP, 2 to 5 percent; anaerobic glycolysis, 20 percent; and aerobic glycolysis, 70 to 80 percent.
- Open-water or long-distance events rely almost exclusively on the aerobic energy system but still rely on small contributions (less than 5 percent) from anaerobic sources.

Keep in mind the premise of training is to challenge the energy continuum so the body can adapt and enhance the way energy is produced and delivered to the muscles. Based on the principle of progressive overload, for these adaptations to take place, swimmers need to train at higher and higher intensities—slow swimming will probably not stress the system enough to produce the desired result. Higher-intensity training will overload the biochemical reactions, the neuromuscular system, and the cardiorespiratory system such that enhanced performance will be the result. Your training should reflect the demands of the races you swim—and this leads to the concept of swimming-specific training.

# SWIMMING-SPECIFIC TRAINING

Engaging in a great deal of aerobic training will help you build your aerobic capacity, or your ability to perform endurance-type activities. But although long, slow distance training may help with the recovery process, it does not improve your ability to perform high-intensity, anaerobic work. In fact, it may do just the opposite. There is a saying: Long, slow distance training trains you to swim long and slow. Studies have shown that endurance training can compromise sprint performance. Similarly, if all you do is sprint your performance, your endurance events will suffer. Although the typical distance swimmer spends most of the time training endurance-type repetitions, some short, high-powered training should be included to enhance the body's ability to buffer pH changes as well as to enhance neuromuscular adaptations—the ability of the nervous system to send messages to the muscle to contract rapidly and forcefully. Again, it is important to match the training to the demands of competition. Think about your races and how much of your training is targeted to preparing your body for competition.

Our philosophy, which governs our training program, is to incorporate race-pace and race-rate training—every day. This involves choosing the right balance between aerobic and anaerobic training. In the workouts we run at USC and the training we've done in the nearly two decades I've coached at the Irvine Novaquatics, we include a lot of passive aerobic activity between bouts of intense activity. Our way of training is more conducive to developing the neuromuscular adaptations that are needed for swimming fast. Swimming at race pace, and *faster* than race pace, helps build neuromuscular adaptations and gets the brain and muscles talking to each other properly. Throughout, swimmers need to focus on maintaining proper swimming technique, even when swimming at race intensity. There is an old-standing debate over what is more important, quality or quantity. In our program, we emphasize quality—we train fast every single day.

The main thrust behind race-specific training is on developing efficiency in the water. Amanda Beard and Aaron Piersol are two great examples of swimmers who have followed a "train to race" program throughout their swimming careers. These two athletes were not exposed to heavy training volumes at any point in their development, but they are two of the best examples of swimmers who have continually progressed as they've grown older; their peak performances have continued to improve well into their 20s, setting world records and winning Olympic gold medals along the way. It would be hard to suggest that their performances over the years have been compromised by a lack of excessive overdistance training. Sure, they are gifted athletes, but they've always been trained to race. You can do the same thing with your training.

## SWIMMING WORLD RECORDS IN PRACTICE

Gennadi Touretsky, renowned coach of several Australian and Russian Olympians, was famous for preparing his swimmers to be able to swim fast at any time in practice. He would sometimes ask his swimmers to step up on the blocks and "race" even before they'd had an opportunity to warm up. Other times, he would stop his swimmers in the middle of a set with no warning whatsoever to have them race. On top of that, the swimmers were expected to be within a small percentage of their best times—not practice bests, but racing bests, and some of these swimmers were world-record holders. His swimmers were expected to swim fast any place, any time.

Leading up to the Sydney Olympic Games, Coach Touretsky was in Colorado Springs, Colorado, training several swimmers, including the 50-meter freestyle world-record holder Alexander Popov. Several USA Swimming staff members were observing practice one day when Coach Touretsky stopped Popov and told him to get up on the blocks for a race-pace 50-meter freestyle. We got out our stopwatches to time the sprint. We started our watches on the go command and looked at each other in amazement at the end of the race. There was no electronic timing, so the time was not official, but both of us who had timed the race had clocked Popov at 0.10 second *under* the world-record time. This was a swimmer who was not tapered, was in the middle of a workout, and was swimming in the altitude of Colorado. Pretty amazing! It begs the question of how many American swimmers could come within a fraction of a second of their best times at any given moment. The answer is likely not very many. There is a difference between training to make it through practice and training to race. That specificity of training, as well as developing a racing mind-set, makes all the difference in the world.

# FOUNDATIONAL AND SWIMMING-SPECIFIC STRENGTH

Strength training should also be geared to developing the specific attributes a swimmer needs in order to race fast. It would be very easy to just start giving you sample exercises or programs at this point; however, before doing this, you need to understand several strength training concepts and how they relate to the design of a strength and conditioning program. These are the concepts of foundational and swimming-specific strength.

*Foundational strength* is a term we use that is synonymous with developing a full-body strength base. When developing general strength, you should focus on building endurance in the major muscle groups throughout the body while also focusing on injury prevention (see chapter 8) and developing strength in the core of the body (see chapter 5). The goal of building foundational strength is not to get as strong as you can but to build a strength base on which you will build power and *swimming-specific* strength.

*Swimming-specific strength* is a term to describe the strength needed to swim the four competitive strokes. Each of the four strokes has specific demands and requires you to use different muscles in different ways. You many hear other strength coaches use the term *functional strength* instead of *swimming-specific strength*, but in essence, both terms are synonymous and refer to developing in-water strength specific to the four strokes.

It's often useful to think of strength training as a pyramid. The base of the pyramid is made up of your foundational strength. On top of that foundation, you develop your muscular power and swimming-specific strength. Realize that developing only foundational strength will not necessarily make you faster. In fact, pure strength rarely equates to fast swimming. It is swimming efficacy, and the ability to transfer that strength to the water, that characterizes most of the best swimmers. However, developing solid foundational strength puts the necessary building blocks in place and increases your potential for developing high levels of swimming-specific strength.

The rest of this chapter presents foundational strength exercises—exercises that are important for all swimmers and that focus on the muscles used in all strokes. We follow this with several sets of exercises geared specifically to the individual strokes. Keep in mind as we go through the general strengthening exercises that the core exercises (described in chapter 5) and the injury-prevention exercises (described in chapter 8) also fall into this category. As much as possible, we have chosen exercises that can be done on the pool deck with a minimal amount of equipment.

# BUILDING FOUNDATIONAL STRENGTH

If you have never engaged in strength training, or you have but are coming back to it after a time away, you will want to take a relatively long time to build your general strength. Typically, you want to take four to eight weeks at the beginning of the season, training two or three times per week, to build your foundational strength. Some swimmers will want to take even longer. To recap, the goals of this type of training are threefold:

1. Build a base of muscular strength and muscular endurance throughout the body.
2. Engage in injury prehabilitation to strengthen the areas that tend to get weak.
3. Develop core strength and stability.

The best way to accomplish these goals is to perform two or three sets of each exercise, completing 15 to 25 repetitions in each set. Be sure to train both sides of the body. Many swim programs will set up a strength-training circuit in which you rotate from one exercise to the next, going through the entire circuit two or three times. This is an effective way to build foundational strength and promote muscular endurance at the same time. Chapter 11 lays out some sample strength and conditioning circuits you can use in your training.

The following are some fundamental strength exercises. It is not important to do every exercise every time you train, but you do want to train the entire body. It is very tempting to focus on only training the upper body and the muscles you can see in the mirror. However, muscular balance is required throughout the body, and strengthening the legs and back is important for swimmers as well.

# LOWER-BODY FOUNDATIONAL STRENGTH EXERCISES

## Squat

**Focus:** Build strength in the gluteal muscles as well as the muscles throughout the lower body. You should use weights or an elastic band, but you can also use body weight for resistance when starting out.

### Procedure

1. Stand on a piece of heavy-resistance elastic band so the feet are approximately shoulder-width apart or slightly wider.

2. Grasp one end of the band with each hand and hold the hands at shoulder level. There should be a strong tension in the band in this starting position.

3. Lower yourself into a squat position so the knees are bent to 90 degrees.

4. Drive with the legs and return to the starting position.

5. Make sure you maintain a normal curvature of the spine, push the chest out and up, and do not let the knees come forward past the toes.

### Variations

- Perform this exercise while using a barbell and a squat rack. Load the barbell with an appropriate weight and step under the bar so it lies across your upper back. Stand and step away from the rack to perform the squat.

- Make the squat more challenging by holding dumbbells in each hand or standing on an unstable surface, such as a balance pad.

Caution: Avoid allowing the knees to come forward past the toes, because this places large stresses on the front of the knee. Swimmers who have lower-back pain should also get approval from a medical professional before doing squats.

# Lunge

**Focus:** Build lower-body strength and core stability.

## Procedure

1. Stand with your feet shoulder-width apart. Step forward with the right leg to initiate the lunge.

2. Maintain an upright posture while bending the right knee 90 degrees. Do not allow your right knee to pass in front of your toes, and your left knee should not touch the ground.

3. Immediately push off the front foot to return to the starting position.

4. Complete the repetition by lunging with the left foot forward.

## Variations

- Dumbbell lunge: Initially perform the exercise using only your body weight, but for greater resistance, hold a dumbbell in each hand or hold a medicine ball behind your head when performing the exercise.

- Oblique lunge: To shift the focus to the muscles of the inner thigh, step outward at a 45-degree angle when performing the lunge.

- Side lunge: Step straight out to the side to shift a greater focus to the muscles of the inner thigh.

- Balance lunge: To challenge your balance, have a teammate stand behind you, holding the ends of an elastic band looped around your waist. The pull of the band will force you to stabilize using your core to perform the exercise without losing your balance. Your teammate should move to the left and right to vary the direction of the pull.

# Monster Walk

**Focus:** Build strength and stability in the muscles on the outside of the hip.

**Procedure**

1. On the pool deck, loop a piece of elastic tubing around the ankles and get into good athletic position: knees bent slightly and not over the toes, body upright and facing forward, and feet slightly wider than shoulder-width apart.

2. Maintain this position while you slowly step 3 to 6 inches (8 to 15 cm) to the side with the right foot.

3. While controlling the band, lift the left foot and step back toward the right foot.

4. Continue this pattern while walking 15 to 20 steps across the pool deck. Reverse direction and walk back to your starting position.

# Ankle Dorsiflexion

**Focus:** Improve strength in the muscles in the front of your calf—the muscles that provide ankle stability and contribute to kicking power.

**Procedure**

1. Attach a loop of elastic band to a stationary object, such as a fence or a table leg.

2. Sit on the pool deck and loop the other end of the elastic band around your toes. Place a rolled-up towel under your knee to help isolate the correct muscles. Bend the knee slightly.

3. With your toes pointed slightly, position yourself so there is tension in the band in this starting position.

4. Pull your toes toward your shin and slowly return to the starting position.

# Calf Raise

**Focus:** Improve the strength of the two muscles in your calf, improve kicking efficiency, and improve your strength off the blocks and walls.

### Procedure

1. Stand so the balls of your feet rest on the edge of a step.
2. Allow your heels to drop below the level of the step.
3. Drive with the calf muscles so you lift your heels and stand on your toes.
4. Hold this for 1 to 2 seconds and slowly return to the starting position.

### Variations

- For added resistance, perform the exercise one leg at a time or hold a dumbbell in your hand while performing the exercise.
- To work the deeper calf muscle, the soleus, keep the knees bent slightly while performing the exercise. You can also sit in a chair with your knees bent 90 degrees. Place a barbell or dumbbell across your thighs to provide resistance. Raise your heels off the ground, hold for 1 to 2 seconds, and return to the starting position.

# Seated Hamstring Curl With Elastic Tubing

**Focus:** Improve the strength of the hamstrings, which will lead to increased kicking strength and hip stability.

### Procedure

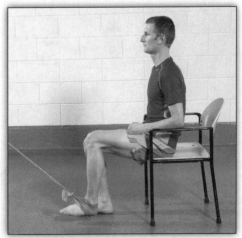

1. Sit on a chair or bench with your knees bent 90 degrees.
2. Loop a piece of elastic band around your ankle or heel and secure the other end to a sturdy object, such as a backstroke flag post or a fence.
3. Position your chair far enough away from the attachment point of the tubing to create moderate tension in the band when your leg is extended straight in front of you.

4. Slowly flex your knee 90 degrees and hold this position for a count of 2.

5. Return the leg to the starting position.

**Variation:** You can also perform this exercise in the weight room using a hamstring curl machine.

# Step-Up

**Focus:** Develop strength and stability through the hips, knees, and ankles.

**Procedure**

1. Stand in front of a step or platform that is approximately 15 inches (38 cm) high.

2. Place the right foot on the platform *(a)* and drive with the right leg until the right knee is straight *(b)*. Try not to push off with the left leg.

3. Touch the step briefly with your left foot before stepping down with your left leg. Perform the step-down movement slowly and under control, again working the right leg.

4. Step down with the right leg.

5. Repeat the movement 15 times leading with the right leg before performing 15 more repetitions leading with the left leg.

**Variation:** You can increase the difficulty of the exercise by holding dumbbells in each hand or by holding a medicine ball.

# Single-Leg Deadlift

**Focus:** Develop strength and stability throughout the core by targeting the gluteal muscles, lower back, and hamstrings.

**Procedure**

1. Start by standing with your feet approximately shoulder-width apart, holding a 3- to 5-kilogram medicine ball straight in front of you. Maintain good posture with ears, shoulders, hips, and ankles in alignment.
2. Balance on your left leg, bending the knee and hip slightly.
3. Keeping the right leg straight, bend forward at the hips until the upper body and right leg are parallel to the floor. Allow your arms and the medicine ball to hang straight down.
4. Slowly return to the starting position, engaging your gluteal muscles to drive the movement.

**Variation:** You can also perform this exercise while holding a dumbbell in the opposite hand (hold the dumbbell in the right hand when standing on the left leg) instead of using a medicine ball.

Caution: Do not perform this exercise if you have lower-back pain.

# Additional Lower-Body Foundational Strength Exercises

All of the lower-body exercises listed in chapter 8 are also appropriate to include in the development of foundational strength:

Single-leg squat (page 160)

Star drill (pages 160-161)

Elastic-band kick (page 161)

# UPPER-BODY FOUNDATIONAL STRENGTH EXERCISES

## Pull-Up

**Focus:** Strengthen the latissimus dorsi and the shoulder adductors that help with power production in the pull.

**Procedure**

1. Use a stool or jump up to grab a pull-up bar with an overhand grip (so your palms face away from you). Your hands should be slightly wider than shoulder-width apart.

2. Hang briefly with your arms straight. Your feet should not touch the ground.

3. Using your arms and the muscles of your upper back, pull your body upward until your chin passes above the bar.

4. Hold this position briefly and slowly lower your body back to the starting position.

5. Do not allow your body to swing; keep the upper body rigid.

**Variation:** The chin-up is performed by reversing the position of the hands on the grip so that the palms face you. This places more emphasis on the biceps muscle of the upper arm.

Note: Swimmers may find they cannot do more than one or two pull-ups. If this is the case, substitute lat pull-downs for pull-ups or enlist the help of a teammate to support your feet as you execute your pull-ups.

# Lat Pull-Down

**Focus:** Develop strength in the latissimus dorsi and the muscles of the upper back—some of the most important muscles for generating the power behind your pull.

## Procedure

1. Loop a piece of strong elastic tubing over a lifeguard chair or through a fence.
2. Sit on a stability ball or kneel on the pool deck so there is tension in the band when the arms are extended overhead *(a)*.
3. Pinch your shoulder blades together and pull your upper arms to your sides until your hands reach about ear level. Keep the elbows pointed out toward the sides throughout the movement. The elbows should be bent 90 degrees in the finish position *(b)*.
4. Hold this position briefly and return to the starting position.

Note: The lats are the muscles that give many swimmers their V shape and are used every time a swimmer pulls. You likely will want to use a fairly heavy resistance when training these muscles since the lats are some of the strongest muscles in the body.

**Variation:** You can also perform this exercise in the weight room using a lat pull-down machine. Sit at a lat pull-down machine and grab the pull bar so that your hands are slightly wider than shoulder-width apart—the wider the grip, the more you will engage the lats. Squeeze your shoulder blades together and pull the bar straight down to your upper chest. Slowly return to the starting position.

# Core Chest Press

**Focus:** Improve strength in the chest muscles while also developing core stability.

## Procedure

1. Attach one end of a piece of elastic tubing to a fence or other stationary object at shoulder height. Grab the other end with one hand and face away from the fence.
2. Hold the tubing at chest level and step away from the attachment point so there is tension in the tubing in this position (a).
3. Contract the core muscles and lock down the pelvis by contracting the abdominal, lower-back, and gluteal muscles.
4. Push the hand straight away from the body (b). Do not lean into the exercise or use the legs—keep a stable posture.
5. Slowly return the hand to the starting position.

## Variations

- You can also perform this exercise using both arms at the same time (this is actually an easier version of the exercise). Loop the elastic tubing around a backstroke flagpole, around another post, or through a fence and grasp one end with each hand.
- You can make the exercise more challenging by standing on one leg or while balancing on a foam pad or a pillow.

# Reverse Fly  ⊙ DVD

**Focus:** Develop strength in the upper back and the rear part of the shoulders.

**Procedure**

1. Lie facedown on a stability ball with your feet on the ground. Hold a light weight in each hand. Your body should be at about a 45-degree angle to the ground.
2. Bend your elbows 90 degrees and allow the arms to hang toward the ground *(a)*.
3. Squeeze the shoulder blades together and lift the arms until they are parallel to the ground *(b)*. Keep the elbows bent throughout the exercise.

**Variation:** You can also perform this exercise by looping a piece of elastic tubing to a fence at chest level. Grasp one end of the tubing in each hand and pull the hands outward to the sides while also squeezing your shoulder blades together.

# Upright Row

**Focus:**  Develop strength in the muscles of the upper back, particularly the trapezius muscle, which helps to stabilize the shoulder blade.

**Procedure**

1. Grasp one end of an elastic band with each hand. Step on the band so there is some tension in it even when your arms hang straight down.
2. Squeeze the shoulder blades together and pull the shoulders back slightly.
3. Leading with the elbows, pull your hands up toward your chin. Keep the elbows pointed outward and lift the hands only until the upper arms reach shoulder level.
4. Hold this position briefly and slowly return to the starting position.

**Variation:**  You can also perform this exercise using dumbbells or a barbell.

# Seated Row

**Focus:**  Build strength in the upper back, including the muscles that stabilize the shoulder blades.

**Procedure**

1. Loop a piece of elastic tubing through a fence or around a backstroke flagpole at chest height. Sit on a stability ball and position yourself so there is some tension in the band when your arms are held straight in front of you.
2. Maintaining an upright posture, squeeze your shoulder blades together and pull your hands to your chest. Keep your elbows up to mimic the position the arms will be in when swimming.
3. Slowly return the hands to the starting position, making sure to contract the core throughout the exercise.

**Variations**

- Perform the exercise bringing the elbows in to your sides. This is a slightly easier form of the exercise, but it will still work the muscles of the upper back.
- You can also perform this exercise while standing.

# Standing Internal Rotation

**Focus:** Develop strength in the internal rotators—muscles that contribute to the catch and propulsion in most strokes.

## Procedure

1. Attach a piece of low- to moderate-resistance elastic tubing to a fence or other stationary object at waist level.
2. Stand with your body sideways to the fence so the right arm is closer to it.
3. Grasp the free end of tubing with your right hand and step away from the fence so there is moderate tension in the band when the elbow is at your side and your hand is pointing forward, away from the body *(a)*.
4. Rotating only the shoulder, move the hand until it lies across your body *(b)* and then return to the starting position.

**Variation:** You can also perform this exercise with the arm in an elevated position. Attach the elastic tubing at shoulder height and stand facing away from the fence. Elevate the upper arm 90 degrees and bend the elbow 90 degrees. Rotate the arm forward, maintaining a constant position of the upper arm.

# Posterior Chain Exercise   ⊙ DVD

**Focus:**   Develop strength in the lower back, shoulder stabilizers, and rotator cuff muscles.

**Procedure**

1. Lie on your front and extend your arms above your head in a streamlined position.
2. Grasp a 2.5- to 5-pound weight (about 1 to 2 kg) in the left hand.
3. Lift the feet, legs, head, and upper chest off the floor and maintain this position throughout the exercise *(a)*.
4. Slowly bring your arms to your side, tracing a wide arc *(b)*. The arms should stay straight during this movement.
5. Pass the weight to the right hand behind your lower back or buttocks.
6. Slowly move the arms back to the streamlined position, making a wide arc.
7. Transfer the weight to the left hand over your head. Complete five repetitions this way and five more in the other direction.

# Triceps Extension

**Focus:** Strengthen the triceps muscles in the back of the upper arm to help with the finish phase of the stroke.

## Procedure

1. Stand on a piece of elastic tubing and grab ahold of the free end with both hands behind your head. Stagger the feet, if necessary, so the tubing runs up the middle of your back.
2. Position your arms so your elbows point toward the sky and are bent 90 degrees or more in the starting position *(a)*.
3. Without moving the upper arms, straighten the elbows so the hands now point to the sky *(b)*.
4. Slowly lower the hands back to the starting position.

## Variations

- You can also perform this exercise while holding a dumbbell instead of using elastic tubing.
- You can also strengthen the triceps by performing only the freestyle finish on a swim bench or simulating the finish of your stroke using elastic tubing.

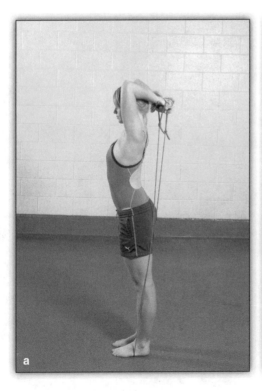

# Wrist Flexion and Extension

**Focus:** Improve strength through the forearm to support proper hand position when pulling.

### Procedure for Wrist Flexion

1. Sit in a chair and rest your forearms on your thighs. Your palms should face upward and the wrists should hang over your knees.
2. Hold a light dumbbell in each hand.
3. Slowly lift the weight by curling your wrists upward (a). Hold for a count of two and slowly lower the weight back to the starting position.

### Procedure for Wrist Extension

1. Perform the exercise in the same way, except start with your palms facing the pool deck.
2. Curl the wrists upward, bringing the back of the hands toward the forearms (b).

**Variation:** You can also do this exercise while holding one end of a piece of elastic tubing in each hand instead of dumbbells.

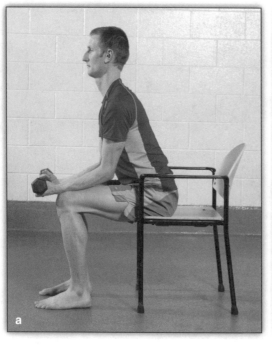

## Additional Upper-Body Foundational Strength Exercises

All of the core exercises in chapter 5 and upper-body exercises listed in chapter 8 are also appropriate to include in the development of foundational strength. Examples include the following:

Prone bridge progression (pages 93-94)

Back bridge progression (pages 95-96)

Back extension (page 108)

Standing external rotation (page 154)

Catch position external rotation (pages 154-155)

Full can (page 155)

Chest punch (pages 156-157)

Upper-body step-up (page 157)

# BUILDING STROKE-SPECIFIC STRENGTH

One of the main goals of your strengthening program is to take the general strength you've developed and transfer it to the water, making your pulling and kicking more efficient. However, this is complicated for these reasons:

- You need to be able to transfer the strength you develop on dry land to the water to help your performance, which can be a difficult process.
- Butterfly, backstroke, breaststroke, and freestyle are all biomechanically different from one another and place different demands on the body.

You can incorporate many stroke-specific exercises into your training plan to address these differences, and you can use methods to facilitate the strength transfer from the weight room to the pool. For example, we do quite a bit of resistance training at USC, both in and out of the water. When our strength session is a dryland session, we try to get in the water immediately to improve the swimmers' ability to transfer what we did in the weight room to the water. In most instances, we find this works very well.

The rest of this chapter identifies the unique characteristics of each stroke and presents several examples of stroke-specific strengthening exercises that will improve performance. If you're an IMer, you're in luck. You get to incorporate the best exercises for each stroke into your training. Before discussing stroke-specific strengthening exercises, however, it is important to address two aspects of swimming-specific training that typically do not receive enough attention in practice or in books or articles: the role of kicking and developing leg strength and building arm strength with sculling.

## Developing Leg Strength With Kicking

Why talk about kicking in a strength and conditioning book? Actually, we view kicking as a form of strength training and do a lot of kicking sets to build lower-body strength. In recent years, more and more coaches are placing greater emphasis on kicking. In part, this is to increase the propulsive capacity of the kicking action—which is seen as significant in swims of every distance (50 to 1,500 free)—but can also be used to improve general physical conditioning. There is a myth that swimmers should rely solely on the upper body when swimming at the expense of the legs, and that kicking is energetically inefficient. Yes, the muscles of the legs are large and use more oxygen when they are activated, but swimmers can and should train to improve the strength and effectiveness of the kick. The majority of the kicking sets in our program are designed to be performed at a very high intensity, and many of the kicking sets are done with snorkels as well as fins. The use of the snorkel allows an athlete to maintain a good body position.

Leg strength contributes a great deal to swimming speed, and we treat it that way at USC. Just watch swimmers like Ian Thorpe and Grant Hackett and see how they put it into another gear when they turn on their kicks in the middle of a race. Is it a coincidence that these two Australians use the legs effectively when they race? In a conversation with an Australian national coach several years ago, the topic turned to kicking. In Australia, he said, kicking makes up roughly a third of the total yardage completed in a given practice. Although we don't make kicking a set percentage of the yardage we put in each day at USC, we do stress its importance.

While sprinters have generally been characterized as very aggressive kickers, several distance swimmers, such as Larsen Jensen and Grant Hackett, maintain a kick-dominated swimming style in their races. We are seeing more and more distance swimmers adopt this style; consequently, they are enhancing their kicking through training. With that said, many swimmers still just let the legs drag behind their bodies and use a two-beat kick only to provide stability and not much else—they do not use the legs for propulsion throughout the race. Swimmers who are able to maintain a six-beat kick throughout the entire race are the ones who seem to swim the fastest. They also have a better distance per stroke and better efficiency in the water.

In our program, we keep track of kicking times and actively monitor what our swimmers are able to do. We have some basic parameters we expect swimmers to be able to achieve. One of those is to kick 100 meters in under 1:05 with a board. That is our "magic marker" for kicking. We also use a lot of unconventional ways to build leg and kicking strength—such as kicking with fins and doing vertical kicking while holding a weight—and we've really seen how it can contribute to swimming speed. You should set up performance goals for your kicking and take steps to build lower-body strength:

- Strive to have kicking make up at least 25 percent of the distance you swim during practice.
- When you kick, be sure to mix things up. Kick with a board sometimes and without a board others. (Note: If you have shoulder pain, take caution when using a kickboard; using a kickboard can aggravate an existing shoulder injury.) Kick on your front, your side, or your back.
- Don't just flutter kick; add some butterfly and breaststroke kicking.
- Work the kick in both directions. Most swimmers emphasize the downbeat of the kick, but propulsion can be generated on the upbeat as well.
- Butterfly kicking, whether it is done on your front or on your back, is a great way to develop full-body coordination and strength in the muscles of the core. We refer to this as *abdominal kicking* to emphasize the contributions made by the abdominal muscles in the butterfly kick and that it's more than just kicking with the legs.

## Kicking Exercises

There are several ways to improve your kicking strength and efficacy, which are outlined here:

**Kicking With Fins**   Kicking with fins is just like doing weight training for the legs: Because the surface area of the fin is larger than your foot, you will have greater resistance when you kick and will have to activate the leg muscles more than normal. When you use fins, you need to kick with the proper speed and intensity. It does no good to kick more slowly and go only as fast as you would without fins. In addition, you need to maintain the most efficient body position possible—the use of a front-mount snorkel will emphasize the proper body position. If you think of this as strength training and treat your kicking just as you would when lifting weights, you should kick with high intensities for short periods while also allowing yourself adequate rest between efforts. Quality is more important than quantity. You can find fins in all shapes and sizes. Several companies make shortened fins (such as Zoomers by Finis Inc., Livermore, California), which allow you to maintain the frequency of your kick while getting greater propulsion. Remember that muscles adapt best when they are subjected to progressive overload—increase the resistance or duration of the exercise slowly and incrementally. Increase things (even kicking) too much too quickly, and you set the stage for an injury.

**Vertical Kicking**   Vertical kicking is done in deep water and can be used with all four strokes to develop leg strength and power. When you kick vertically, against gravity, you place a greater demand on your legs. The goal of vertical kicking should be to keep your head and upper body out of the water as much as possible. Depending on your leg strength and experience, this may be easier said than done. We like to kick for 30-second intervals, resting an equal amount between sets. At the end of your rest, go down to the bottom, push off, and perform a pull-out to start your next set. As you kick, focus on using your leg drive and maintaining a good body position; try to limit the amount of upper-body movement. Many times, a lot of back-and-forth movement indicates a weakness in the core of the body.

There are several ways to perform vertical kicking, and you should choose the best one for you depending on your present strength and level of expertise.

- *Vertical kicking with fins.* This is the easiest since the increased propulsion that comes from the fins assists in keeping your head out of the water.
- *Vertical kicking with hands at the sides.* Keeping your hands at your sides, or sculling lightly in front of you will place less demand on the legs than the next option.
- *Vertical kicking with hands in streamlined position above the head.* This places a greater demand on the legs and develops greater core stability.
- *Vertical kicking against resistance.* It is possible to add resistance either by holding a weight over your head or by tethering a weight to a piece of elastic tubing or rope and tying it to your waist. This will provide the added load that you need to overcome to perform the kicking correctly.
- *Reverse vertical kicking.* This involves kicking in the vertical position but against the bottom of the pool. It is made difficult by the breath-control component. Whenever performing breath-control work, you must do so under the supervision of a coach.

## Developing Upper-Body Strength With Sculling and Hand Paddles

Another in-water strengthening exercise that is specific to swimming is sculling. Sculling is the process of moving the arms and hands back and forth in short loops while continually adjusting the pitch of the hands to generate propulsion. Sculling is used to some degree in all of the swimming strokes, and using sculling as a strengthening exercise can help build forearm strength while also improving your feel for the water. When you perform sculling, you will want to use motions that most accurately reflect the demands of that stroke. As in the examples for kicking, sculling drills can be done both horizontally and vertically. One of the most important considerations when designing training sessions is to use variety in the training to maintain interest and intensity.

Hand paddles are another in-water strengthening device, but you need to use caution with them. Using hand paddles typically places greater stress on the upper body than when swimming without paddles. This can translate to a greater risk of shoulder injury if you do not use proper swimming technique. As with fins, if you use hand paddles, use them as a strengthening exercise, not as a way to swim the same speed with less effort. Structure pulling sets as a series of shorter intervals, trying to swim fast while maintaining your race stroke rates. This can be challenging, but the payoff is that you improve strength more than you would by simply going through a long set of easy swimming.

## Freestyle- and Backstroke-Specific Exercises

Freestyle and backstroke are known as long-axis strokes because the body rotates around an imaginary axis that extends from the head through the pelvis and to the feet. Every stroke you take involves rotation, so many of the freestyle and backstroke exercises have been chosen because they also incorporate rotation about the long axis of the body. What follows are some of the specific demands of freestyle and backstroke.

Swimming freestyle places great demands on the shoulder and upper-back musculature; you should train these areas to handle the loads seen in the sport. For both strokes, you need to focus on building a strong kick. And, of all the strokes, backstroke performance seems to be the most closely tied to stroke rate—meaning that the faster the arms turn over, the faster you swim. Accordingly, you will see that some of the exercises in this section involve high rates of speed.

The exercises presented here are marked FR or BA to indicate whether they are appropriate for freestyle or backstroke training, respectively. As you will see, many of the exercises are appropriate for both strokes. Unless otherwise noted, perform two or three sets of these exercises, with each set including 15 to 25 repetitions, and be sure to train both sides of the body.

# Walking Lunge With Rotation (FR, BA)

**Focus:** Improve the strength of the lower body while coordinating lower-body movements with rotation in the core.

### Procedure

1. Stand and hold a medicine ball at shoulder level with the arms extended in front of the body.

2. While maintaining proper posture, take a step forward with the right leg and drop into a lunge position.

3. From this position, rotate the upper body and trunk to the left, pausing briefly, and then turn to the right, pausing briefly again.

4. Return to a position in which you are facing forward, and stand while stepping forward with the left leg.

# Kicking With Ankle Weights (FR, BA)

**Focus:** Improve strength in the hip flexor muscles to help with kicking strength and core stability.

### Procedure

1. Place small ankle weights around your ankles.

2. Lie on your back for BA or on your front for FR and lift your feet about 12 inches (30 cm) off the ground.

3. Perform a kicking motion with the legs, making sure the feet do not touch the ground.

4. Continue this motion for 30 seconds.

5. Hold the hands over your head in a streamlined position or place them under the hips to make the exercise easier. However, doing this reduces the benefit to the core.

6. As you are able to handle this weight, increase the duration of the exercise to build endurance, or increase the amount of weight attached to the ankles to improve strength.

# Back Extension With Rotation (FR, BA)

**Focus:** Increase lower-back strength and core stability during long-axis rotation to maintain body position in the water. This is a progression of the back extension exercise described in the section on foundational strength.

## Procedure

1. Set up as if you were performing a back extension exercise (page 108).
2. Perform several repetitions lifting the body straight up and then alternate, rotating to the left and right as you extend the back.
3. Increase the difficulty of this exercise by holding a weight across your chest.

Caution: Do not hyperextend the back—only lift until there is a straight line from the ankles to the head.

# Medicine Ball Handoff (FR, BA)

**Focus:** This exercise develops rotational power through the core and is performed using two swimmers standing back to back.

## Procedure

1. Using a 3- to 5-kilogram medicine ball, one swimmer rotates to the right to pass the medicine ball while the teammate rotates to his or her left to accept the pass.
2. Continue passing the ball in this clockwise direction for 10 to 15 seconds, making the passes as quickly as possible.
3. Rest and repeat the exercise in the opposite direction.

**Variation:** You can make this exercise more difficult by standing 4 to 6 feet (about 1 to 2 m) from the other swimmer and tossing the medicine ball to him or her instead of handing it off.

# High-to-Low Chop (FR, BA) 🔘 📀

**Focus:** Develop strength through the entire kinetic chain using the legs, core rotation, and arms simultaneously.

## Procedure

1. Attach a piece of low- to moderate-resistance elastic tubing to a fence or other stationary object above head height.

2. Position your body with the right shoulder closer to the fence. Grasp the handle with both hands—you should have to rotate your torso to reach the handle in its starting position *(a)*.

3. Use your torso rotation and the muscles of the upper back to bring the hands down and across the body so they end up outside the left hip *(b)*.

4. Perform this exercise explosively but return to the starting position in a controlled manner between each repetition.

**Variation:** You can also perform this exercise in a weight room using a cable column machine.

# Alternate-Arm Superman (FR, BA)

**Focus:** Strengthen the muscles of the lower back while developing independent control of the arms and legs.

## Procedure

1. Lie facedown on the floor with your arms stretched overhead. Place a towel, mat, or pillow under your pelvis for comfort.
2. Keeping your limbs straight, simultaneously raise your right arm and left leg several inches off the ground. Hold this position for a count of three.
3. Lower back to the ground, pausing briefly, and repeat the exercise, lifting the left arm and right leg.

**Variation:** You can also perform this exercise by lifting both arms and legs simultaneously, but be sure to warm up beforehand to limit the stress placed on the lower back.

# Russian Twist (FR, BA) 💿 📀

**Focus:** Improve trunk rotation, stabilization, and balance through the core while also improving coordination between the core and upper-body musculature. You perform the Russian twist using a stability ball and a small medicine ball.

## Procedure

1. Lie faceup with an exercise ball under your shoulder blades. Your feet should be shoulder-width apart on the floor and your knees bent 90 degrees.
2. Hold a medicine ball away from the chest with the arms straight.
3. Lock down the pelvis and maintain a flat back. There should be a straight line through the knees, hips, and shoulders.
4. Slowly rotate the upper body (don't just drop the arms) to the right until the arms are parallel to the pool deck.

5. Return to the starting position and complete the repetition by rotating to the left.

6. Perform the exercise slowly and maintain control of the movement.

7. Start by performing two or three sets of 5 repetitions to each side and build to sets of 15 repetitions over time.

Note: The stability ball will move across the upper back, but you must control the core and the shoulder and upper-back muscles to execute the exercise properly.

## Straight-Arm Row (FR)

**Focus:** Build strength in the muscles that adduct the shoulder—important muscles for generating power in the pull.

**Procedure**

1. In a standing position, attach a piece of elastic tubing to a fence or other solid object several feet above your head.

2. Grab one end of the tubing with each hand and step away from the fence so there is a moderate to strong tension in the band when the arms are extended in front of you *(a)*.

3. Pinch the shoulder blades together and pull both hands toward your thighs *(b)*.

4. Hold briefly and slowly return to the starting position.

**Variation:** You can also perform this exercise using a lat pull-down machine found in most weight rooms. Perform the exercise the same way by grasping the pull-down bar with both hands approximately shoulder-width apart.

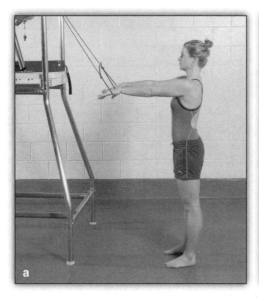
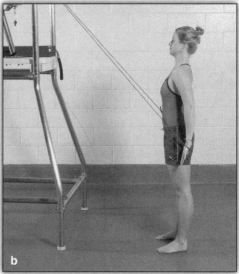

# Freestyle Sculling, Midpull Position (FR)

**Focus:** Increase strength in the muscles of the forearm while also improving propulsion and developing an improved feel for the water.

## Procedure

1. While floating on your front, position your arms in a midpull position. Your arms should be out to the sides at roughly chest level with the elbows high and the fingers pointing to the bottom of the pool.

2. Make a small sculling motion for 30 seconds, moving the hands from side to side while maintaining the position of the upper arms. You should propel yourself forward in the pool.

3. You should kick only enough to maintain your body position and turn your head to the side or use a snorkel if you need to take a breath.

# One-Arm Medicine Ball Throw-Down (BA) 💿 📀

**Focus:** Develop strength and power in the arm and core, using the muscles in the same way they are used when finishing a backstroke pull.

## Procedure

1. Stand with the feet shoulder-width apart.
2. Hold a small (2 to 3 kg) hand-sized medicine ball in your right hand.
3. Bend the elbow so that the medicine ball is at chest level.
4. In one motion, throw the ball to the pool deck while rotating your body to the left, just as you would in the backstroke pull.
5. Pick up the medicine ball and repeat, performing three or four sets of six repetitions with each arm.

Caution: Throw the medicine ball slightly to the side so you do not hit your feet. Additionally, swimmers who have not yet gone through puberty should not perform this exercise.

## Backstroke Sculling (BA)

**Focus:** Increase strength in the muscles of the forearm while also improving your feel for the water and the propulsive force of the backstroke pull.

### Procedure

1. While floating on your back, position your arms in at your sides with your hands near your hips.
2. Make a small sculling motion with your wrists for 30 seconds, moving the hands from side to side. You should be able to propel yourself down the pool headfirst.
3. Try not to kick, but if you need to, kick only enough to maintain your body position in the water.

**Variation:** Perform this same drill one arm at a time. However, rotate the body into the position you would be in if you were finishing the backstroke pull (rotate slightly to your left when finishing the pull with the right arm).

## Additional Exercises for Freestyle and Backstroke

Additional exercises described in this chapter are appropriate for developing strength for freestyle or backstroke:

Medicine ball leg lift (pages 67-68)

Hip extension (page 69)

Hip flexion (page 70)

Medicine ball V crunch (page 71)

Bent-over row (page 71)

### Butterfly- and Breaststroke-Specific Exercises

Butterfly and breaststroke are what are known as *short-axis* strokes in that the body tends to rotate, or undulate, around an axis that passes through the hips (a shorter axis than the one the body rotates around in freestyle and backstroke). As such, it is important for butterfly and breaststroke swimmers to have well-developed strength throughout the torso and core to drive the necessary undulation while also maintaining a good body position in the water.

Butterfly places significant demands on the shoulders, arms, and upper back, so many of the butterfly-specific exercises will develop strength in these areas. As mentioned, the kick is also critical to butterfly performance, and you should include exercises to develop a strong and symmetric kick, meaning you emphasize generating propulsion on both the downbeat and the upbeat of the kick.

Breaststroke-specific drills also target the muscles throughout the torso and the legs to allow the body to knife through the water and undulate with efficiency. Both strokes, breaststroke in particular, derive some propulsion from sculling actions. As such, we've incorporated several sculling drills that take into account the various ranges of motion and arm positions relative to the body that are seen in the strokes. So, in the following exercises, you will see a greater focus on building chest and forearm strength as well as developing strength throughout the hips and legs for generating a strong and powerful kick.

Each exercise here is marked FL or BR to indicate whether it is appropriate for butterfly or breaststroke, respectively. You can do many of these exercises on a pool deck with minimal equipment. You can also do most of the exercises in the weight room using traditional strength-training equipment. Unless otherwise noted, perform two or three sets of 15 to 25 repetitions of these exercises, and make sure to train both sides of the body.

# Medicine Ball Leg Lift (FL, BR)  ◉ DVD

**Focus:**  Improve strength in the hip flexors and core stability, specifically as they relate to the butterfly kick and body position in breaststroke.

## Procedure

1. Lie on your back on the pool deck.
2. Hold a 1- to 5-kilogram medicine ball between your feet and lift it approximately 12 inches (30 cm) off the ground.

3. Lift and lower the medicine ball 6 to 12 inches (15 to 30 cm) in each direction. Continue for 15 seconds, building to 30 as strength and stability improve. Increase the weight of the medicine ball to improve strength.

4. Ideally you will hold your hands out to the sides, but you can place them under the hips to make the exercise easier. Doing this reduces the benefit to the core, however.

**Variation:** You can also perform this exercise on a bench. Position your body so the legs hang off the end of the bench and increase the range of motion so the legs lift 12 inches and then drop below the bench 6 to 12 inches.

# Good Morning (FL, BR)

**Focus:** Build strength in the lower back and hip extensors to help with body position and kicking efficiency.

**Procedure**

1. Stand with your feet slightly wider than shoulder-width apart and place your hands behind your head.

2. Keeping the back flat, slowly bend at the waist until you feel a stretch in the hamstrings in the back of your thighs.

3. Slowly return to the starting position.

Caution: Be sure to warm up before doing this exercise, and do not perform it if you have back problems.

**Variations**

- To make the exercise easier, bend the knees slightly.

- Add difficulty by using a barbell across the shoulders. Increase the weight on the bar to make the exercise more challenging. You do not have to use large weights to see the benefit from this exercise.

# Hip Extension (FL, BR)

**Focus:** Develop strength in the gluteal muscles for a strong upward kick in butterfly and body position in breaststroke and butterfly.

## Procedure

1. Attach a piece of heavy-resistance elastic tubing to a fence or other stationary object at ankle level.
2. Stand facing the attachment point and place the free end of the band around your left foot.
3. Step back from the fence so there is moderate to heavy tension in the band when the foot is slightly in front of the body *(a)*. It is best if you have something to lightly hold onto for balance.
4. Keeping the leg straight, extend the hip and pull the leg backward *(b)*. Keep a good upper-body posture and do not lean forward when performing the exercise.
5. Slowly return the leg to the starting position.

**Variation:** You can also perform this exercise by using a pulley or a multihip machine found in most fitness centers.

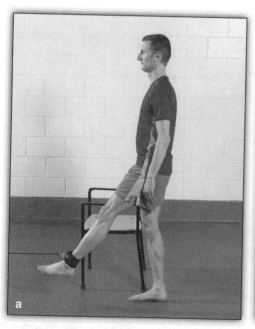

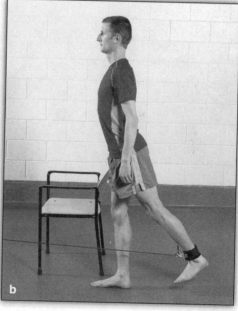

# Hip Flexion (FL, BR)

**Focus:** Improve strength in the hip flexor muscles to develop a strong downbeat in your butterfly kick and to maintain body position in breast-stroke. This exercise also strengthens the core.

## Procedure

1. Attach a loop of heavy-resistance elastic tubing to a fence or other stationary object at ankle level.

2. Stand facing away from the attachment point and place the free end of the band around your right foot.

3. Step away from the fence so there is moderate to heavy tension in the band when the foot is slightly behind the body *(a)*. It is best if you have something to lightly hold onto for balance.

4. Keeping the leg straight, flex the hip, pulling the leg forward *(b)*. Keep a good upper-body posture and do not lean forward when performing the exercise.

5. Slowly return the leg to the starting position.

**Variation:** You can also perform this exercise by using a pulley or a multihip machine found in most fitness centers.

# Medicine Ball V Crunch (FL, BR)

**Focus:** Build stability through the core while performing simultaneous upper-body and lower-body movements.

**Procedure**

1. Start by lying down on the pool deck and holding a light medicine ball between your ankles. Extend your arms over your head.

2. Keeping the legs straight, perform a crunch, simultaneously lifting the shoulders, arms, and legs off the ground.

3. At the top of the movement, transfer the medicine ball from your feet to your hands.

4. Lower the legs back toward the pool deck and the arms to the chest.

5. Repeat the movement and transfer the ball back to your feet.

6. Perform 15 complete repetitions of this exercise, focusing on maintaining stability in the core and perfect form.

# Bent-Over Row (FL)

**Focus:** Strengthen the muscles of the upper back that control the shoulder blades.

**Procedure**

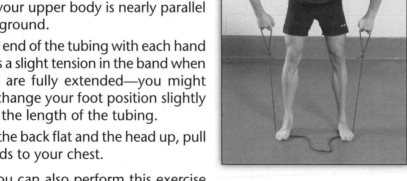

1. Start by standing on a short piece of elastic tubing with the feet slightly wider than shoulder-width apart.

2. With the knees slightly flexed, bend at the waist so your upper body is nearly parallel with the ground.

3. Grab one end of the tubing with each hand so there is a slight tension in the band when the arms are fully extended—you might need to change your foot position slightly to adjust the length of the tubing.

4. Keeping the back flat and the head up, pull your hands to your chest.

**Variation:** You can also perform this exercise by using a barbell or dumbbells instead of the elastic tubing.

# Bent-Over Lateral Raise (FL)

**Focus:** Develop strength in the back of the shoulders to help with arm recovery.

## Procedure

1. Stand on a short piece of low-resistance elastic tubing, grabbing one end of the tubing in each hand.

2. Flex the knees slightly and bend at the waist so the torso is essentially parallel to the ground (*a*). There should be some light tension in the band when the arms hang down toward the ground.

3. Keeping the back flat, lift the arms out to your sides until they are parallel to the ground. Simultaneously pinch the shoulder blades together (*b*).

4. Hold this position briefly and slowly lower the arms to the starting position.

## Medicine Ball Throw to the Ground (FL)

**Focus:**  Develop explosiveness and power through the middle part of the butterfly stroke. Focus on the finish of the stroke.

### Procedure

1. Stand with your feet shoulder-width apart and hold a 2- to 5-kilogram medicine ball in your hands at chest level.
2. Using both arms, accelerate the medicine ball and throw it into the ground.
3. Catch the ball on the bounce and immediately perform another repetition.
4. Complete two to three sets of 15 to 20 repetitions.

## Sumo Squat (BR)

**Focus:**  Build strength in the inner thigh and gluteal muscles. This exercise is performed in the same way as the classic squat except the foot position places greater demands on the muscles of the inner thigh.

### Procedure

1. Stand on a piece of heavy-resistance elastic band so the feet are wider than shoulder-width apart and the toes are pointed slightly outward.
2. Grasp one end of the band with each hand and hold the hands at shoulder level. There should be a strong tension in the band in this starting position.
3. Lower yourself into a squat position so the knees are bent to 90 degrees.
4. Drive with the legs and return to the starting position.
5. Make sure you maintain a normal curvature of the spine, push the chest out and up, and do not let the knees come forward past the toes.

**Variation:**  You can also perform this exercise by using a barbell and a squat rack. Load the barbell with an appropriate weight and step under the bar so it lies across your upper back. Stand and step away from the rack to perform the squat.

# Chest Fly (BR) 🔘 DVD

**Focus:** Build strength through the chest for the inward sweep of the breaststroke pull.

**Procedure**

1. Loop a piece of elastic tubing through a fence at chest level.
2. Grasp one end of the tubing with each hand and face away from the fence.
3. Step forward so there is tension in the band when the arms are held out to the sides (*a*).
4. Keeping the elbows bent slightly, move the hands in a steady arc until they come together in front of your chest (*b*).
5. Hold this position briefly and slowly return to the starting position.

**Variation:** You can also perform this exercise in the weight room using a cable column or while lying on a stability ball using dumbbells.

# Sculling in the Catch Position (BR)

**Focus:** Build strength and a feel for the water during the outward sweep of the breaststroke pull.

## Procedure

1. In the water, lie on your front with your arms extended above your head.
2. With your hands, scull outward about 12 inches (30 cm) and then scull inward to the starting position.
3. Adjust the orientation and pitch of your hands throughout the motion so you move forward down the pool.
4. Try not to kick, and lift your head slightly to breathe when necessary.

# Ways to Add Swimming-Specific Training

There are other ways to add swimming-specific strength training to your program. Several of these involve swimming against resistance. We use these training methods with our swimmers to build strength and work on developing efficiency in the pool. These methods are described in greater detail in chapter 6.

Swimming against elastic-tubing resistance (page 128)

Swimming while pulling buckets or parachutes (page 128)

Using a swim bench (pages 129-130)

Dryland swimming (page 130)

# Chapter 4

# Building Endurance

Some athletic records are so phenomenal they border on legend. Two records in particular stand out in the world of swimming—the 1,500-meter freestyle record of 15:52.10 set by Janet Evans in 1988 and the seven gold medals won by Mark Spitz in the 1972 Olympics. At the time these records were set, they seemed untouchable, and for the most part they have been. However, two current swimmers are taking swimming into uncharted waters, breaking or matching these records—two of the oldest in the books. Kate Ziegler, a distance swimmer and USA Swimming national team member, came within 0.20 second of eclipsing the women's 1,500-meter freestyle record at the 2007 World Championships before shattering the standard and establishing a new world record of 15:42.54 several weeks later. In her record-setting performance, Kate turned in splits that pushed unknown limits of her ability, yet she was able to maintain her level of performance throughout the entire race. At the 2007 World Championships, Michael Phelps swam an unbelievable eight events—five individual events and three relays. Not only did he compete in this previously unheard-of number of events, but he came away with seven gold medals (a feat matched only by Mark Spitz in a major international competition) while setting five world records in the process. Unlike Spitz, however, who swam each event only twice in a trials–finals format, Phelps had to swim each of his individual races three times (with the exception of the 400 IM) as part of the trials–semifinals–finals format introduced in 2000.

What allows some swimmers to tap into energy reserves and get stronger and stronger as a race goes on? What allows others to exhibit a seemingly superhuman ability to recover after a race and turn in stellar performance after stellar performance? The answer to both of these questions, at least in part, is muscular and cardiorespiratory endurance.

# TRAINING FOR ENDURANCE IN SWIMMING

Swimming is a unique mixture of endurance and power—both are needed for success in the pool. Even distance swimmers need power to be able to drive the kick a bit harder or pick up the tempo to negative-split a race or finish strong. Similarly, sprinters need to have well-developed aerobic systems to facilitate recovery after a swim. The relative balance between power and endurance training may be different for each event, but one thing is true: Building on the information presented in chapter 3, we believe it is important for all swimmers to develop muscular endurance and build a well-developed base of cardiorespiratory conditioning, since this serves as an essential building block for future power and strength development. A well-developed aerobic energy system allows your body to be able to generate the energy to sustain long-duration exercise, and it also enhances recovery after intense exercise.

At the University of Southern California and the Irvine Novaquatics, we take a somewhat unique approach to training for endurance and developing the aerobic energy system. Endurance can be built in one of two ways:

1. By swimming at a constant, moderate intensity for a long period
2. By swimming at race paces using high-intensity intervals while using appropriate rest periods to challenge and develop the aerobic energy system

Depending on the methods you employ to build endurance, you will likely see different results. It is a common saying in the strength and conditioning field that long, slow distance training conditions an athlete to swim long and slow. While this may be the goal for someone training simply to stay fit, a swimmer interested in racing fast needs to develop his or her endurance through high-quality training.

We make a concerted effort to bring race specificity to our training; a large part of that involves matching our training to the demands of competition. As a result, we do not do a great deal of what many would call overdistance training—or long, long sets of submaximal-intensity swimming. Technically, we do not even have a distance group at USC; we like to call them the long sprinters, and their training has as much high-intensity, short-duration training as it does conventional distance training. In other words, we emphasize quality over quantity, fast swimming over completing a certain training volume or a set distance. There is also a lot of passive aerobic activity between bouts of intense activity, and that helps build swimmers' endurance as much as anything.

Is there ever a time for overdistance training? There can be, but how much volume do you truly need to do to maintain a feel for the water and enhance swimming performance? Some coaches think it's 10,000 meters a day; others think it's 15,000 meters or even 20,000 meters a day. There are swimmers who thrive on this approach to training, but is it the best

© Human Kinetics

Training should develop the ability to use efficient strokes throughout the entire race—not just when fresh at the start. This, in turn, will result in faster times.

model for everyone? One of the problems we have had in our sport is that the training is too general in nature. It has focused so much on swimming thousands and thousands of meters when it should be focused as much, if not more, on developing an efficiency that involves preparing the body to race. We do have our swimmers swim longer distances or longer sets in practice on occasion, but when they do, the focus during those sets is on technique, not necessarily endurance. The result of this? Well, if you look at the overall status of distance swimming in the United States, an argument could be made that swimmers have the goal of surviving the workout rather than swimming fast. Technique, including how the swimmers kick, is adapted to conserve energy and help the swimmers make it through a certain volume of work. Then, once they see the light at the end of the tunnel, whether it's the end of a workout or the end of a race, they kick it into gear. As an example, many swimmers lengthen their strokes and kick well when they get to the last 100 meters of a race. If they trained to swim the entire 800 or 1,500 meters the way they swim that last 100 meters, their swims would be amazing. However, their training is not geared toward developing efficiency; therefore, many distance swimmers are not able to maintain that awesome stroke for the entire race. When you look at what distance swimmers from other countries do, you see there is a real efficiency in the way they swim. They are not driven by an interval that is beyond their capacity. It all comes back to the idea of training for the race you want to swim. Specificity is the key, and you want to focus your endurance training on swimming at race-pace stroke rates.

## TRAINING WITH SWIMMING SPECIFICITY

Jon Urbanchek, who coached for years at the University of Michigan and trained numerous Olympians, and I are closely related in the way we approach training. He is considered by many to be a distance coach, but really, he is a specificity coach. He doesn't do huge volumes of distance, but a lot of shorter-distance, high-quality distance training. This approach is more efficient than simply swimming to be able to make an interval or completing a set volume of work. This approach has worked very well for his teams, and we have seen this approach work at the Novaquatics and are starting to see the benefits at USC.

# USING HEART RATE TO GAUGE TRAINING INTENSITY

Heart rate (HR) is a good tool for gauging the intensity of your training and can provide some general guidelines for structuring your endurance training. To measure your heart rate, simply count the number of times your heart beats in 10 seconds and multiply by 6, or use a heart rate monitor when you train to keep track of how fast your heart is beating. If you are not using a heart rate monitor and measure your heart rate yourself, one of the easiest places to feel your pulse is the carotid artery in the neck. You should measure heart rate immediately after a swim to give you the most accurate representation of your heart rate while swimming. In some instances you might even have the time to measure heart rate between repeats in a set.

Many experts suggest that to develop the aerobic energy system and build endurance, you should train with a heart rate that falls between 65 and 85 percent of your maximum HR. While training in this zone will improve cardiorespiratory fitness and endurance, consistent training at the high end of this range is what is recommended for enhancing your racing performance. Most health clubs and pools have posters showing what your heart rate should be, based on your age, for training in the aerobic zone. An example of a heart rate chart is shown in figure 4.1.

This introduces another question—what is your maximum heart rate? To *accurately* determine your maximum heart rate, you need to go through a specialized step test in which HR is monitored as you complete a series of increasingly harder swims. You can estimate your maximum HR in one of two ways:

1. Conduct your own version of the step test. Perform a series of 5 × 200s on a 5:00 interval, swimming the first at approximately 60 percent effort. Get progressively faster on each one so the fifth is a maximum-effort swim. At the end of each swim measure, write down your HR.

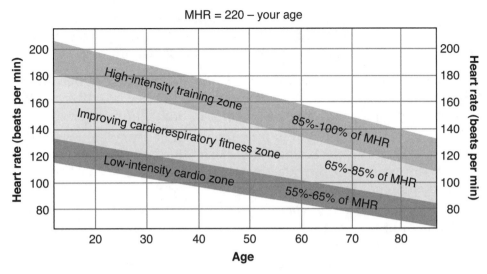

MHR = 220 – your age

Figure 4.1   Heart rate can be used for estimating training intensity, and heart rate training-zone tables are available to help you fine-tune your training.

Adapted with permission from the Cardio Tennis Program. www.CardioTennis.com

The HR you measure at the end of the fifth 200 should be a pretty good indicator of your maximum HR.

2. Use a formula that has been developed to estimate maximum heart rate. Two formulas are provided here; the first is easier to remember, but the second is thought to be more accurate:

$$HRmax = 220 - Age$$

$$HRmax = 205.8 - (0.685 \times Age)$$

Note that these formulas do not take into account any individual characteristics but can give you an idea of what your maximum HR is and can help you establish your aerobic training zone. For reference, these formulas tend to underestimate the maximum HR for people with above-average fitness.

Whichever method you choose, you should measure your maximum HR while swimming, not while running or cycling. Maximum HRs in the water might be as many as 20 beats below what you might measure when performing a land-based test. This is because your weight is partially buoyed by the water and you do not have to deal with the full effects of gravity.

## CROSS-TRAINING FOR SWIMMERS

Sometimes you might not have access to a pool or just need a break from swimming. How can you still work on developing your cardiorespiratory endurance outside of the pool? Cross-training, or using activities other than swimming to maintain your conditioning, is a great way to improve your aerobic base while adding variety to your training. Cross-training provides several physical and mental benefits for swimmers:

- *Improve or maintain your physical conditioning.* You do not need to just swim to improve your aerobic endurance. Other activities, such as cycling, jogging, and playing soccer, can build endurance.

- *Build mental breaks into your training.* It can become tedious to swim every day of the week. Engaging in an alternative activity can help mix things up and provide a spark, if it's needed, to maintain your enthusiasm for training.

- *Maintain conditioning when recovering from an injury.* If you have a shoulder injury, you can ride a stationary bike during recovery and not lose fitness.

- *Help balance the body.* Swimming uses the same muscle groups continuously. In many areas of the body, it is essential to maintain a strength balance so no one muscle group gets too strong in relation to the other muscles in the body.

- *Build strength in muscles important to swimming.* It has been said that you can't maximize the strength you need for swimming simply by swimming. To really get the most out of your body, you need to do something else. Adding a cross-training exercise such as cycling can help build leg strength and endurance, which can lead to improved performance in the pool.

- *Develop a better overall level of fitness and conditioning.* Research has shown that participating in a variety of activities improves overall athleticism. In fact, research on young athletes indicates that those who participate in a variety of sports and activities at younger ages perform better in the long run when they do decide to specialize compared to those athletes who specialize in a sport at an early age.

- *Add flexibility to your training.* It is not uncommon for lap-swimming times to be changed or for a pool to close for maintenance. Having a cross-training option at your disposal can help you adapt to times when you do not have access to a pool.

## Considerations for Cross-Training

With all of the potential benefits of cross-training, you would think it would be a no-brainer for swimmers. However, there are risks involved, and you should take the following suggestions into account when you start your cross-training regimen.

- *Fitness can be activity specific.* Just because you are in great swimming shape and can complete an hour-long workout in the pool does not mean you're ready to go out and run or bike for an hour. Build into any new activity gradually. Remember, you will likely use different muscle groups than you use in swimming, so don't expose them to too much too soon.

• *Don't add cross-training to an already-full training schedule.* If you already have a full swimming schedule, substitute a cross-training workout for a swim workout—don't simply add another workout to your training week. Remember, rest is critical for staying fresh and recovering properly between training sessions. You cannot make any gains if you do not allow your body to recover.

• *Avoid activities that aggravate an existing injury.* This should be common sense, but if you have a shoulder injury, for example, avoid sports that involve overhead movements (such as volleyball or tennis) that will place stress on the injured muscles and tendons in the shoulder. Additionally, if you feel your new cross-training activity is creating a new injury, *stop.* That's the last thing you want from an activity intended to add some variety to your training.

• *Cross-training is not a substitute for swimming.* Specificity is key to any athletic performance, and swimming is no exception. If you want to see your swimming performance improve, in-water and strengthening workouts will still need to make up the bulk of your training. Additionally, when you are out of the water for an extended time, detraining can occur, and it is not uncommon for swimmers to lose their feel for the water. The bottom line is that, when used appropriately, cross-training can be an effective tool for enhancing your swimming performance.

## Cross-Training Options for Swimmers

Many cross-training options are available that build cardiorespiratory and muscular endurance while maintaining or even improving your fitness level. The following list provides a brief description of several activities and how they can improve your swimming performance. Before starting any exercise or activity you have not done before, make sure you know how to use the equipment properly. Also, be sure to use proper technique to minimize the risk of injury.

**Cycling** Cycling is a great form of exercise for building muscular strength and endurance. To get the best workout on the bike, make your cycling session into a session of interval training. Many stationary bikes give you the ability to choose an interval or random program. Choose a resistance level that allows you to spin the pedals easily at a rate of 80 to 110 revolutions per minute.

**Deep-Water Running** Deep-water running works as a great conditioning exercise, especially for swimmers with upper-body injuries. In deep-water running, your feet should not touch the bottom of the pool—you are essentially running in place, although you will slowly make your way down the pool. Use a flotation device to assist with this exercise, or increase the level of difficulty by choosing not to use one.

**Jogging** Jogging and walking are some of the easiest forms of cross-training because you can do them virtually anywhere at any time, and you really do not need any special equipment. Take caution, however, because running can subject the lower body to large stresses you don't normally experience in the pool. Get fitted for a good pair of running shoes to help protect against injury.

**Upper-Body Ergometer** The upper-body ergometer, sometimes known as a UBE, provides a cardiorespiratory workout while using the upper body. Using a UBE is like pedaling a bicycle with your hands. It is one of the few cross-training alternatives that involves only the upper body and is a great complement to any of the lower-body activities.

**Elliptical Trainer** Elliptical trainers can be found in virtually every health club and offer a low- or no-impact form of training. The motion of the machines resembles that of running and cross-country skiing. These machines can provide a total-body workout because many allow you to involve the arms as well as the legs.

# DEVELOPING MUSCULAR ENDURANCE

In many ways, strength training can be viewed as a form of cross-training since it provides a different way to stimulate and challenge the body above and beyond what you achieve in the pool. However, when building muscular endurance, be sure to approach it in the right way. Muscular endurance refers to a muscle's ability to generate a relatively high level of force repeatedly without fatigue. This is important in every swimming race since even in the 100-meter freestyle, a distance commonly thought of as a sprint in swimming, the average swimmer will take 40 to 50 strokes with each arm and kick continuously throughout the race. Doing this without fatiguing requires some level of muscular endurance.

In chapter 3, we discussed the need to build a foundation of full-body strength. The emphasis of this general strength training is to build a level of muscular endurance. When this is established, it is possible to build swimming-specific strength and power. You should also follow the muscular endurance model of training when building core strength and performing exercises to prevent injury.

A strengthening program that emphasizes muscular endurance should use moderate levels of resistance, and you should perform several sets of an exercise. Each set should consist of 15 to 25 repetitions. Your muscles must get used to contracting often against a light resistance and recovering quickly; consequently, the amount of rest between sets should be minimal. The following are some general guidelines when using strength training to build muscular endurance:

- Endurance-based exercises should make up the bulk of your early season. You should continue to use the exercises, although to a lesser degree, as you move closer to your competitive season (see chapter 11 for more information related to seasonal planning).

- Use relatively light weights or resistance when building muscular endurance. You should be able to lift the weight 15 to 25 times while maintaining correct form throughout. If you are not able to maintain correct form or you fatigue quickly, lower the resistance. Strive to perform two or three sets of each exercise.

- Circuit training is a great way to emphasize muscular endurance, and training circuits can easily be set up on the pool deck. Circuit training, however, is better suited for performing exercises for a set period than for performing a certain number of repetitions. In this case, perform each exercise for 20 to 30 seconds before resting.

- Take short rests between sets, typically less than 30 seconds. The work-to-rest ratio should be 1:1 or less—if the set takes 25 seconds to complete, you should take a maximum of 25 seconds before you start the next set. Remember, you are training both your muscular and cardiorespiratory systems to recover quickly. To do this, you need to maintain the appropriate work-to-rest ratio.

- Incorporate variety into your training. There are many exercises you could use to build leg strength, for example. Mix them up so your program does not become stale.

# Chapter 5

# Training
# for Core Stability

**B** alancing and maintaining a streamlined body position are critical in swimming. Being able to control your body improves efficiency and allows you to knife through the water with minimal resistance. However, to achieve this position, you need to have strength and control of the muscles through the middle part of your body—the area known as the *core*. A weak core can lead to poor technique and even increased risk of injury. Think about how you use your core when you swim—body position, body rotation in freestyle and backstroke, undulation in butterfly and breast-stroke, and so on. Because of the various functions performed by the core muscles, building core stability to enhance swimming performance means more than simply doing crunches to strengthen the abdominal muscles. When it comes to strength and conditioning, the core is arguably *the* most important area of the body to focus on, and training needs to address the *entire* core, incorporating balance and rotation as well.

You will notice throughout the chapter that we focus on building core *stability,* not core *strength*. On the surface there may not seem to be much of a difference between strength and stability, but there actually is: Core stability incorporates both muscular strength and muscular control. Strong core muscles are important, but even the strongest muscles are useless if they are activated at the wrong time or in the wrong order. Because of this, swimming-specific core exercises need to challenge you to maintain balance and control of the muscles while also developing strength. This will help make the core training work you do transfer to your performance in the pool. This chapter introduces exercises and drills that will challenge your core and improve core stability both in and out of the water.

# UNDERSTANDING THE CORE

Before we dive into exercises for the core, it's important to get a better understanding of the muscles that make up this important area of the body. What comes to mind when you hear the word *core*? If you're like most people, you think of the abdominal muscles and a set of six-pack abs. While this definition is technically correct, at least in part, it's important to recognize that the core is more than just your abs. Think of the core as a muscular cylinder surrounding the middle third of your body composed of *all* the muscles that surround the body's center of mass:

- *Erector spinae* muscles in the lower back extend, or straighten, the lower back and provide stability to the pelvis.
- *Internal and external oblique* muscles in the abdomen work together to rotate the torso and assist in side bending. They also provide stability to the pelvis. The right internal oblique and the left external oblique contract simultaneously to produce rotation to the right, and vice versa.
- *Transverse abdominis* in the lower abdominal region runs laterally across the abdomen and acts as a corset to provide stability to the pelvis.
- *Rectus abdominis* forms the six-pack and flexes the trunk (produces forward bending).
- Many other muscles attach to and control the pelvis and spine, such as those that flex and extend the hip.

Taken together, these muscles allow for a range of movements throughout the middle third of the body, but they also provide stability to the pelvis and spine. But how exactly does a strong and stable core help a swimmer? Most important, the core links the upper and lower halves of the body. When the upper and lower halves of the body are linked, you will be able to attain the following:

• *Maintain a streamlined body position in the water.* Most swimmers think of streamlining as something to focus on only off the starts and turns. However, being streamlined essentially means "punching" as small a hole as possible through the water to reduce drag, whether you are coming off the wall or swimming at the surface. With poor core stability, the legs will drop and you will waste energy moving through the water simply because you are not as streamlined as you could be. This is one of the great things about developing core stability—you'll be able to swim faster without having to pull or kick any harder simply by being able to maintain a better body position in the water.

## PERFORMANCE TIP

When you're swimming at race speeds, even a small drop of the hips can increase the amount of drag you have to overcome by as much as 25 percent.

Core stability improves many swimming skills, including maintaining a streamlined position in the water.

AP Photo/Mark J. Terrill

• *Establish a stable base of support that will help you develop a stronger pull and kick.* It's been said that core stability allows for limb mobility. In other words, having good core stability allows you to use your arms and legs for what they're meant for—to generate propulsion. This is more important in swimming than it is in land-based sports where you have an interaction with the ground. The grounding effect seen in land-based sports allows for large forces to be generated between the feet and the ground that can then be transferred through the body. This energy can power a forehand in tennis or help an offensive lineman drive into his block. In swimming, there is no rigid surface to push against—you are essentially trying to pull or kick against a surface that is always trying to move out of your way. It's your core stability that provides the base of support you need to generate efficient movement and propulsion from the arms and legs.

Knowing your arms and legs can do only so much, would you rather use them to stabilize the body or generate propulsion? Hopefully you said you want to generate propulsion. Yet, many swimmers who lack core stability often rely on their arms and legs to provide balance in the water—especially when breathing. Because of this, they cannot tap into the full propulsion-generating power of the upper body. Think about your own strokes: Do you pull wider with one arm than the other? Do your legs spread farther apart when you breathe? If so, you might need better core stability.

• *Increase the effectiveness of your kick.* Have you ever tried to push a piece of cooked spaghetti across the dinner table? While pulling it across the table is pretty easy (like pulling the body through the water), it's very difficult to push the wet noodle because of its floppiness. This is like trying to use your kick to push you across the pool when you have poor core stability. Creating a rigid link between upper and lower body allows your legs to push you through the water rather than rely entirely on your arms to pull you.

• *Generate body roll in freestyle and backstroke.* If you're like most swimmers, you've probably had a coach who told you to rotate from the hips when swimming freestyle and backstroke. Where do you think that rotation comes from? While some rotation is produced by the kick, a large part comes from the muscles of the core—particularly the oblique muscles. This body rotation is necessary for efficient pulling (and kicking) in freestyle and backstroke.

• *Drive your undulation in butterfly and breaststroke.* Core stability is not just important for freestyle and backstroke. A strong core allows the propulsion of the kick to drive the body forward and adds to the power from the upper body.

• *Control lateral (side-to-side) movement of the body.* Swimmers who have a weak core will often fishtail, or produce side-to-side movements of the hips with every pull and kick, creating extra drag and reducing swimming efficiency.

Overall, having a stable core will help you swim faster by allowing you to generate larger forces, and do so more efficiently, while reducing the amount of drag you experience in the water.

## KINETIC CHAIN AND SWIMMING

The body is made up of a series of segments that are all linked together to function as one unit—what is known as the *kinetic chain*. Figure 5.1 shows how parts of the body can be linked together in the kinetic chain. Because these segments are all linked together, what happens in one link affects what happens everywhere else in the body. This offers a tremendous benefit, because you can tap into the strength of your entire body when swimming. But there is also a downside: If there is a weak or a broken link, it can compromise the integrity of the entire chain. The saying "You're only as strong as your weakest link" is true when it comes to strength training and sport performance. When the kinetic chain is intact, power can flow

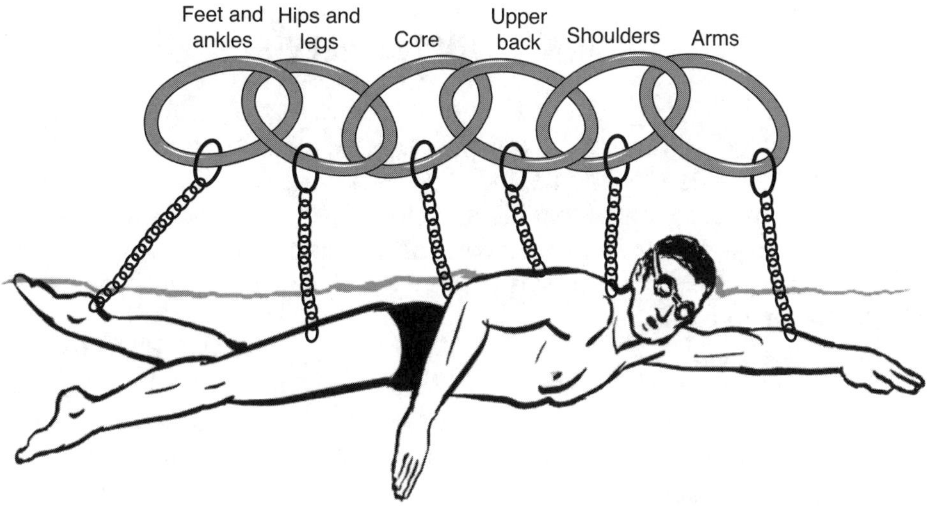

Figure 5.1   The segments of the body are linked together, much as the links in a chain. Because of this, a weak or broken link can affect another part of the body.

Adapted, by permission, from E.W. Maglischo, 2003, *Swimming fastest* (Champaign, IL: Human Kinetics), 124.

from the legs and torso to the upper body. A broken link, whether it results from a lack of strength, poor muscular control, or fatigue, blocks this flow of power and places demands on the smaller muscles of the shoulder. The demands placed on these relatively small muscles increase the risk of fatigue, technique breakdown, and injury. Can a swimmer still swim fast with a broken link? In some cases, yes, but it always comes at a cost. The tradeoff for a weak link in the kinetic chain, particularly when it occurs in the core, is an increased risk of injury.

Let's look at the idea of the kinetic chain within the context of a swimming stroke. With poor core stability, your body position will change in the water, meaning to swim the same speed, you will have to pull harder to overcome the increased drag. This will place more stress on the muscles in the shoulder. Additionally, because you are not maintaining balance in the water, you will likely have to pull deeper, wider, or with a straight arm to get the balance you need, especially when you breathe. This too will place stress on the shoulders. All of this together can contribute to an increased risk of shoulder injury.

## DRYLAND PROGRESSIONS FOR THE CORE

Swimming places extra demands on the core and increases the need for dynamic stability—or stability while the body is moving—compared to other sports. Because water is a fluid, the body can essentially move any way it wants with little opposition; there is no ground pushing back to constrain the way the body can move. This is a difficult scenario to

# LOCKING DOWN THE PELVIS

Strength and conditioning coaches have described how to activate the core in many ways, including pulling the navel in toward the spine and flattening out the lower back. We use the idea of locking down the pelvis. In other words, we want you to think about activating the muscles of the core to lock everything in place so the pelvis will not move. Locking down the pelvis is a critical concept for building stability in this area of the body, and to do this you will have to activate the entire muscular cylinder.

So, how does this conceptualization of activating the core differ from the other ways strength and conditioning coaches have described it? For one, by locking down the pelvis, you will maintain the normal curvature of the spine. The spine is strongest and most stable when it maintains its normal curvature; this means there should still be a small curve in the lower back when you perform core exercises as well as when you swim. This way of thinking also puts the emphasis on the pelvis, which really is the essential component in linking the upper and lower parts of the body together. When you have locked down the pelvis, you should be able to use your fingers to feel that your abdominal muscles, lower-back muscles, and even gluteal muscles are all contracting.

duplicate on land, but luckily some pieces of equipment allow swimmers to experience a similar unstable feeling when training the core on dry land. Our swimmers at USC and the Irvine Novaquatics do a lot of unbalanced training out of the water, but we also do similar exercises in the pool. We do a lot of work that emphasizes maintaining body position and posture as well as building core strength against resistance. We find when we do this, the benefits carry over to the pool more effectively than with some other exercises.

Most of the exercises discussed here are presented as a series of progressions, taking you through beginning, intermediate, and advanced versions of an exercise. As the exercises get more difficult, the demands placed on the core increase. Many of the advanced progressions are dynamic exercises, requiring the core to stabilize the body during movement. We present exercise descriptions for all of the basic and intermediate exercises here in the book and refer you to the accompanying DVD to watch the advanced exercises being performed. When going through these exercises, it is important that you start with the beginner-level exercises first and work to increase the time or number of repetitions. Remember, the quality of the exercise is much more important than the number of repetitions. If there is weakness in the core, you still might be able to do the higher-level exercises. However, it is likely that you will attempt to generate the necessary stability by substituting other muscles to compensate for the weakness in the core. The problem here is that these muscles were not designed to be stabilizers, and using them in this way may result in technique problems when you get in the water. Follow the progressions laid out in this book to teach your body to use the correct muscles. As you get stronger, you can progress to the more difficult exercises.

## PERFORMANCE TIP

Although many people enjoy doing core workouts early in the morning, it has been shown that doing sit-ups and lower-back exercises before the body has a chance to warm up can place up to three times as much stress on the vertebral disks of the lower back as performing the same exercises later in the day. These higher stresses could contribute to lower-back pain.

# Prone Bridge Progression

Prone bridging involves controlling the core to maintain a consistent body line, much as you need in the water. The focus of these exercises is on maintaining a straight line from the ankles through the hips to the shoulders while balancing on your forearms and your feet. Work to maintain this form even as your balance becomes challenged and the stabilizing muscles become more fatigued.

## Beginner Level

1. Start with your toes and knees in contact with the ground and your forearms resting on the ground.
2. Lock down the pelvis and lift your body off the ground so that the only points of contact with the ground are your toes and forearms.
3. Maintain a flat back so there is a straight line from your ankles to your shoulders (a).
4. Hold this position for 15 seconds, and repeat two or three times, taking 15 seconds of rest between each set.
5. Build your endurance until you can hold the position for 30 to 45 seconds in each repetition.
6. If you are unable to hold this position for even one set, start with the knees and forearms on the ground to make the exercise a bit easier to control.

## Intermediate Level

You will need an inflatable stability ball for this exercise.

1. Rest your forearms on the stability ball.
2. Lock down the pelvis and maintain a straight body line from ankles to shoulders (b).

Prone bridge: (a) beginner and (b) intermediate level.

3. Try to hold this body position for 15 seconds, and repeat two or three times with 15 seconds of rest between each effort.

4. Build to the point where you can hold each set for 30 to 45 seconds.

To further increase the difficulty of this exercise, roll forward slightly so only your elbows are in contact with the ball. As the contact area between your body and the ball decreases, you will increase the demands on the core.

### Advanced Level

The first advanced exercise builds on the intermediate exercise. Lift each foot off the ground alternately, simulating a kicking motion.

### Alternative Advanced Level

This additional advanced exercise also builds on the intermediate exercise and requires simultaneous core and shoulder stability as you balance with your hands on the exercise ball instead of resting on your forearms.

# Back Bridge Progression

Back bridge exercises target the entire core, requiring these muscles to maintain a consistent body line from the shoulders through the hips to the knees and ankles. Again, as the exercises increase in difficulty, the core will be required to stabilize the body in increasingly demanding and dynamic situations.

### Beginner Level

1. Start by lying on your back with the knees bent, both feet flat on the ground close to your buttocks, and your arms on the floor at your sides.

2. Lock down the pelvis and use the core and the gluteal muscles (not the quadriceps muscles in the front of your thighs) to lift your hips to the sky so a straight line is formed from the shoulders to the knees. At the same time, pull your toes toward your shins. Focus on activating your gluteal muscles by imagining you are squeezing a penny between your cheeks.

3. Hold this up position for a count of three before lowering the hips.

4. Allow your buttocks to touch the ground and immediately lift the hips again.

5. Perform two to three sets of 15 repetitions, building to sets of 25 as stability improves, with 15 seconds of rest between each set. As you get stronger, hold the up position for increasingly longer times with a goal of holding each repetition for a count of 10.

### Intermediate Level

For this variation of the exercise, you will reduce the amount of contact you have with the ground. This exercise duplicates the demands of

Back bridge: beginner level.

swimming since the body needs to maintain a consistent body line while the legs act independently.

1. Start in the same way as you started the beginner exercise, except you should extend the right leg so only the left foot is on the ground.
2. Lock down the pelvis and use your gluteal muscles to lift the hips to the sky. There should be a straight line from the shoulders through the hips to the right ankle. You will need to activate the entire core to maintain this body line while also keeping the body from twisting.
3. Hold this up position for a count of three.
4. Lower the hips until your buttocks touch the ground, and immediately start the next repetition. The right leg should remain straight throughout.
5. Perform two sets of 15 repetitions with each leg, resting 15 seconds between each set.

### Advanced Level

Place your heels on an inflatable stability ball while you bridge. Hold this position for 15 seconds to start, and build to two or three sets of 30 to 45 seconds. Cross your hands across your chest or cross your feet on the ball to really challenge yourself.

### Alternative Advanced Level

To add a level of difficulty, alternately lift each foot off a stability ball to dynamically challenge the core.

# Side Bridge Progression

Side bridging develops strength in the muscles that make up the sides of the core. Since these muscles also help a great deal with initiating and controlling body rotation, developing strength and stability in this area is critical.

### Beginner Level

1. Lying on your left side, bend your left arm 90 degrees and place it under your upper body.
2. Lock down the pelvis and contract the muscles of the core to lift your hips toward the ceiling. In the up position, there should be a straight line between your feet, hips, and head.
3. Hold this position for 15 seconds and perform two sets on each side, resting 15 seconds between each set.
4. As you get stronger, increase the amount of time in the up position until you are able to hold the position for 30 to 45 seconds at a time.

Side bridge: beginner level.

### Intermediate Level

This version of the exercise increases the need for dynamic stability.

1. Start the exercise as you did in the beginner exercise.
2. From the up position, slowly lift the right leg 12 to 24 inches (30 to 60 cm) toward the sky.
3. Hold this position for a count of three before slowly lowering the leg back to the starting position.
4. Perform two sets of 15 repetitions of this exercise on each side, resting 15 seconds between sets.
5. Gradually build to performing 25 repetitions in each set as stability improves.

### Advanced Level

This version of this exercise builds on the beginner exercise, but it requires you to perform a rowing motion while holding the up position, building dynamic stability.

# Dying Bug Progression

The dying bug exercise is so named because it is done on your back while moving the arms and the legs in a way that resembles a dying insect. This exercise requires a great deal of dynamic stability, and we will approach it in pieces before putting the entire movement together in the advanced stage of the exercise. If at any time during this exercise you feel the lower back arching off the floor or pressing into the floor, you should stop; at that point you are no longer working the correct muscles.

### Beginner Level

1. Lying on your back, bend your knees while keeping both feet on the ground.

2. Lock down the pelvis by activating the core muscles and slowly lift the right foot 6 to 8 inches (15 to 20 cm) off the ground. There should be no movement in the pelvis as you lift the right foot.

3. Hold this position for a count of three before lowering the foot back to the ground. Lift the left foot off the ground in the same way.

4. Perform three or four sets of this exercise, trying to execute 15 repetitions in each set.

If you are unable to complete the exercise without letting the pelvis move, perform only as many repetitions as you can successfully. As you become stronger, hold the up position for as long as 15 seconds.

### Intermediate Level

To increase the difficulty of this exercise, keep the legs off the floor at all times.

1. Start the exercise by lying on your back with the hips and knees bent 90 degrees.

2. Lock down the pelvis by activating the core muscles. Be sure to maintain the normal curvature in the lower back and not press it into the ground.

3. Slowly lower and straighten the left leg until the foot is approximately 6 inches (15 cm) off the ground.

4. Hold this position briefly before bringing the left leg back to the starting position.

5. Lower the right leg in the same way.

6. Perform two sets of 5 repetitions with each leg to start; as you get stronger and gain more control over the core, progress to three sets of 15 to 20 repetitions with each leg, taking 30 seconds between each set.

### Advanced Level

At this point you can incorporate arm motion into the exercise to require even greater dynamic stability from the core, much as you would see when swimming freestyle or backstroke. Alternate lowering the right arm with the left leg and the left arm with the right leg.

Dying bug: intermediate level.

# Bird Dog Progression 🔘 DVD

This exercise improves strength and control of the core muscles, particularly in the muscles of the lower back, while also controlling movement of the arms and legs. It is a great exercise that requires the core to provide dynamic stability.

## Beginner Level

1. Start the exercise on all fours. Keep the head in line with the spine by looking down during the exercise.
2. Lock down the pelvis and lift the right arm and left leg until they are parallel to the ground. Keep a flat back throughout the exercise *(a)*.
3. Hold this position for a count of three and slowly return to the starting position.
4. Repeat while lifting the left arm and right leg.
5. Perform two sets of 15 cycles (both sides) of this exercise.

## Intermediate Level

You will need an inflated stability ball. This exercise is more difficult because you are required to balance on the ball throughout the exercise.

1. Place the stability ball under your torso and hip region and position your body so both hands and feet touch the ground.
2. Lock down the pelvis and slowly lift the right arm and left leg until they are parallel to the ground *(b)*.

Bird dog: *(a)* beginner and *(b)* intermediate level.

3. Hold this position for a count of three before lowering the arm and leg back to the starting position.

4. Repeat, lifting the left arm and right leg.

5. Perform two sets of 15 cycles (both sides) of this exercise.

**Advanced Level**

At the advanced level you are required to use the core to prevent body rotation as you simultaneously lift the arm and leg on the same side of the body.

## Seated Medicine Ball Chest Pass Progression

This progression involves two swimmers, each sitting on an inflatable stability ball. Using a small medicine ball, the partners alternate throwing chest passes to each other; as the points of contact with the ground are removed, the exercise becomes more difficult.

**Beginner Level**

1. This exercise starts with both partners sitting on a stability ball, facing each other. Both feet should be on the ground and the partners should be approximately 6 to 12 feet (2 to 4 m) apart.

2. Alternate throwing and catching chest passes. As you catch the ball and return it to your partner, you will need to engage your core to avoid falling off the stability ball.

3. Continue the chest passes for 15 seconds and repeat the set three times.

4. Gradually increase the time until each set lasts 30 to 45 seconds.

Seated medicine ball chest pass: intermediate level.

### Intermediate Level

1. Perform the exercise with only one foot on the ground.
2. Continue the chest passes for 15 seconds and repeat the set four times, twice with the right foot on the ground and twice with the left foot on the ground.
3. Gradually increase the time until each set lasts 30 to 45 seconds.

### Advanced Level

To challenge your core stability and balance, progress to doing the exercise with both feet off the ground.

# Seated Medicine Ball Toss Progression

This exercise is much like the medicine ball chest pass exercise, except it becomes even more swimming specific since it requires the core to provide stability during rotation. Perform this exercise with a partner, yet instead of throwing chest passes, you and your partner should rotate the hips and torso while catching and throwing a small medicine ball from the side.

### Beginner Level

1. Both partners start by sitting on stability balls, facing each other. Both feet should be on the ground and the partners should be approximately 10 to 12 feet (3 to 4 m) apart. Both feet should be on the ground as you use the core to provide stability to the pelvis while also producing the rotation for throwing or catching the ball.

Seated medicine ball toss: beginner level.

2. Alternate throwing the medicine ball to each other. Decelerate the ball when you catch it by rotating the body; then rotate in the other direction to toss the ball back to your teammate.

3. Continue the tosses for 15 seconds and repeat the set four times—two times throwing and catching from the right side and two from the left.

4. Gradually increase the time until each set lasts 30 to 45 seconds.

### Intermediate Level

Perform this exercise while keeping only one foot in contact with the ground.

### Advanced Level

Eventually you may be able to perform the exercise while keeping both feet off the ground. Just so you don't think you're embarking on an impossible task, take heart: We have been able to get swimmers to do the advanced form of this exercise in our collegiate and age-group swimming programs.

## Leg Drop

This exercise requires core stability with rotation and carries over to performance in the pool. The premise of the exercise is that you will allow the knees to drop to the side of your body in a controlled manner, requiring activation of the obliques and other core muscles.

### Beginner Level

1. Lying on your back with your arms extended by your sides, place both feet on the floor near your buttocks.

2. Lock down the pelvis and slowly lower your knees toward the floor on your left side. Go as far as you can until you feel your right hip start to lift off the ground (a).

3. Hold this position briefly before slowly bringing the knees back to the starting position.

4. Repeat the movement to the right side.

5. Perform two to three sets of 10 to 15 repetitions to start with and gradually build to sets of 25 as core stability improves.

### Intermediate Level

1. Lying on your back with your arms extended by your sides, lift the feet off the ground by flexing the hips and knees 90 degrees (b).

2. Lock down the pelvis and lower the knees to the floor on your left side. Go as far as you can until you feel your right hip start to lift off the ground.

Leg drop: *(a)* beginner (finish position) and *(b)* intermediate level (start position).

3. Hold this position briefly before slowly bringing the knees back to the starting position.
4. Repeat the movement to the right side.
5. Perform two to three sets of 10 to 15 repetitions to start with and gradually build to sets of 25 as core stability improves.

**Advanced Level**

Perform this level of the exercise in much the same way as the other levels, except hold the legs straight throughout the movement.

# Knees to Chest Progression

This progression improves coordination between the lower body and core while developing core strength and stability through rotation.

**Beginner Level**

1. Place your hands shoulder-width apart on the pool deck and rest your legs on a stability ball so the ball rests midway between your knees and ankles.

Knees to chest: beginner level.

2. Lock down the pelvis and draw the knees straight to the chest.
3. After a brief pause, extend your legs slowly, returning to the starting position.
4. Repeat, performing two or three sets of 15 repetitions.

### Intermediate Level

This level of the progression introduces rotation and engagement of the oblique muscles to a greater degree. Perform the exercise in exactly the same way, except instead of pulling the knees straight to the chest, do the following:

1. First pull the knees along a diagonal path toward the chest and right shoulder.
2. Return to the starting position and repeat the movement, drawing the knees toward the left shoulder.
3. Perform two or three sets, completing 10 cycles (both sides) in each set.

### Advanced Level

This advanced exercise, also called the diagonal leg tuck, improves coordination between the lower body and core while developing core strength through rotation. Keeping the right leg on the ball, draw your left knee toward your right shoulder. Return and repeat, bringing the right knee toward the left shoulder.

## IN-WATER PROGRESSIONS FOR THE CORE

Since swimmers train and compete in the water, it is beneficial to engage in some core strengthening exercises that actually take place in the water.

# Front Balance Drill

This drill requires you to maintain a streamlined position on your belly while balancing on a flotation device designed to introduce greater instability than what the water provides on its own.

## Beginner Level

The beginner level of this exercise uses one or several kickboards.

1. In the water, position one or two kickboards (stacked on top of each other) under the chest and hold the body in a streamlined position.
2. Lock down the pelvis and activate all the muscles in your core to maintain the streamlined position and keep the legs at the surface while staying on the kickboard. The buoyancy of the kickboard will cause it to shoot out from under you if your body posture deviates from a balanced, streamlined position.
3. Hold this position for 15 seconds, slowly turning the head to the side when you need a breath.
4. Repeat this set three or four times and gradually increase the time you hold the streamline until you are able to consistently hold the position for 30 to 45 seconds.

As you become more proficient at this exercise, add more kickboards to the stack under your chest. The increased buoyancy will provide more instability while challenging the core.

## Intermediate Level

Add difficulty by incorporating arm and leg movements. When you are comfortable holding a streamlined position while balancing on a kickboard, you can start to move your arms and legs in various patterns.

1. From the streamlined position, slowly move your arms from overhead along a wide-arcing path to your sides, as if you are making a snow angel. Maintain control and body posture while making these movements.
2. Return the arms to a streamlined position.
3. Keeping the arms overhead, slowly separate your legs and return them to the starting position.
4. Finally, put both actions together.
5. Repeat this pattern for two or three sets of 5 complete cycles (all movements), gradually building to 10 cycles in each set.
6. You can also move the arms slowly through a freestyle-like stroke.

Front balance: intermediate level.

### Advanced Level

Lie on a foam roll or half of a foam roll instead of a kickboard while maintaining a streamlined position.

## CHALLENGING THE CORE

You are limited only by your imagination in choosing or designing core training exercises, and you can take the in-water core training to incredible levels of difficulty if you choose. We have asked the Irvine Novaquatics swimmers to try to hold a streamlined position while balancing on an inflated stability ball *in the pool*. We started by throwing several stability balls in the pool and asking the swimmers to play around with them. It took some time, but after several practice sessions, many of the swimmers were able to balance on the ball in a streamlined position without falling off. It just goes to show what control you can have over your body position when you have a stable core.

## Back Balance Drill

This drill is much like the previous exercise, except it requires you to maintain a streamlined position on your back while balancing on a flotation device. Because much of the exercise description is the same as in the previous exercise, the descriptions are brief.

### Beginner Level

1. On your back, position one or two kickboards under your torso and middle back.
2. Lock down the pelvis and get into a streamlined position without falling off the kickboard.
3. Perform three or four sets, holding this position for 15 seconds each time.
4. Gradually increase the time you hold your streamline to 30 to 45 seconds in each set.

As in the front balance drill, you can add more kickboards to make the exercise more difficult.

### Intermediate Level

Perform the movement while maintaining the balanced, streamlined position on the kickboard.

1. Move the arms in sweeping motions to your sides, as if making a snow angel.
2. You can also lift them out of the water, as in a backstroke recovery.
3. Alternate moving the arms and separating the legs to further challenge your balance.

### Advanced Level

Balance your body on a half foam roll.

Back balance: intermediate level.

# ADDITIONAL CORE TRAINING EXERCISES

Some core training exercises do not lend themselves to being a part of a progression. This section presents several stand-alone exercises that build core strength and control.

## Back Extension

**Focus:** Target the muscles of the lower back, an area critical to swimming performance.

**Procedure**

1. Position yourself over an exercise ball so your thighs and abdomen are in contact with the ball and the feet are on the ground.
2. Place your hands at the sides of your head with the elbows out to the sides or cross your arms across your chest.
3. Contracting the muscles of the lower back, lift the torso until there is a straight line between the feet, hips, shoulders, and head.
4. Slowly lower the upper body back down to the ball.
5. Increase the difficulty by crossing your arms and holding a weight across your chest.

Caution: Do not hyperextend the back; go only to the point where there is a straight line from the ankles to the head.

Back extension.

Do not neglect the lower-back muscles when training the core. These muscles are critical for core stability. Be sure to integrate exercises that strengthen the extensors of the lower back and spine into your core training plan.

# T Exercise

**Focus:**   This exercise is performed in much the same way as the Russian twist (pages 63-64), except it does not use a medicine ball. However, it does place greater demands on the muscles of the upper back that stabilize the shoulder blades. Maintaining a flat tabletop-like posture during the exercise requires great strength and control throughout the core and upper body.

## Procedure

1. Position your body on the stability ball so you feel the contact with the ball in the middle of your upper back.
2. Extend your arms out to your sides while maintaining a straight line from your knees to your shoulders.
3. Gradually roll off the ball to the left, keeping the body flat (not rotating). As you move to the left, the ball will appear to roll to your right.
4. Keep rolling until the ball is just past your right shoulder, and slowly return to the starting position.
5. Make the movement to the opposite side and perform two to three sets of 10 repetitions to start, building to 15 repetitions over time.

T exercise.

# Abdominal Crunch With Rotation

**Focus:** This exercise is a staple in most core training plans. It builds strength and stability in the rectus abdominis and oblique muscles, especially when done with rotation.

## Procedure

1. Lie with the middle of your back on a stability ball and both feet flat on the floor. Place your arms across your chest. There should be a straight line from your knees to your shoulders *(a)*.
2. Contract your abdominal muscles and curl upward and to your left. Do not lift your torso past 45 degrees *(b)*.
3. Slowly lower your body back to the starting position and repeat, this time rotating to the right.
4. Perform two or three sets of 15 repetitions to each side.

**Variation:** Make this exercise more challenging and power oriented by having a teammate throw a medicine ball to you every repetition.

Abdominal crunch with rotation.

# Chapter 6

# Developing Explosive Power

**P**ower is the combination of strength and speed. Have you ever noticed how Natalie Coughlin always seems to come up half a body length ahead of her competitors off the start and turns, or the way Michael Phelps is able to shift into another gear and just pull away from his competitors? Watching these two swimmers, you begin to appreciate the importance of having power when you swim. There is not a race where the ability to generate power does not come into play. Even distance swimmers, long thought to need only endurance, can benefit by adding power-improving exercises into their training plans. The mathematical definition of power is force multiplied by velocity. The ability to produce power is directly related to swimming efficiency and your ability to maximize propulsive forces by accelerating the hands and arms through a stroke cycle. Power is essential to being able to explode off the blocks or drive off the wall on each of your turns. Power distinguishes the medalists from the nonmedalists, the elite performances from the mediocre.

The focus of power training needs to be on finding the optimal balance between strength and speed and then being able to carry that power to your athletic performance. Sport-specific power development is difficult in any sport, but because swimmers need to be able to generate the power against water (an unstable surface), as opposed to the ground, power training can become even more complicated. In other words, when a runner applies force to the ground, it translates into nearly 100 percent propulsive force, but in swimming, some of the force applied to the water puts the water in motion, resulting in a lower percentage going toward propulsion. One of the most difficult tasks for swimmers is learning how to apply force in a manner that maximizes the resultant propulsive action. This chapter focuses on exercises and training strategies you can use for developing power and explosiveness. It also presents practical ways of transferring that power from the weight room to the pool. Refer to chapter 10 and chapter 11 to discover how to integrate these exercises with the others presented earlier in this book to develop a comprehensive, season-long training plan.

## COMPONENTS OF A STRENGTH AND CONDITIONING PROGRAM FOR POWER

So, how do you build and develop strength, speed, and power for swimming? The first step is to establish a general full-body strength base, as discussed in chapter 3. Exercises that boost power are meant to be performed at 100 percent intensity—a maximum effort—and it is important for the body to be prepared to handle the physical demands these exercises bring with them. With a foundation of strength in place, you will be able to focus on performing shorter-duration, high-intensity exercises that develop explosiveness and produce forces rapidly.

In the past, it was thought that power was best developed by lifting heavy loads for a small number of repetitions. However, this way of training addresses only the force component, not the speed component, of the power equation. Recent thinking about building power in athletes has changed to incorporate several new paradigms. Now, strength and conditioning programs for maximizing swimmers' power should contain three components:

1. *Some* strength training using heavy resistance
2. Plyometric exercises that develop the rate of force, or how quickly the muscles can contract and produce force
3. Speed-based strengthening that uses lower resistances but emphasizes performing the exercises through the greatest range of motion as quickly as possible

Many of the exercises in chapter 3 can be performed with heavier loads to address the first component of power development—strength training with heavy resistance. The rest of this chapter describes in greater detail how to develop components 2 and 3.

## GUIDELINES FOR DEVELOPING POWER

Training for power places greater demands on the body than training for muscular endurance, and it is important not to overstress the body when focusing on power development. We've emphasized that quality of training is more important than quantity of training. This holds true when training to develop power.

When you set out to build power, you should take several safety and performance considerations into account as you set up your program. From a safety perspective, you should be aware of these issues:

- Perform explosive exercises at the start of a workout (after a warm-up) while your body is fresh. Fatigued muscles can negatively affect technique and cause injury. Fatigue also limits the gains you can expect to achieve.

- Set up your training program using exercise progressions so that exercises increase in complexity and intensity as you become more experienced with power-based exercises. As an example, start with low-level plyometric exercises and master them before progressing to more demanding exercises.

- Power exercises are meant primarily for physically mature athletes. Prepubescent swimmers can easily handle low-level plyometric exercises, such as jumping rope and skipping, but swimmers should avoid moderate- and high-intensity exercises until they have gone through puberty, and even then they should do those exercises with caution.

You should be aware of these issues concerning performance when building power:

- Each repetition should be an all-out effort. Perform the exercises at 100 percent intensity, working to get the most out of each repetition and each set.

- Perform the exercises as rapidly as possible to train the neuromuscular system to produce force quickly and efficiently. As an example, when doing lower-body plyometric exercises (described in the next section), minimize the amount of time your feet are in contact with the ground.

- Endurance training focuses on doing several sets that include many repetitions, but when training for power, you should do three to five sets, each containing 3 to 10 repetitions, to maximize gains.

- When trying to maximize your power, use loads that are 30 to 60 percent of the maximum load you could lift one time. In other words, the loads should seem fairly light. But remember, the emphasis is on performing these movements quickly. The body cannot move heavy loads fast.

- Use power exercises sparingly early in the season; these should make up an increasingly greater part of your training as you move closer to your competitive season (see chapters 10 and 11 for more information).

- Do power exercises two times per week. But if you do some form of strength training every day, you can increase the frequency to three times per week; make sure to allow adequate recovery time between training sessions.

- Make the exercises as swimming specific as possible. Many of the exercises presented in this chapter are full-body exercises that involve the legs, arms, and core—just as in swimming. Many also involve some degree of rotation and others are actually performed in the water.
- Add variety. There are several exercises you can use to build power. Use them to keep your training interesting and new.

At USC we believe that swimmers should schedule the strength and conditioning sessions as separate and distinct training sessions rather than perform them before or after intense pool training sessions. However, following a dryland session with a brief, 30- to 45-minute pool session is valuable for developing neuromuscular adaptations that occur with strength and power training. We even incorporate some in-water power training during this time. It is likely that body composition and body density will change as the result of a progressive strength and conditioning program. If there is not an accompanying increase in efficiency, this increased density has the potential to negatively affect performance rather than enhance it. This is why maintaining technique is so important to the overall success of swimmers, and we've found that when our swimmers are able to follow a power training session with a 45-minute session in the water, they are able to enhance their efficiency and consolidate the strength gains made in the weight room.

Power gives you an edge in competition, as demonstrated here by Natalie Coughlin.

# PLYOMETRICS AND POWER DEVELOPMENT

Plyometrics is a category of exercises commonly used for building explosive power in athletes. The word literally means "greater measure," and you can expect to see marked improvements in your strength and power when you include these types of exercises in your training plan. The idea behind plyometrics is that you ask the muscles to contract while lengthening (an eccentric contraction) to decelerate a movement and then quickly shorten (a concentric contraction) to produce another movement, usually in the opposite direction. For example, when running, many of your leg muscles contract eccentrically each time your foot hits the ground. This lengthening contraction helps absorb the shock of impact and, as you'll see, actually stores energy in the muscles that are lengthening. These same muscles then contract concentrically and shorten to propel you into your next stride.

Plyometrics takes advantage of two of muscle's unique properties that can be used in enhancing explosiveness. Muscle is elastic, much like a rubber band. When it is stretched or lengthened during an eccentric contraction, it stores energy. This energy can then be returned when it shortens to produce a greater amount of force than the muscle could normally.

The muscle has a stretch reflex. When activated, the stretch reflex can put additional force and power into a movement. You likely know what the stretch reflex is already. When you go to the doctor for a physical exam, he or she checks the stretch reflex by tapping on your knee with a rubber hammer. The tap with the hammer causes the quadriceps muscle and tendon to lengthen rapidly. This in turn tells the quadriceps muscle to contract, causing the knee to extend.

When muscles in the body are stretched rapidly, as the leg muscles are when pushing off the wall or the core muscles are when rotating in freestyle or backstroke, it is possible to tap into the extra force these two mechanisms provide.

## EXPERIMENT WITH ENERGY STORAGE

To prove to yourself that muscles can store energy when stretched, perform a simple experiment by doing two vertical jumps. On the first jump, get into your starting position with the knees and hips bent. Hold this position for several seconds and then execute your jump, measuring the height. On the second jump, perform what is called a countermovement before you jump. From a standing position, drop your body's center of mass toward the ground by bending the hips and knees slightly. Now, instead of stopping in the down position, immediately explode upward into your jump. You likely will jump 1 to 2 inches (about 2 to 5 cm) higher on the second jump than on the first. Is this because your muscles were stronger on the second jump? No. It's because you stored energy in the leg muscles as you performed your countermovement, and it helped you to jump higher.

# Guidelines for Performing Plyometric Exercises

As you have likely already gathered from the points mentioned previously, the key to performing plyometric exercises correctly is to do them quickly, minimizing the amount of time between the muscle lengthening and the subsequent concentric contraction. When a muscle is stretched and then immediately forced to contract, very little of the stored energy is lost. However, if you wait to use the stored energy, it will be lost and converted to heat. After as little as one second, as much as 50 percent of the stored energy is lost. Performing these exercises with an emphasis on speed and quickness also trains the body's neuromuscular system to produce force rapidly. When doing lower-body plyometric exercises, this means minimizing the amount of time the foot is in contact with the ground. For upper-body exercises, it means minimizing the amount of time you are in contact with the medicine ball or weight.

Plyometric exercises come in various levels of intensity, and it is important to progress from low- to moderate-level and then high-intensity exercises. These exercises can place your joints under a great deal of stress, and you need to build into them gradually. It has been recommended that you be able to squat two times your body weight and bench press one time your body weight before engaging in high-level plyometric exercises for the legs and upper body, respectively.

For safety, perform any lower-body plyometric exercises on a soft surface, such as grass, a hardwood basketball court, or rubberized flooring instead of concrete or asphalt. This will reduce the stress placed on the legs. You also should not perform these exercises on the pool deck (if there is water on it) or any other slippery surface. Many of these exercises involve jumping, and taking this precaution will reduce the risk of slipping and falling. Build into things gradually and emphasize quality over quantity. Keep in mind that these are power-based exercises, and you do not need to do a large number of repetitions to see an effect.

The following pages show examples of low-, moderate-, and high-intensity plyometric exercises that you can use to help your performance in the water. A variety of exercises are presented, and you should not use all of these as part of a single training session. Instead, use these to add variety to your training and to target various areas of the body. Unless otherwise stated, you should perform two or three sets of these exercises, completing 6 to 10 repetitions in each set.

# LOW-INTENSITY PLYOMETRIC EXERCISES

## Jumping Rope

**Focus:** Develop lower-body power as well as full-body coordination.

Jumping rope is a great low-level plyometric exercise, and there are many variations you can use to spruce up your jump rope routine (such as single-leg jumps and crossovers). Ease into a jump rope program gradually, starting with only 100 jumps your first few times, and build from there.

## Skipping

**Focus:** Develop single-leg explosiveness. Skipping is a low-level plyometric exercise that can build explosive leg strength.

### Procedure

1. From a standing position, bend the left knee and raise the right arm while pushing off the ground with the right foot.
2. Land on the left foot and take a small hop on that foot before pushing off for the next skip.
3. Alternate landing on the right and left feet. With experience and strength, you can try to get as high as possible off the ground with each skip.

## Lateral Line Hop

**Focus:** Develop strength and power in the legs and core.

### Procedure

1. Draw a line on the floor and stand to the left of the line.
2. From an athletic position (feet shoulder-width apart, knees and hips slightly bent, chest up and facing forward), jump over the line with both feet landing 12 to 18 inches (30 to 45 cm) to the right.
3. When you land, minimize the ground contact time and quickly jump back across the line to the starting position.

**Variation:** Start on your left foot and jump over the line so you land only on your right foot. Alternate landing on the left and right feet as you jump over the line.

## Standing Broad Jump

**Focus:** Develop lower-body explosiveness for starts and for coming off the wall after a turn.

**Procedure**

1. Draw a line on the ground to serve as the starting position.
2. Starting with your toes touching the line, bend the hips and knees slightly (your countermovement) and then swing the arms and jump as far forward as you can. It is best to land on a soft surface such as sand or grass.

## 90-Degree Jump Turn 

**Focus:** Build lower-body strength while also incorporating rotation.

**Procedure**

1. From an athletic position, jump in the air and rotate the body 90 degrees to the right before you land again.
2. When you touch down, immediately jump up and rotate 90 degrees back to the left. Use the core muscles, not the legs, to initiate the rotation.

# Seated Medicine Ball Twist

**Focus:** Develop rotational power in the core.

**Procedure**

1. While in a seated position, hold a 3- to 5-kilogram medicine ball in both hands.
2. Extend the arms so they are straight in front of you and rotate your torso to the left so the medicine ball touches the ground to the left of your body.
3. Immediately rotate to the right and touch the ball to the ground on your right side.
4. Repeat this movement as rapidly as you can for 15 to 20 seconds.

**Variation:** Make the exercise more difficult and challenging for the core by lifting the feet off the ground.

# Shoulder Pullover

**Focus:** Develop power in the shoulders and pectoral muscles that are used when pulling.

**Procedure**

1. Lie on your back with the knees bent and both feet on the ground.
2. With the arms extended, hold a small (2- to 3-kilogram) medicine ball above your head.
3. While keeping the arms slightly bent and without lifting the body, throw the ball to a partner standing at your feet, as in a soccer throw-in.
4. Catch the medicine ball when your partner throws it back to you and repeat the throw almost immediately.

**Variation:** Make the exercise more difficult by having your partner stand farther away.

# MODERATE-INTENSITY PLYOMETRIC EXERCISES

## Bounding

**Focus:** Build power in the lower body by doing long-stride running.

**Procedure**

1. From a standing position, start by jumping upward and outward using your left leg. Try to bound as far as you can.
2. Land on your right foot and immediately jump off your right foot. Try to minimize contact time with the ground.
3. Continue in this way, alternating legs, until you perform 6 to 10 bounds with each leg.

## Streamline Jump

**Focus:** Develop explosive power in the legs.

### Procedure

1. Start by standing in a streamlined position with the arms overhead and squeezed tightly over your ears.
2. Flex the hips and knees slightly and explode upward into a streamlined vertical jump.
3. Land with the hips and knees slightly flexed and repeat the jump, performing 6 to 10 jumps in total.

**Variation:** If you have access to a basketball court, you can perform these jumps while trying to touch the backboard.

## 180-Degree Jump Turn

**Focus:** Build lower-body strength and power while generating and controlling rotation.

### Procedure

1. From an athletic position, jump in the air and rotate the body 180 degrees before you land again. Use the core muscles, not the legs, to initiate the rotation.
2. When you touch down, immediately jump up and rotate back in the other direction.
3. Perform a total of 10 to 12 jumps in this way.

# Figure-Eight Medicine Ball Pass and Throw

**Focus:**   Develop rotational power through the muscles of the core. This exercise is similar to the medicine ball rotational pass, except it requires an additional degree of rotation as the ball is passed in a figure-eight pattern instead of in a circle.

## Procedure

1. Stand back to back about 2 to 3 feet (0.6 to 1 m) from a partner.
2. Holding a 3- to 5-kilogram medicine ball, your partner rotates to the right to pass the ball to you.
3. You simultaneously rotate to the right to receive the pass.
4. Both partners then rotate left to pass the ball.
5. Continue in this way for 10 to 15 seconds.
6. Rest and repeat the exercise, passing the ball in the opposite direction.

**Variation:**   Stand 4 to 6 feet (1.2 to 2 m) apart and throw the medicine ball to each other instead of handing it off.

# Plyometric Sit-Up

**Focus:** Develop upper-body and abdominal strength while also building core stability.

**Procedure**

1. Get into a sit-up position with both feet on the ground.
2. Lift the shoulders and upper body off the ground.
3. A teammate tosses a 2- to 3-kilogram medicine ball toward your chest.
4. Catch the ball and decelerate it into your chest as you simultaneously lower your shoulders toward the ground.
5. Explosively perform a sit-up with a chest pass, throwing the ball back to your partner.
6. Perform 10 to 15 repetitions.

# Plyometric Leg Lift

**Focus:** This exercise develops power in the lower abdominal muscles.

**Procedure**

1. Lie on your back with a partner standing at your head.
2. Grab onto your partner's legs with your hands for stability and lift your legs off the floor.
3. The partner pushes your legs back toward the floor.
4. Decelerate the movement as quickly as possible and lift the legs again.
5. Perform 6 to 10 repetitions.

## Explosive Wall Chest Pass

**Focus:** Develop upper-body power and explosiveness in the chest muscles.

**Procedure**

1. Holding a 3- to 5-kilogram medicine ball at chest level, stand about 6 feet (2 m) away from a concrete wall or other rigid surface.
2. Rapidly extend the arms and throw the ball into the wall.
3. Catch the ball off the rebound and immediately throw it again.
4. Perform 10 to 12 repetitions.

---

# HIGH-INTENSITY PLYOMETRICS

## Explosive Rotational Throw

**Focus:** This exercise builds leg and rotational power throughout the torso.

**Procedure**

1. Stand 4 to 6 feet (1.2 to 2 m) away from a concrete wall and hold a 3- to 5-kilogram medicine ball in your hands.
2. Standing with your body perpendicular to the wall and with your left shoulder closest to the wall, load the legs and rotate the torso to the right as you prepare to throw the ball.
3. Explode with the legs and the core as you throw the medicine ball into the wall.
4. Catch the medicine ball on the rebound and immediately load the legs and rotate the torso to get set for another repetition.
5. Perform 8 to 12 repetitions from the right side and an additional 8 to 12 repetitions from the left side.

# Medicine Ball Squat With Chest Throw

**Focus:** Develop lower-body power and use of the kinetic chain.

**Procedure**

1. Starting in a standing position, hold a 3- to 5-kilogram medicine ball at chest level.
2. Drop into a deep squat and immediately explode upward, performing a chest throw that launches the ball straight up in the air.
3. Land in a balanced position with the weight on the balls of the feet and the knees and hips slightly flexed.
4. Let the ball bounce once; as you catch the ball, immediately drop into a squat position and repeat the movement.
5. Perform 6 to 12 repetitions.

# Medicine Ball Squat Jump

**Focus:** Build explosive leg power for great starts and turns.

**Procedure**

1. Holding a 3- to 5-kilogram medicine ball behind your head, drop into a full squat position.
2. Explode upward, jumping off the ground.
3. Land with the knees and hips slightly bent and drop immediately into another squat.
4. Perform 6 to 12 repetitions.

# 360-Degree Jump Turn

**Focus:** Build lower-body strength and power while generating and controlling rotation.

**Procedure**

1. From an athletic position, jump in the air and rotate the body 360 degrees before you land again. Use the core muscles, not the legs, to initiate the rotation.
2. When you touch down, immediately jump up and rotate back in the other direction.

# Power Drop

**Focus:** Build explosiveness in the muscles of the chest.

**Procedure**

1. Lie on your back with your arms extended toward the ceiling. A partner stands over you holding a 2- to 3-kilogram medicine ball.

2. When your partner drops the ball toward your chest, catch it, decelerate the ball as you bend the elbows and bring them closer to your chest, and then quickly throw it back to your partner.

# External Rotator Catch and Toss

**Focus:** This exercise requires a partner. It strengthens the muscles of the upper back and rotator cuff.

**Procedure**

1. From a kneeling position, bend the elbow 90 degrees and lift the upper arm so it is parallel to the ground. Your fingers should point to the sky.

2. Your partner stands several feet behind you and throws a small medicine ball (0.5 to 1 kg) over your shoulder for you to catch.

3. In one movement, catch the ball, decelerate the movement, and throw it back to your partner. The only motion should be internal and external rotation of the shoulder, and the upper arm should not move as you catch and return the ball.

# Plyometric 90/90 Ball Drop ⊙ DVD

**Focus:** Improve the strength of the external rotators and scapular stabilizers.

**Procedure**

1. Lie facedown on an exercise ball, bending the elbow 90 degrees and lifting the arm to your side.
2. Hold a small (0.5 to 1 kg) medicine ball in your hand.
3. Drop and quickly catch the ball, maintaining an elbow bend of 90 degrees and keeping the upper arm in a constant position.
4. Repeat this motion as quickly as possible for 30 seconds.
5. Perform two or three sets with each arm in this way, resting 15 seconds between each set.

**Variation:** Perform this exercise while lying on the edge of the pool or on a tabletop.

# Overhead Medicine Ball Throw

**Focus:** This exercise builds power and stability in the shoulder and upper-back muscles.

**Procedure**

1. Stand approximately 2 feet (0.6 m) away from a concrete wall or other rigid surface.
2. With the arms straight, hold a 2- to 3-kilogram medicine ball over your head.
3. Pound the medicine ball into the wall as hard as you can.
4. Catch the ball on the rebound, decelerate the motion, and throw the ball back into the wall again.
5. Continue this pattern for 15 seconds.

# IN-WATER SWIMMING-SPECIFIC POWER EXERCISES

Many of the exercises described so far are dryland exercises, but you can do exercises and drills in the water to improve your swimming power.

**Swimming Against Resistance** Swimming against extra resistance provides the benefit of training for power in the pool. This allows you to use proper stroke mechanics while maintaining a feel for the water. There are many ways you can add resistance to your swimming. We use the following methods in our training programs:

• *Elastic tubing.* Attach one end of a 10-yard-long piece of elastic tubing to your waist and attach the other end to the end of the pool or starting blocks. Push off the wall and swim as you normally would. Eventually you will get to a point where you cannot stretch the cord any farther. When you reach that point, swim in place for 15 to 30 seconds and allow yourself at least 1 minute of rest between efforts. Work on trying to develop more stroking and kicking power while improving your efficiency to stretch the cord as far as possible.

• *Pulling buckets or parachutes behind you.* It is easy to tether a bucket to the end of a rope that is tied to your waist. The water caught in the bucket or parachute will add to the resistance you must overcome, increasing your need to develop greater propulsive force. We use swimming parachutes since they allow swimmers to vary the amount of resistance (drag). It is also possible to replicate the added resistance provided by a parachute by tying a rope to a small bucket and securing the other end around your waist. One of the most important aspects of resistance training using a bucket or parachute in the water is that it is specific to swimming and will enhance swimming strength. In contrast, most weight room work enhances foundational strength.

• *Vertical resistance work.* You can use vertical kicking sets for developing power by holding a small medicine ball above your head. Additional information on vertical kicking can be found in chapter 3 (page 58).

• *Power rack.* Many clubs have access to a power rack, which is a weight stack that can be tethered to a belt placed around your waist. As you swim down the pool, you lift the weight stack.

Any of these approaches allow you to develop power while using proper stroking mechanics and maintaining your feel for the water. Coaches can be innovative when creating resistance sets. The only guidelines we insist on are that the training should be safe and should not negatively affect your stroke technique. For example, we tend not to use devices such as weight belts while swimming, since the downward force tends to upset balance in the water and consequently has a negative effect on technique.

## MAKING IN-WATER RESISTANCE TRAINING FUN

Strength training is usually an individual activity, but you can introduce competition and make it into a fun team event. One of the strength activities we do is swimming tug-of-war races. In this drill, two swimmers are connected by a 10-yard length of elastic tubing. The swimmers wear belts around their waists that the elastic tubing is connected to. The swimmers both start in the middle of the pool; on the coach's signal, they square off against each other in a race to opposite ends of the pool. At some point, each swimmer will pull against the resistance produced by the swimmer racing in the opposite direction. This tug-of-war continues until one swimmer reaches the wall or a 30-second time limit is reached, whichever occurs first.

Another strength activity is swim brick races. On the coach's command, two swimmers start at opposite ends of the pool and race to a pair of swim bricks, or other weights, placed on the bottom of the middle of the pool. They dive for the swim bricks and then kick back to the wall where they started. The swimmers lie on their backs while holding the swim bricks on their chests. You can make this exercise more challenging by tethering each swimmer to the wall using elastic tubing or having them swim to the brick while towing a swim parachute.

**Assisted Swimming**  Swimming against resistance makes sense when it comes to developing strength and power, but how does swimming with assistance help develop power? It works on developing speed and getting the body accustomed to the feel of swimming fast. Swimming with assistance trains the neuromuscular system for race-pace performances. The easiest way to perform assisted swimming is to attach a long piece of elastic tubing to one end of the pool and the other to your waist. Pull yourself or swim to the other end of the pool, let go, and allow the band to pull you along as you swim. It helps if you have a partner to remove the tubing from the pool and pick up the slack as you swim. Swim the way you want to in your race, using the proper stroke rate while maintaining correct technique.

**Kicking With Fins**  While this was discussed briefly in chapter 3, it is important to readdress this topic here since kicking with fins can develop lower-body power. Kick all out for 15- to 30-second intervals with a 1:2 or a 1:3 work-to-rest ratio. So if you kick for 15 seconds, take 30 to 45 seconds of rest before starting your next interval.

**Using a Swim Bench or Swim Ergometer**  Several companies make swim benches, or pieces of equipment that allow you to mimic your strokes on dry land while pulling against resistance. Some swim benches allow you to set a resistance you pull against, whereas others (such as Vasa Trainer) involve using your body weight to create the resistance as you pull yourself up an incline. These machines give you an opportunity to build strength while maintaining perfect technique. It is important to maintain your stroke technique when doing intervals on the swim bench. Train for 15- to 30-second intervals and allow two or three times as much rest between sets. If you partner with another swimmer, you can alternate and get your rest while the other person swims. Swim benches can be found on deck at many swim clubs.

**Dryland Swimming**   You can also build strength on dry land by pulling against elastic tubing looped through a fence. Grab one end of the tubing in each hand and start by performing several pulling sets of 30 seconds and build up to several minutes of continuous exercise.

When doing any of these exercises, keep in mind that you should try to mimic the stroke you will race with. This means maintaining the appropriate stroke rate to engrain the proper neuromuscular patterns. It can be tempting to slow your stroke to generate more force with each pull, but your goal is to improve efficiency. To do that, you need to swim at the proper rate.

Additionally, be sure to look at swimming against resistance as you would any other training exercise. It can be tempting to think that swimming against added resistance all the time will produce even greater benefits than normal swimming. Our thoughts are to use everything in moderation. No matter how hard you try to prevent it, swimming against added resistance will alter your stroke mechanics. Doing brief bouts of these exercises can build strength. However, doing these exercises in large doses can lead to stroke alterations and the development of bad habits in technique.

# ADVANCED POWER TRAINING: MODIFIED OLYMPIC LIFT

Olympic lifts, like the snatch and the clean and jerk, are a class of exercises that are used in Olympic weightlifting competitions. These are multijoint exercises that build strength and full-body explosive power. Because of the technical expertise required in performing these exercises correctly, they are difficult to describe in a book format. However, on the DVD we present several modified Olympic lifts that will help you to develop your power and explosiveness. The advanced power exercises on the DVD are the hang clean, the high pull, and the push press.

# Chapter 7

# Enhancing Flexibility for Better Strokes

**M**uscular function is based on a balance between strength and flexibility. Muscular strength is important, but the ability to produce force through a full range of motion is what allows you to become truly proficient in the water. You ask your body to do some pretty amazing things in the pool—just think about the range of motion the shoulder must go through in the butterfly or the ankle flexibility you need in order to produce an efficient freestyle kick. Flexibility training is just as important to your performance as strength training. Not many people think of stretching as *training*, but that is exactly how you need to approach it. If you make stretching an integral part of your overall training program, you will start to see results.

Let's say you start a full-body stretching program and because of your improved flexibility you are able to add an inch (about 2.5 cm) to every stroke you take in freestyle. If nothing else changes, you will gain approximately *2 feet* (0.6 m) every 50 meters you swim. This can equate to precious tenths of seconds that could be the difference between finishing first and finishing second, making the final heat and swimming in the consolation heat, or making the cut and not making the cut. In addition to improving performance, adequate flexibility can prevent injuries throughout the body. This is especially true for several key areas where swimmers tend to exhibit deficits in flexibility, which are addressed later in this chapter.

# TYPES OF FLEXIBILITY

Flexibility relates to the elasticity, or stretchiness, of the joints and other structures that surround the joints. Two kinds of flexibility are important to swimmers:

1. *Static flexibility* is the range of motion measured at a joint while maintaining a stationary position. In other words, there is no movement. Most athletes are familiar with static stretching, which typically involves stretching a muscle or muscle group and holding that position for 20 to 30 seconds.

2. *Dynamic flexibility* is flexibility with movement and can be thought of as the range of motion that's available to you while you're actually swimming.

**PERFORMANCE TIP**

Pilates and yoga are two great ways to improve flexibility. In addition, these programs build strength and core stability as well as coordination of muscle groups throughout the body.

Which is more important to a swimmer? While it might seem that dynamic flexibility is the more important component, regular static stretching is also a necessary first step toward developing great dynamic flexibility and improving your swimming performance.

# BENEFITS OF FLEXIBILITY

So, why should you make static stretching a part of your training plan? There are a number of compelling reasons:

• *Stretching can maintain or increase joint range of motion, allowing for longer and more efficient strokes.* When muscles are used frequently, they can lose elasticity and develop tightness. Over time, stiffness can continue to increase and, if not addressed, will limit joint range of motion and compromise function.

What's it like when joint range of motion is limited? Think of a dog chained to a fence when suddenly a cat walks by. The dog takes off after the cat, quickly using up more and more of the leash. Eventually the dog reaches the end of the leash—the end of his range of motion—and comes to a violent stop. The dog may not get hurt doing this one time, but doing this repeatedly can result in injury because of how the stresses are distributed through the body at the time of impact. When flexibility is limited and a joint reaches the end range of motion, larger-than-normal forces can be generated as well, which over time can lead to injury.

• *Stretching improves a muscle's ability to generate force and allows for greater force production through a full range of motion.* Good flexibility means you will be able to generate more force throughout your entire stroke cycle.

• *Stretching improves circulation to your muscles.* The increased blood flow that occurs after stretching can speed up the recovery process after a workout or a meet.

• *Stretching improves posture both in and out of the water.* Tight muscles can lead to postural changes that place stress on various parts of the body. When you picture a swimmer, you likely think of someone whose shoulders are rolled forward. While some of these postural changes can be due to muscular weakness, many of them are due to tightness in the chest and shoulder muscles. Additionally, poor flexibility in the hip flexors in the front of your pelvis can place added stress on the lower back.

• *Regular stretching can help you overcome some of the bad habits you engage in throughout the day.* Sitting for long periods, something you might do at work, can lead to muscular tightness throughout the lower body and back. You've probably felt this stiffness when standing up and walking after a long car ride. If you have a desk job or spend long periods sitting, this tightening happens day after day, and your joint range of motion eventually becomes limited to the point that it causes pain or places restrictions on what you can do in the water. Regular flexibility training can negate this effect.

• *Stretching promotes relaxation.* Who can't use more of that?

Keep in mind that while flexibility is important, swimmers will progress through periods of relative inflexibility as they develop. As children hit their growth spurts, for example, the bones actually grow faster than the muscles,

Flexibility is necessary for achieving full range of motion and developing efficiency as well as proper technique.

Icon Sports Media

and it is not uncommon for swimmers to go through a period of inflexibility. Additional stretching may be needed during this time to improve, or even maintain, range of motion. Also, males tend to be less flexible than females, and older swimmers tend to have greater challenges in flexibility than younger swimmers. In any of these situations, it is important to place an additional emphasis on flexibility training.

Taking all of this into account, you would think that stretching would be a part of every swimmer's training program. But unfortunately, it is not; flexibility is probably the most overlooked component of an effective conditioning program. Swimmers will complain that they don't have the time or it takes too long and they don't want to take time away from their swimming. However, you need to realize that regular stretching is an important part of your comprehensive training plan. And we're not just talking about stretching only when your muscles feel tight after a hard set. You should do flexibility training every day. If you start stretching regularly, you will feel better both in and out of the water.

## STRETCHING GUIDELINES

The following are a few guiding principles that relate to flexibility training. By following these guidelines, you will be amazed at how quickly your flexibility can improve.

**You should stretch at the end of your practice, not before.**   Let that sink in a minute before we move on. Most athletes stretch before practice, but there are several reasons why stretching after you swim is advantageous.

Muscles are most pliable when they are warm, making the end of practice an ideal time to work on flexibility training. In addition, static stretching before a practice or event can actually impair a muscle's ability to generate peak forces and power for as long as an hour after the stretch is performed. In a sport like swimming, which requires virtually all the muscles in the body to produce force and power, static stretching before a workout has the potential to limit performance. While the research on this topic has not been done on swimmers specifically, there is no reason to believe a swimmer's muscles function any differently than the muscles of athletes competing in other sports.

Please don't misinterpret this message. Static stretching is still very important for you as a swimmer. You should just do it at the end of a practice or after your cool-down from a race.

As an alternative, perform your stretching throughout the day or in the evenings. While the muscles may not be warm at this time, you can still improve your flexibility. If you still think you need to stretch before your swim, make sure there is at least one hour between your stretching session and the start of your race or practice.

**Perform each stretch two or three times and hold each stretch for 20 to 30 seconds.**   This will produce the greatest gains in flexibility. Holding the stretch for a longer time does not seem to produce any additional benefits.

**Make stretching a regular part of your routine.**   Flexibility does not improve overnight, and making a change requires making flexibility training a part of your daily routine. Try to devote 10 to 15 minutes every day to stretching. A single stretching session can improve flexibility for up to 90 minutes, but you are looking for long-term flexibility gains, and that comes with time.

**Stretch both sides of your body.**   Unlike some sports, swimming is a bilateral activity, so it is important to stretch the muscles on both sides of the body.

**Stretch within your limits.**   Do not try to do too much or stretch a muscle group too vigorously. Enter the stretch gradually and go only to the point that you feel a slight to moderate level of tension. Continue to breathe deeply and normally throughout the stretch—do not hold your breath. You may find you can go a little deeper into the stretch each time you exhale.

**Stretching should never be painful.**   You should feel tension in the stretched muscle, but it should never hurt. If you do feel pain, *stop* the stretch.

> **PERFORMANCE TIP**
>
> Avoid bouncing when you stretch, because this creates large forces in the muscles that could lead to injury.

## STRETCHES FOR SWIMMERS

There are more than 600 muscles in the body. If you are creative, you can find stretches for most of them. With that said, swimmers typically have a limited amount of time to devote to stretching, so it's important to make every stretch count. The stretches presented in the following pages target areas of the body that often become tight in swimmers or are important for swimming performance. You can do all of these stretches on the pool deck or at home—and you can actually do some in the pool.

# Hip Flexor Stretch 💿 📀

**Focus:** Improve flexibility in the hip flexors in the front of the hip. Flexibility in the hip flexors is important for maintaining a good body posture in the water, particularly in the breaststroke as the feet are drawn up toward the buttocks.

**Procedure**

1. Start this stretch in a lunge position, with the right foot forward and the left knee on the ground.

2. Maintaining good posture with the upper body upright, gradually move the body's center of mass forward and downward so the hips drop slightly toward the floor. You will feel a stretch in the front of the left hip. Place a towel under the knee for comfort, if necessary.

## PERFORMANCE TIP

Poor flexibility in the hip flexors (found in the front of your hips) can lead to added stress on the lower back, possibly contributing to low back pain or injury.

# Calf Stretch

**Focus:** Improve flexibility in the two muscles in the back of the calf. As you gain flexibility in these muscles, you will see your kicking efficiency improve. While the calf stretch can be performed many ways, the method presented here consistently elicits a deep stretch.

## Procedure

1. Start the stretch in a pike position, contacting the ground with your hands and toes.
2. Keeping your legs straight, unweight one foot and use your body weight to press the opposite heel toward the ground *(a)*.
3. Bend the knee slightly; you should feel the stretch move into the second muscle deeper in the calf *(b)*.
4. Repeat by stretching the muscles in the other leg.

**Variation:** You can stretch both legs at the same time by simply keeping the legs straight and pressing both heels toward the ground.

## Ankle Stretch 🔘 📀

**Focus:** Improve the flexibility in the muscles in the front of the calf. This stretch will improve kicking efficiency by allowing you to point your toes and create a much more effective foot surface to kick against.

**Procedure**

1. From a standing position, place the top of your left foot on the floor slightly behind your body—you should feel the pressure on the top of your foot just above your toes. Your leg will have to rotate inward slightly to get into this position, and that is fine; in fact, you want that.

2. Gently transfer some of your body weight to the left foot. You will feel the stretch in the front and outside of the calf.

## Hip Adductor Stretch

**Focus:** Increase flexibility in the muscles of the inner thigh. This is important for executing a strong breaststroke kick and maintaining strength and range of motion throughout the hip.

**Procedure**

1. Stand on both feet and separate the legs so your feet are wider than shoulder-width apart. Both feet should face forward.

2. Keeping both feet on the ground, gradually bend the left knee and shift your body weight to the left. As you do this, your hips will drop slightly toward the floor and you should start to feel a stretch through the inner part of the right thigh.

# Figure-Four Stretch

**Focus:** Improve the external rotation of the hip by stretching the piriformis muscle. Having good range of motion in the hip is essential for being able to execute an efficient breaststroke kick while also maintaining a good body position in the water.

## Procedure

1. Lie on your back and cross the right ankle over the left knee. The left knee can be bent 90 degrees. However, to stretch the hamstrings of the left leg simultaneously, keep the leg straight. Your legs will look like the number 4.

2. Grab behind the left knee with both hands and pull it toward your chest. You will feel a stretch deep in the right hip.

# Hamstring Stretch

**Focus:** Improve the flexibility of the hamstring muscles and the gastrocnemius muscle in the calf.

## Procedure

1. Lie on your back and loop a towel around your left foot.

2. Keeping the left leg straight and the right leg on the floor, pull the towel to bring the thigh closer to your body. You should feel a stretch in the back of the thigh.

## Standing Quadriceps Stretch

**Focus:** Stretch the quadriceps muscle and hip flexors in the front of the thigh.

### Procedure

1. Stand on the left leg, bend your right knee, and grasp the right foot with your right hand.

2. Maintaining good posture, pull the foot toward your buttocks. By grabbing the foot and not the ankle when you pull, you will also stretch the muscles in the front of the calf.

3. One of the quadriceps muscles also flexes the hip, and you can stretch this a bit more by extending the hip and allowing the knee to move backward slightly.

## Seated Groin Stretch

**Focus:** Improve the flexibility of the groin and inner-thigh muscles. This stretch is especially helpful for the breaststroke kick.

### Procedure

1. Sit on the pool deck with the soles of your feet together in front of you.

2. Grab your toes and place your elbows on your knees.

3. Gently pull the chest toward the feet while simultaneously pushing the knees toward the pool deck with your elbows.

# Knees to Chest Stretch

**Focus:** Improve flexibility in the muscles of the lower back. Lower-back flexibility is important for maintaining body position in the water as well as lower-back health.

## Procedure

1. Lie on your back and bring both knees toward your chest.
2. Grab your knees with both arms and pull them tightly to your chest (*a*). You should feel a moderate stretch in your lower back and gluteal region.

**Variation:** Perform this stretch one leg at a time. To target the right lower back, keep the left leg straight and on the ground while you grasp the right knee with both arms and pull it to your chest (*b*). Repeat, stretching the left leg.

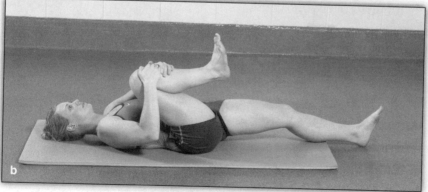

# Spinal Twist

**Focus:** Develop rotational flexibility through the hips and spine.

**Procedure**

1. While in a seated position, extend the left leg.
2. Bend the right knee and place the right foot on the outside of the left knee.
3. Place the left elbow outside the right knee.
4. Maintaining a good upper-body posture, simultaneously rotate the body to the right while pressing the knee to the left. You should feel a stretch in the lower back and torso and also through the hips.
5. Use the right hand to provide balance throughout the stretch.

# Hip Twist

**Focus:** Improve flexibility in the muscles of the hip and lower back.

**Procedure**

1. Lie on your back with your knees bent and feet flat on the pool deck.
2. Place your arms out to the sides to stabilize the upper back or cross your arms over your chest.
3. Place your right ankle across the left knee.
4. While keeping the upper back flat on the ground, use the right leg to pull the left leg toward the pool deck. You should feel a stretch along the outside of your hip or lower back.

# Upper-Back Stretch

**Focus:** Improve flexibility in the latissimus dorsi and upper-back muscles. The muscles of the upper back are engaged every time you execute a pull, and over time they will become tight. The upper-back stretch improves flexibility in these muscles while improving shoulder range of motion and pulling efficiency.

### Procedure

1. Standing near a lifeguard chair or in a doorway, reach out with the right arm and grasp the chair or door frame above shoulder level.

2. Gradually sit back and allow your body weight to stretch the muscles in the upper back.

3. You can modify the focus of the stretch by adjusting where you grab the chair or door frame.

**Variation:** Perform this stretch in the water by grabbing onto a ladder and stretching the muscles in the same way.

# Streamline Stretch

**Focus:** Improve flexibility of the upper-back muscles.

### Procedure

1. Stand in a streamlined position, stretching upward with your hands and squeezing your arms over your ears.

2. Slowly bend at your waist to the right—you should feel a stretch in the muscles in the upper back on your left side.

3. Return to the starting position and slowly bend to the left.

# Triceps Stretch

**Focus:** Improve flexibility in the triceps muscles. These muscles straighten the elbow and are active primarily during the finish of the freestyle, butterfly, and backstroke pulls.

### Procedure

1. From a standing position, grasp the left elbow with the right hand over and behind the head. The left hand should be pointed straight down the center of your back.

2. Push with the right hand, moving the left hand down the spine toward the ground. You should feel a moderate stretch in the back of the left upper arm.

# Chest Stretch

**Focus:** Improve flexibility in the chest muscles, which often become tight in swimmers.

### Procedure

1. Perform this stretch from a standing position by resting your forearm against the pole of the backstroke flags or a door frame with the hand pointed toward the ceiling. The elbow should be at shoulder height.

2. Gently lean your body forward, allowing your body weight to perform the stretch.

3. You should feel the stretch through the front of the shoulder and into the chest.

# STRETCHING AND INJURY PREVENTION

One of the common beliefs about stretching is that it prevents injury. And it can—within reason. Flexibility addresses some of the imbalances seen in swimmers. But recognize that the benefits of stretching come over the long term, not from any single stretching session. Stretching before a practice does not reduce the risk of injury during that practice. What you need to focus on is achieving a normal range of motion around your joints. There is an optimal range of flexibility in which swimmers are at the lowest risk of injury. If you fall outside this normal range because your muscles are extremely tight or because you are hyperflexible, the risk of injury actually increases. Most swimmers need additional flexibility in some areas, but if you already have extremely flexible joints, additional stretching is not recommended.

The following stretches are geared toward injury prevention in the shoulder and are described in detail in chapter 8.

Cross-arm stretch (page 158)

Sleeper stretch (pages 158-159)

Towel stretch (page 159)

## INAPPROPRIATE STRETCH FOR SWIMMERS

It is somewhat strange for a book to specify things swimmers should *not* do. However, one stretch is so ingrained in swimming culture that it is important to highlight it and describe why it can actually be harmful to swimmers—the partner-assisted shoulder stretch. In this stretch, a partner grasps the hands of the swimmer and tries to touch them behind the swimmer's back. Athletes can also perform this without a partner by using a doorway to assist with the stretch. This stretch places a great deal of stress on the structures in the front of the shoulder, and performing it can increase shoulder instability and the risk of developing a shoulder injury. An acceptable alternative is the chest stretch, described on page 144. On the surface, the chest stretch looks much like the shoulder stretch. However, the positioning of

The partner-assisted shoulder stretch shown here is not recommended for swimmers.

the arm focuses the stretch more on the muscles in the chest rather than the structures holding the shoulder together.

# Chapter 8

# Preventing, Coping With, and Returning From Injury

**B**y this point, it should be clear that strength and conditioning can enhance performance. However, strength training is also an integral part of any injury-prevention program. Like it or not, injuries and sports go hand in hand, and swimming is no exception. In fact, it's been estimated that as many as 80 percent of all swimmers will experience an injury at some point during their careers. Even though swimming is a non-weight-bearing, low-impact sport, the repetitive nature of the strokes contributes to overuse injuries as well as flexibility and strength imbalances.

An elite freestyler, for example, may take 20 to 25 stroke cycles every 50 meters. If a swimmer trains 10,000 meters per day, he or she will take 4,000 to 5,000 stroke cycles *every day* (since each stroke cycle equals one pull with each arm, that equates to between 8,000 and 10,000 individual arm strokes). If that same swimmer trains six days a week over the course of a year, each arm will pull more than 1,500,000 times. Is it any wonder overuse injuries occur or that strength and flexibility imbalances develop throughout the body? Although you might not engage in this much training, consider this: Even if you swim three times a week, completing 3,000 meters in each practice session, you will take approximately 250,000 stroke cycles, or half a million individual strokes, over the course of a year. That is a lot of repetitive stress placed on the body, particularly if you do not swim with perfect technique. While any one stroke will not necessarily cause an injury, the damage that builds up over time with each incorrect stroke can easily sideline a swimmer. The good news is that strength training and conditioning can prevent many of the most common injuries seen in swimming.

AP Photo/Chuck Stoody, CP

The repetitive stress placed on a swimmer's body can lead to overuse injuries—the result of small amounts of damage adding up over time.

## TYPES OF INJURIES IN SWIMMING

When you look at the types and numbers of swimming injuries that occur, most are soft-tissue injuries that result from overuse. Here are the most common types of injuries:

- Tendinitis is the inflammation of a tendon, which joins a muscle to a bone. An example is swimmer's shoulder.
- A ligament sprain occurs when a ligament (which joins a bone to a bone) becomes stretched or partially torn. An example is breaststroker's knee.
- Muscle strain or pull occurs when a muscle is pulled or partially torn. An example is lower-back pain.

All of these injuries occur when too much force is applied to the tissue—sometimes from one large force, but more often over time as small amounts of damage build up each time the tissue is stressed. The rest of this chapter examines three specific injuries—swimmer's shoulder, breaststroker's knee, and lower-back pain—and discusses how strength and conditioning can be used as part of an injury-prevention plan.

# Swimmer's Shoulder

The term *swimmer's shoulder* refers to many conditions that result in shoulder pain while swimming. In most instances, however, swimmer's shoulder involves the impingement, or pinching, of one or more of the rotator cuff tendons (most commonly the supraspinatus muscle) or the biceps tendon within the shoulder. Figure 8.1 shows the inner workings of the shoulder. As you look at this figure, you might be struck with the realization that there's not a whole lot of space in the shoulder. Because of this, any abnormality, whether it is improper technique, muscular weakness or inflexibility, or even an overly loose shoulder, can cause the shoulder to move improperly, resulting in a tendon getting pinched between structures.

> **PERFORMANCE TIP**
>
> Of the estimated 80 percent of all swimmers who will experience an injury at some point in their swimming careers, 66 percent of these will experience an injury to the shoulder.

Many of the swimming strokes put the shoulder into what has been called the impingement position, in which the arm is fully extended overhead and the shoulder is internally rotated. (With your right arm extended over your head, rotate your arm so your palm faces to the right.) You likely recognize this as the position of your hand and arm as they enter the water in freestyle, butterfly, and backstroke. Being in this position, especially while trying to produce force at the start of a stroke, increases the chance of impingement. But even with all these things seemingly stacked up against the shoulder, if all the muscles are functioning properly, it is unlikely that impingement will occur just because of how the arm is positioned. Other factors, such as muscular weakness, fatigue, or inflexibility, come into play.

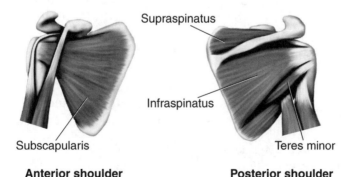

Supraspinatus

Infraspinatus

Subscapularis

Teres minor

**Anterior shoulder**   **Posterior shoulder**

Figure 8.1   The muscles that make up the rotator cuff.

Reprinted from R.S. Behnke, 2006, *Kinetic anatomy*, 2nd ed. (Champaign, IL: Human Kinetics), 50-51.

## Weakness, Fatigue, and Strength Imbalances

Improper technique definitely contributes to shoulder injuries, but so do strength and flexibility imbalances in the shoulder and upper back as well as the core. In swimmers, the muscles that externally rotate the shoulder are often weaker than the muscles that internally rotate the shoulder. This makes sense, since the internal rotators are active and are strengthened with virtually every stroke you take, whether it is the catch and pull in freestyle, butterfly or breaststroke, or the finish in backstroke. The external rotators, on the other hand, do not get strengthened to the same degree when swimming. This is important, because the internal and external rotators form a force couple that helps to stabilize the shoulder. Both muscle groups contract to keep the ball-and-socket joint properly aligned. When the normal force balance is upset in the shoulder, the ball no longer stays centered in the socket and the chance of impingement increases. Additionally, the external rotators tend to fatigue more quickly when this strength imbalance exists. Swimmers need to take deliberate steps to strengthen the external rotators to restore a normal strength balance in the shoulder while also building endurance to allow the shoulder to function properly.

Side-to-side strength imbalances can also develop that place stress on the shoulder. Many swimmers breathe only to one side in freestyle or have one arm that pulls harder or more efficiently than the other. Although it is not known how these imbalances contribute to injury, swimmers who consistently breathe to one side frequently develop an asymmetric stroke that can place increased stress on the shoulders. One way to offset these imbalances is to develop a bilateral breathing pattern when you train.

## Other Muscles Contributing to Shoulder Problems

When shoulder pain occurs, it is natural to assume that the cause of the pain lies in the actual ball-and-socket joint itself. But remember that a weak link, or break in the kinetic chain, can contribute to injuries in other parts of the body. Many times weakness in the muscles of the upper back and chest—the muscles that control how the shoulder blades move—is what contributes most to the shoulder pain. For the ball-and-socket joint to function properly, you need to have excellent strength and control of the muscles that direct the shoulder blades. To get a better sense for how much the shoulder blade moves during arm movements, watch a teammate

> **PERFORMANCE TIP**
>
> When you lift your arm, the first 30 degrees of motion comes primarily from the movement in the shoulder ball-and-socket joint. After that, most of the motion comes from the movement of the shoulder blades. In fact, the shoulder blade contributes 2 degrees of motion for every 1 degree contributed by the ball-and-socket joint.

lift and lower the arms, starting with the arms at the sides and finishing with them in a streamlined position overhead. You should see the shoulder blades move throughout the entire movement, particularly once the arms get above shoulder height. In a healthy shoulder, where the scapular stabilizers are strong, the shoulder blades will stay flush against the torso throughout the movement (see the scapular stabilization test in chapter 1). However, in most swimmers, particularly after muscles become fatigued, you will see the shoulder blades pop off the torso (a phenomenon called *scapular winging*), which signifies weakness in the muscles that control the shoulder blades. When the shoulder blades start moving improperly, injury risk to the shoulder increases.

One scapular stabilizer that deserves special attention is the serratus anterior muscle (figure 8.2). This muscle wraps around the rib cage and is active throughout much of the freestyle stroke cycle. The serratus anterior has been found to fatigue quickly in swimmers with shoulder pain; this is particularly problematic since most traditional exercises do not strengthen this muscle. In the following section are exercises that target this muscle as well as the external rotators in the rotator cuff.

## Injury-Prevention Exercises for the Shoulder

You have many exercise options for protecting the health of the shoulder, and some of them are presented here and in the accompanying DVD. These

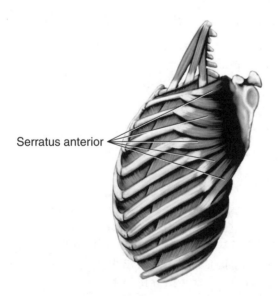

Serratus anterior

**Figure 8.2** The serratus anterior muscle is important in swimming—it attaches to the rib cage and helps control the shoulder blade.

Reprinted from R.S. Behnke, 2006, *Kinetic anatomy*, 2nd ed. (Champaign, IL: Human Kinetics), 132.

exercises target the strength imbalances and areas of weakness most often seen in the shoulders and upper back, and they promote healthy joint function while also strengthening the kinetic chain. Follow some general guidelines when performing these exercises:

- *Use very light weights.* The muscles you are training are pretty small. Using weights that are too heavy will engage other muscles.
- *Focus on building endurance.* Perform two or three sets of 15 to 25 repetitions of each exercise.
- *Control the movement.* It is not a race to see who can perform these the fastest. Use slow, deliberate movements and focus on setting the shoulder blades at the start of each exercise.
- *Develop consistency.* Perform these exercises at least two times per week. Remember, just because you are not injured does not mean the exercises are not important. Injury prevention should be a priority at all times of the year.
- *Maintain proper form.* If you cannot maintain the correct technique, stop the exercise.
- *Avoid pain.* If you have a preexisting injury or any of these exercises cause pain, stop the activity. These exercises should produce a muscle burn, but they should never cause pain.

## Shoulder Blade Pinch: Setting the Shoulder Blades

**Focus:**  Strengthen the scapular stabilizers in the upper back. This is the most basic of the upper-back exercises and serves as the starting point for many of the rotator cuff and upper-back exercises that follow.

### Procedure

1. Loop a piece of elastic tubing around the backstroke flagpole or through a fence, and grab one end with each hand.
2. Step backward so there is a light tension in the band when the arms are fully extended in front of you (a).
3. Without bending your arms, pinch your shoulder blades together (b). To help with this, have a partner place a hand on your upper back; you should try to squeeze the hand with your shoulder blades.
4. Hold this position for a count of 3 before slowly returning to the starting position. The stretch felt in the band is due entirely to the activation of the muscles controlling the shoulder blades.

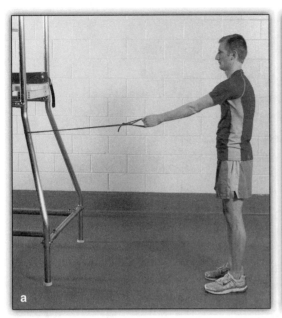
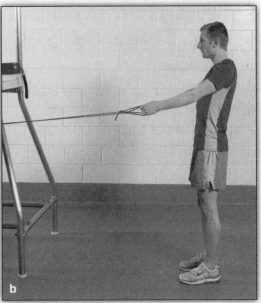

## Shoulder Retraction With External Rotation

**Focus:**   Strengthen the external rotators in the rotator cuff and the muscles in the upper back that control the shoulder blades.

**Procedure**

1. Stand with your arms at your sides and the elbows bent 90 degrees.

2. Grasp each end of an elastic band or tubing in each hand so there is a slight tension on the band when the hands are pointed forward.

3. Pinch the shoulder blades together and rotate the arms outward several inches.

4. Hold this position for a count of 3 and return to the starting position.

5. To activate the appropriate muscles, push the chest forward slightly as you perform the exercise.

## Standing External Rotation

**Focus:** Build strength in the external rotators of the rotator cuff.

**Procedure**

1. Secure a piece of elastic tubing to a fence or the backstroke flagpole.
2. Place a small towel under the left arm and grab the free end of the tubing with the left hand.
3. Stand with your right side closer to the fence and keep the left arm at your side with the elbow bent 90 degrees. The tubing should now come across the body.
4. Step to the left so there is a slight tension on the band at the start of the movement.
5. Set the shoulder blades and slowly rotate the left shoulder until the hand and forearm point away from the body.
6. Hold this position briefly and return to the starting position.
7. Perform the exercise with both arms.

**Variation:** Lie on your right side and hold a small (1 to 2 kg) hand weight. Slowly rotate the shoulder until the fingers of the left hand point toward the sky, and then lower the weight back to the starting position.

## Catch Position External Rotation

**Focus:** Strengthen the rotator cuff muscles that externally rotate the shoulder. This movement is more complicated than the standing external rotation exercise because you are required to stabilize the shoulder and shoulder blades to a greater degree. But this exercise is more swimming specific because it mimics the shoulder motion used in the freestyle and butterfly catch.

**Procedure**

1. Attach a piece of elastic tubing to a fence at waist level.
2. Facing the tubing attachment, point and grab the free end with the left hand.
3. Lift the arm out to the side and bend the elbow 90 degrees *(a)*. There should be a slight tension on the band at the start of the exercise.
4. Set the shoulder blades and rotate the shoulder so the hand and forearm point to the ceiling in the end position *(b)*.

5. Hold this position briefly before returning to the starting position.

6. Repeat the exercise with the right arm.

Note: The upper arm should not move when you perform this exercise correctly.

# Full Can

**Focus:** Strengthen the muscles of the rotator cuff and improve shoulder stability.

**Procedure**

1. Stand on a piece of elastic tubing and grasp each free end with each hand.

2. Set the shoulder blades and point your thumbs toward the sky.

3. Slowly lift the arms out to your sides and slightly forward until they reach shoulder level. Keep the thumbs pointed upward throughout the movement, just as if you were holding a full can and trying not to spill the contents of the can.

4. Slowly lower the arms back to your sides.

Caution: Avoid the empty-can exercise, in which the thumbs are pointed downward through the movement, since this can actually irritate tendons in the shoulder.

## Ball Rotation

**Focus:** Build strength and stability throughout the muscles of the rotator cuff and upper back.

**Procedure**

1. Standing approximately an arm's length away from a wall, hold a tennis ball or a 1-kilogram medicine ball between your hand and the wall.
2. After setting the shoulder blades, slowly roll the ball in small clockwise circles on the wall at a rate of one rotation per second. The arm should remain straight throughout the movement.
3. After 15 to 20 seconds, switch directions and make small counter-clockwise circles.
4. Switch arms and perform three sets with each arm.

## Y Exercise

**Focus:** Strengthen the back of the shoulder and upper-back muscles.

**Procedure**

1. To start the exercise, lie facedown with your arms out to the sides and slightly toward the head; your body should look like a Y when viewed from above.
2. Pinch the shoulder blades together and lift the hands toward the ceiling.
3. Hold this up position for a count of 2 before lowering the hands back to the floor.
4. Start by using only the weight of the arms as the resistance but progress to using light hand weights as you get stronger.

## Chest Punch

**Focus:** Build strength in the serratus anterior muscle that runs around the rib cage and controls the shoulder blades.

**Procedure**

1. Perform this exercise while lying on your back.
2. Hold a moderate-weight (3 to 5 kg) medicine ball in your hands above your chest. Extend the arms away from the body (a).
3. Without bending the arms or lifting the back off the ground, push the medicine ball toward the ceiling (b). Even though the arms are straight, you should still be able to lift the ball several inches toward the ceiling as the shoulder blades move.
4. Hold the up position for a count of 2 and slowly return to the starting position.

**Variation:** Perform this exercise while using a slightly lighter weight or medicine ball.

# Upper-Body Step-Up

**Focus:** Improve strength in the serratus anterior muscle that runs around the rib cage and controls the shoulder blades.

## Procedure

1. While on your hands and knees, position your body alongside a 6- to 8-inch (15 to 20 cm) step.

2. Place the right hand up on the step and press up with the right shoulder as you bring the left hand up onto the step.

3. With both hands on the step, arch your back like a cat, pushing the upper back toward the ceiling.

4. Return the left hand and then the right hand back to the floor.

5. Keep the arms straight throughout the movement and perform the exercise to the left as well.

### Injury-Prevention Stretches for the Shoulder

Flexibility imbalances can also be seen in the shoulders of many swimmers, particularly in the direction of internal rotation. Nonathletes commonly have 70 degrees of internal rotation at the shoulder, but research conducted on a group of collegiate swimmers showed they averaged only 49 degrees of internal rotation—a loss of more than 20 degrees. In other sports such as tennis, similar internal rotation deficits develop over time and are linked to an increased risk of injury. It is reasonable to assume that deficits in internal rotation flexibility will continue to worsen in swimmers unless flexibility training is used in improving range of motion.

Three stretches that maintain or enhance internal rotation are the cross-arm stretch, the sleeper stretch, and the towel stretch. When performing these stretches, follow the stretching guidelines first mentioned in chapter 7:

- Perform these stretches at the end of a practice.
- Perform each stretch two or three times with each arm.
- Hold each stretch for 20 to 30 seconds.

## Cross-Arm Stretch

**Focus:**   Stretch the upper-back muscles and the posterior shoulder.

**Procedure**

1. In a standing position, hold your right arm straight out in front of you.
2. Lean backward against the backstroke flagpole or fence to stabilize the right shoulder blade. By minimizing the motion of the shoulder blade, you will enhance the effectiveness of this stretch.
3. Grasp the elbow with the left hand and pull the arm across the body.
4. You will feel the stretch through the back of the shoulder.

## Sleeper Stretch

**Focus:**   Maintain or improve internal rotation in the shoulder.

**Procedure**

1. Lie on your right side as if you were sleeping or watching TV.
2. Flex the right elbow 90 degrees and position the right arm so it is perpendicular to the upper body. The hand should point to the ceiling.
3. With the left hand, push the right hand downward toward the floor, internally rotating the shoulder.

4. You should feel the stretch deep in the muscles of the shoulder.
5. Repeat with the left arm.

## Towel Stretch

**Focus:** Improve internal rotation of the shoulder.

**Procedure**

1. With the right hand, hold a towel above your head and let it hang down the middle of your back.
2. Grasp the other end of the towel with the left hand.
3. Pull upward with the right hand and hold the stretch. You should feel a stretch in the front of the left shoulder. Next, pull downward with the left hand to stretch the right shoulder.
4. Repeat with the arms in the opposite positions.

Note that in some people, it is not tightness but excessive looseness in the shoulder (a condition called hyperlaxity) that can contribute to injury. The shoulder joint is surrounded by a joint capsule, and this structure provides some stability to the joint and keeps the ball and socket positioned correctly. When the front part of the shoulder joint capsule becomes overly stretched, the shoulder becomes loose and impingement is more likely to occur. Many swimmers unknowingly contribute to this condition by performing the partner-assisted shoulder stretch. This stretch can actually be detrimental to the health of the shoulder since it primarily stretches the joint capsule and not the chest or shoulder muscles. Refer to the sidebar on page 145 of chapter 7 for more information on this stretch.

## Breaststroker's Knee

One of the more common swimming injuries in the lower body has been termed *breaststroker's knee*. Breaststroker's knee is actually a strain of the medial collateral ligament on the inside of the knee and seems to result from a combination of overuse, muscular weakness, and poor flexibility. About 27 percent of all swimmers and 75 percent of breaststrokers will experience this knee pain at some point in their swimming careers. In the breast-stroke, the legs are extended rapidly and rotated outward during the kick. While this position puts the feet into the best position to generate propulsion, it also places a great deal of stress on the inside of the knee as the legs are brought together forcefully during the kick. Not surprisingly, knee pain increases with use; as training age and volume increase, so does the risk of developing knee pain. A kick that is directed straight back will place less stress on the inner side of the knee.

### Injury-Prevention Exercises for the Knee

Developing leg strength, muscular endurance, and flexibility, particularly in the muscles around the hip and knee, can prevent lower-body injuries such as breaststroker's knee. By using the exercises and stretches described here and earlier in the book, you should decrease your risk of injury. Please note, however, that while strengthening and improving flexibility are important for all strokes, you should avoid any of these exercises if they aggravate a preexisting injury or cause pain.

## Single-Leg Squat

**Focus:** Develop single-leg strength and stability. This exercise is like the squat, but standing on one leg develops an added level of strength and stability that can help prevent injury to the knee.

### Procedure

1. Stand on the left leg and bend the right knee slightly.
2. Maintaining an upright upper posture, drop into a squat with your left leg, bending the right knee approximately 45 degrees. Drop deeper into the squat as the legs get stronger.
3. Perform two or three sets of 15 repetitions on each leg.

## Star Drill  o DVD

**Focus:** Develop single-leg strength and stability with movement. The star drill is similar to a single-leg squat, except that balance is challenged to an even greater degree. If this becomes too easy, increase the difficulty by standing on a foam pad.

### Procedure

1. Start the exercise by balancing on the left leg. Imagine you are standing in the middle of a compass facing north.

2. Slowly drop into a single-leg squat while lightly tracing a line on the floor with your right heel in the direction of north. Extend the right foot as far forward as you can, making sure to keep good posture and control of your body. Do not bend forward at the waist; keep the upper body upright.

3. Return to the starting position and repeat the motion, except this time trace a line to the northeast.

4. Complete additional repetitions tracing a line with your heel to the east, southeast, and south on the imaginary compass.

5. Go through that entire exercise three to five times and repeat while standing on the right leg and moving in a north, northwest, west, southwest, and south pattern.

# Elastic-Band Kick

**Focus:** Improve strength and stability in the hips and core. Even though one leg is doing the kicking, the leg that remains on the ground is strengthened the most by this exercise.

## Procedure

1. Stand with your feet about shoulder-width apart and loop an elastic band around the left ankle and the other end around a pole or table leg.

2. Turn so your right shoulder is closer to the pole and lift the left leg. All of your weight should now be on the right leg. There should be a slight tension on the band.

3. Quickly move the left leg out to the side 6 to 12 inches (15 to 30 cm) and back while maintaining a good posture and a slight bend in the stance leg.

4. Continue this pattern for 15 seconds initially, building to 30 seconds as you become stronger.

5. Rest and repeat the exercise, this time kicking forward and again kicking backward, keeping the kicking leg straight in both instances. You will have to turn the body each time so you kick away from the tubing attachment point.

6. Go through the same series of exercises with the other leg.

**Variation:** Increase the demands of this exercise by standing on a foam stability pad or a pillow.

### Additional Exercises for Lower-Body Injury Prevention

Additional exercises emphasizing lower-body strength and flexibility are discussed earlier in the book. Please refer to the appropriate pages and follow the guidelines presented with the exercise descriptions.

Squat (pages 40-41)

Hip flexor stretch (page 136)

Hamstring stretch (page 139)

Standing quadriceps stretch (page 140)

Hip twist (page 142)

## Lower-Back Pain

Core strength is another essential component in any injury-prevention program. A weak core and poor balance in the water can lead to all types of mechanical breakdowns that can contribute to injury, such as lower-back pain. Lower-back pain is most commonly seen in breaststroke and butterfly swimmers because of the undulation that occurs in these strokes. It is also common in triathletes who have to lift the upper body out of the water when sighting in the open water. This book devotes an entire chapter to developing core strength and improving balance and stability in the water. The exercises described there strengthen the core and help prevent injuries throughout the body. A number of lower-back and core strengthening and flexibility exercises have already been presented in the book, and we refer you to them to help avoid lower-back injury.

Prone bridge progression (pages 93-94)

Back bridge progression (pages 95-96)

Bird dog progression (pages 99-100)

Knees to chest progression (pages 103-104)

Back extension (page 108)

Hip flexor stretch (page 136)

Figure-four stretch (page 139)

Hamstring stretch (page 139)

# IMMEDIATE TREATMENT FOR INJURIES

Unfortunately, even with the best preparation and injury-prevention efforts, injuries can still occur in swimming. The initial treatment for a soft-tissue injury, such as a strain, sprain, or tendinitis, should be to follow the PRICE principle. Each letter stands for one aspect of treatment you should follow:

**Protection.** Immediately after an injury, immobilize the injured area to encourage healing and to minimize any additional damage that could occur until the injury can be evaluated by a qualified health-care provider.

**Rest.** Avoid performing any activity that causes pain in the injured area. If your shoulder hurts when you are swimming, change strokes or get out of the water and look for other ways to maintain your conditioning, such as cycling or jogging. Pain is your sign to stop what you are doing.

**Ice.** Ice is your ally in the initial phases of injury. Apply ice to the injured areas for 15 to 20 minutes every 2 to 3 hours you are awake for the first 72 hours after the injury has occurred. Ice helps control the inflammation. It is also a good idea to ice an injured body part immediately after swimming or any other physical activity. Do not apply heat to a soft-tissue injury—even though it might feel really good. Heat will only induce more swelling and is counterproductive during the initial phase of healing.

**Compression.** Even when not applying ice, compression will help to minimize swelling. You can use an Ace bandage to wrap the injured area firmly, but not so tightly that blood flow is restricted. Start by wrapping at the point farthest from the heart and move toward the torso. Loosen the bandage if you feel any numbness or tingling.

**Elevation.** To reduce swelling, elevate the injured area above the level of the heart, especially at night or when you are lounging on the couch.

It is always advisable to seek the advice of a medical professional whenever pain is involved, especially if the pain does not go away with rest. It's important to be able to distinguish pain from soreness. Muscle soreness is a normal result of training. Pain signifies something more severe is going on. An orthopedist familiar with swimming should be able to evaluate any potential injury and prescribe more aggressive treatments if warranted.

# ACTIVITY MODIFICATIONS WHEN INJURED

Swimmers adjusting to injuries often ask whether they can still swim while the injury heals. It depends. Let's use the shoulder as an example. Shoulder injuries often respond well with rest if they are not exposed to stresses that will aggravate the injury. A treatment approach might involve decreasing the training load, restricting the use of paddles, and avoiding upper-body strength training that stresses the shoulder joint. If light swimming does not aggravate the condition, do some light swimming. Similarly, if you develop knee pain, you might want to avoid kicking for some time. Regardless of the injury, if you feel pain while doing a certain activity, stop.

An injury is not a free pass to stop your training, however. There are many things you can do to maintain fitness and conditioning. For example, when any of our swimmers have shoulder pain, they kick or swim with fins. When kicking, however, take care when using a kickboard, because kickboards can place the arm in the impingement position. Consider kicking on your side if using a board causes pain. It is not uncommon for swimmers to come away from a shoulder injury with a more powerful kick and the ability to swim times they could not reach before—all without having taken a stroke.

## TRAINING ALTERNATIVES WHEN RECOVERING FROM AN INJURY

Leg strength and kicking efficiency can have a huge impact on swimming speed and efficiency, and here is one example of that. Several years ago, one of our swimmers suffered a shoulder injury and was instructed by his doctor to take six weeks off to allow the shoulder to recover. However, rather than stop swimming all together, the athlete decided he would kick. For the full six weeks, he kicked with fins, doing the same distances and the same intervals as the rest of the team did on their swimming sets. When the swimmer was finally given the doctor's permission to start pulling again, the team was well into its taper and we had only two weeks to get ready for the season-ending championships. There was really very little opportunity to do a lot of in-water shoulder strengthening before the meet. In spite of that, the swimmer swam lifetime bests while qualifying for junior nationals for the first time in several events. He dropped six seconds in his 400 IM and qualified for his first nationals. All of this happened even though he had essentially gone two months without taking a stroke. The only thing that had changed during that time was his improved leg strength. Better yet, the swimmer went on to earn a Division I college swimming scholarship and qualify for nationals in several events. It shows just how important leg strength is to swimming—and it's a great example of being creative with training so you can maintain fitness even while injured.

# Chapter 9

# Nutrition and Hydration for Swimmers

S wimming is a sport that presents some unique challenges in nutrition and hydration. You might practice every day, and in some instances several times a day, training for hours at a time and covering many thousands of meters. How should you prepare the body to recover between practices? Swim meets, on the other hand, offer a completely different nutritional challenge—you might race multiple times a day, each race lasting three minutes or less. How are you supposed to fuel your body to perform in this scenario? These are important questions. The answers will directly affect your performance in the pool and your enjoyment of the sport. Entire books are devoted to the topic of nutrition, and it is beyond the scope of this chapter to cover every detail about proper nutrition. However, this chapter does cover some of the nutrition basics for swimmers and highlights some essential information on what you should do before, during, and after a practice or race to optimize your performance and recovery. Nutrition is something you can control, and it will directly affect your performance in the pool.

## ESSENTIAL NUTRIENTS FOR SWIMMERS

Think of your body as a finely tuned race car. If you've ever watched an auto race, you quickly realize the importance placed on the pit stop—getting the right kind and the right amount of fuel into the car quickly and at the appropriate times during the race. Waiting too long to refuel the car or using the wrong type of fuel can have disastrous consequences. Just as with a car, how your body performs depends to a large degree on the fuel you put into it. If you give it the right kinds of fuel and fill your tank at the right times, you will put yourself in position to perform at your best.

There are specific things you need to look for in the foods you eat, just as there are certain things you need more of than nonswimmers. You need to be aware of what you eat while making sure you get enough of certain nutrients. At the same time, you need to limit your intake of certain other nutrients. Six basic nutrients provide the body with the fuel it needs, help the body repair itself after a strenuous practice, and facilitate recovery.

## Carbohydrate

Carbohydrate is broken down by the body into sugar (such as glucose), and contrary to what you may hear from the proponents of low-carbohydrate diets, carbohydrate is *critical* to swimming performance. The sugar that enters the bloodstream is stored in the muscles and liver as glycogen. This stored glycogen is, in turn, used as the primary energy source for providing energy to the brain and nervous system as well as to working muscles. If you are engaged in any level of strenuous activity or want to optimize your performance in the pool, consider the following:

- You should consume 3 to 5 grams of carbohydrate for every pound of body weight *every day*. For a 150-pound (68 kg) athlete, this is approximately 80 to 120 grams of carbohydrate per day. These amounts are average values and in reality should be periodized (just as your training is) to match your energy expended in training and where you are in your training cycle. Guidelines for various training cycles are provided in table 9.4 later in the chapter.
- When trying to determine how much carbohydrate to eat, think of your dinner plate: Carbohydrate-rich foods should cover roughly two thirds of your plate.
- Good sources of carbohydrate are fruits, vegetables, cereals, grains, beans and legumes, nuts, and dairy products such as milk.

### PERFORMANCE TIP

While you may see some books quote specific percentages for various nutrients (for example, carbohydrate should make up 55 to 60 percent of the calories consumed in a given day), most sport nutritionists now advocate periodizing nutrition and make individualized recommendations based on body weight, the training phase, and training goals.

# Protein

Protein provides little energy to the body but is essential for building muscle and repairing damage that can occur during training. As a general rule, sport nutritionists recommend the following:

- You should strive to eat 0.5 to 0.7 gram of protein per pound of body weight each day during periods of moderate-intensity training. As with all nutrients, protein intake should be adjusted based on your training phase, and intake can increase to as much as 0.9 gram of protein per pound of body weight during times of strenuous resistance training and during the competitive season.
- Good sources of dietary protein are lean red meat, chicken, fish, lower-fat dairy products, and soy products such as tofu, soy milk, and hummus.

Recreational swimmers who engage in lower-intensity training will have lower protein needs. Most athletes regularly exceed the recommended amount of protein in their diets, and protein shakes and other protein supplementation are often unnecessary.

iStockphoto/dswebb

It's important to develop a plan for fueling your body during practice and performance so that you will have the energy you need to perform at your peak.

## Fat

Contrary to popular belief, dietary fat is essential to athletes; it provides a dense source of energy, contributes essential fatty acids, allows fat-soluble vitamins (vitamins E, D, and A) to be absorbed in the digestive tract, and supports many physiological functions (see table 9.1).

- It is recommended that swimmers consume 0.35 to 0.7 gram of fat per pound of body weight during much of the season (see table 9.4 on page 173), adjusting the intake throughout the year to match the demands of training or competition.

- Avoid saturated and trans fat found in foods like red meat, full-fat dairy products, egg yolks, hydrogenated vegetable oils, fried foods, and processed foods such as cookies, crackers, and doughnuts. The American Heart Association recommends that saturated and trans fat make up less than 7 percent and 1 percent of your total caloric intake, respectively. These types of fat elevate LDL cholesterol (the bad cholesterol) while lowering HDL cholesterol (the good cholesterol).

- Focus on consuming monounsaturated and polyunsaturated fat because they can actually be beneficial by lowering LDL and raising HDL cholesterol levels. Unsaturated fat is typically a liquid at room temperature or in the refrigerator and includes plant oils as well as omega-3 and omega-6 fatty acids. Swimmers should focus on consuming omega-3 fatty acids because they carry the greatest health and performance benefits—they actually have anti-inflammatory effects, reduce the risks associated with heart disease, and may inhibit the growth of certain cancers. Omega-6 fatty acids, while having

### Table 9.1   Types of Fat

| Type of fat | Characteristics | Examples | Health effects |
|---|---|---|---|
| Saturated fat and trans fat | Typically solid at room temperature | Butter, coconut oil, beef tallow, palm oil, and lard | Raise blood cholesterol levels |
| Monounsaturated fat | Typically liquid at room temperature | Olive oil, canola oil, peanut oil, almonds, avocados, sesame seeds | Help lower blood cholesterol levels, reduce risk of heart disease |
| Polyunsaturated fat | Typically liquid at room temperature | Safflower oil, sunflower oil, corn oil, soybean oil, cottonseed oil, fish oil, walnuts, flax oil, grains, fish, soybeans | Help lower blood cholesterol levels, decrease risk of heart disease |

some beneficial attributes, can actually contribute to inflammation, asthma, allergies, and other conditions when you consume too much in relation to your intake of omega-3 fatty acids. It is recommended that omega-6 and omega-3 fatty acids be consumed in a ratio of 4:1, yet most Americans consume them in a ratio of 20 to 50:1, creating an imbalance that can lead to illness.

- Many swimmers think fat should be eliminated from the diet completely. However, research has shown that dropping fat intake below recommended levels does not produce any additional health or performance benefits.

## Vitamins

Vitamins are organic compounds that allow the body to produce energy during exercise while also supporting a variety of other physiological functions. Vitamins cannot be produced by the body and therefore must come from the foods you eat. If possible, it is best to get your vitamins directly from the foods you eat. Many athletes do take daily multivitamins to supplement what they get from their food. When choosing a multivitamin, look for a reputable brand containing pharmaceutical-grade vitamins and do not consume more than the 100 percent recommended daily allowance (RDA) for any vitamin. Supplemental vitamins are needed most during times of heavy training and during the competition phases but are not necessarily needed during periods of active rest or light exercise. Table 9.2 provides a selected list of vitamins that are important for swimmers, gives a brief description of what they do, and provides you with several examples of foods that contain the vitamins.

## Minerals

Minerals are inorganic substances (such as iron, calcium, and sodium) that assist in the breakdown of food and support many bodily functions. Like vitamins, minerals are not produced by the body and must be consumed in the foods you eat. The body needs over 20 minerals to function properly, and these minerals must be available in sufficient amounts to ensure health and athletic performance. Table 9.3 lists minerals that are important to swimmers, offers a brief description of what they do, and provides some examples of food sources that contain the minerals.

Swimmers typically consume adequate amounts of most minerals, but deficiencies can occur when consumption is not sufficient to support the demands of training. When a deficiency does occur, it is usually in iron or calcium, and either one can negatively affect health and performance. While these deficiencies are most often seen in female swimmers, it is not unheard of for them to show up in male swimmers as well.

- *Iron.* Iron is an important mineral for athletes. It is a critical component of hemoglobin, the binding site for oxygen in blood. Low iron stores means

## Table 9.2 Selected Vitamins and Their Functions in the Body

| Vitamin | Function | Good food sources |
|---|---|---|
| Vitamin A | Promotes growth and repair of body tissues, bone formation, and healthy skin and hair. Essential for night vision. | Liver, cheese, egg yolk, whole milk, butter |
| Beta-carotene | Acts as an antioxidant. | Sweet peppers, carrots, sweet potatoes, broccoli, greens, spinach, apricots, papaya, watermelon, peaches, asparagus, winter squash, cantaloupe |
| Vitamin D | Aids in the absorption of calcium and helps to build bone mass and prevent bone loss. Helps maintain levels of calcium. | Fish (herring, salmon, oysters, catfish, sardines, tuna, shrimp, mackerel), milk, margarine, fortified breakfast cereals, egg yolks, eggs, butter |
| Vitamin E | Serves as an antioxidant. Needed for normal growth and development. | Peanut butter, mayonnaise, fortified breakfast cereals, nuts (almonds, hazelnuts, peanuts, hickory nuts, pistachios), margarine, wheat germ |
| Vitamin C | Promotes healthy cell development, wound healing, and resistance to infections. Serves as an antioxidant. | Broccoli, cauliflower, strawberries, oranges, orange juice, limes, grapefruit, papayas, cantaloupe, tomatoes, asparagus, spinach, pineapple, raspberries, potatoes, onions |
| Thiamin ($B_1$) | Essential in carbohydrate metabolism. Needed for normal functioning of the nervous system and muscles. | Fortified breakfast cereals, sunflower seeds, peas, pork, orange juice, lima beans, pecans, enriched rice |
| Riboflavin ($B_2$) | Helps in red blood cell formation, nervous system functioning, and metabolism. Needed for vision. | Liver, wheat germ, cheese, fortified breakfast cereals, whey protein, milk, eggs, lamb, pork, veal, beef, broccoli, yogurt |
| Niacin | Involved in carbohydrate, protein, and fat metabolism and proper functioning of nervous system. | Soy protein, whey protein, beef, peanuts, peanut butter, sunflower seeds, fortified breakfast cereals |

# Table 9.3 Selected Minerals and Their Functions in the Body

| Mineral | Function | Food source |
| --- | --- | --- |
| Calcium | Essential for healthy bones and teeth. Assists in blood clotting, muscular function, and nerve transmission. | Dairy products (cheese, milk, cottage cheese, yogurt, ice cream), vegetable greens |
| Magnesium | Helps with nerve and muscular function. Needed for healthy bones and teeth. May help prevent cramping. | Bran, fortified breakfast cereals, soybeans, nuts (almonds, pine nuts, hazelnuts, cashews, walnuts, peanuts), spinach |
| Manganese | Involved in the metabolism of carbohydrate. | Wheat germ, wheat bran, rice bran, fortified breakfast cereals, rice cakes, nuts (peanuts, pecans, pine nuts, walnuts, almonds, hazelnuts), soybeans, mussels, whole wheat (pasta, breads, and crackers) |
| Chromium | Aids in glucose metabolism and may help regulate blood sugar and insulin levels in people with diabetes. | Mushrooms (white), raw oysters, wine, apple, beer, pork, chicken |
| Iodine | Helps regulate growth, development, and energy metabolism. | Iodized salt, saltwater fish, and seafood |
| Iron | Necessary for red blood cell formation and function. | Beef, pork, veal, poultry, clams, oysters, fortified breakfast cereals, enriched bread products, nuts (pine nuts, cashews, almonds), beans (kidney, green, garbanzo), spinach |
| Zinc | Essential for digestion, metabolism, reproduction, wound healing, and immune function. | Oysters, beef, veal, lamb, pork, chicken, lima beans, black-eyed peas, white beans |

oxygen will be transferred less efficiently from the blood throughout the body. Iron also aids in energy release and helps maintain a healthy immune system. Iron is lost from the body primarily through bleeding (such as in a female swimmer's menstrual cycle) and perspiration. If you do not maintain a sufficient iron intake to offset losses, you can develop iron depletion followed by iron-deficient anemia. When this happens, you might have sensations of increased fatigue, weakness, and an overall loss of endurance.

A blood test is the best way to assess your iron status; this can be done as part of a yearly physical exam or if you have symptoms of extreme fatigue. The best way to ensure proper iron intake is to eat a well-rounded diet that includes red meat, seafood, and poultry. Even if you do eat an iron-rich diet, it still might be necessary to take iron supplements if you already have low iron stores. Any iron supplementation should be done under the direction of a physician or sport dietitian. And if you are iron deficient, it is also recommended that you have your iron levels measured via a simple blood test several times per year. If you're a vegetarian, you can get iron from cereals, spinach, nuts, and some beans; you should eat these foods with a source of vitamin C (such as an orange or fortified orange juice) to enhance absorption.

• *Calcium.* Calcium is another mineral that is often deficient in female athletes. Calcium is one of the building blocks of bone, and low calcium intake has been shown to increase the risk of osteoporosis later in life. Bone formation is stimulated by skeletal loading, and calcium supplementation could be more important for swimmers than for other athletes due to the low-impact nature of the sport. Calcium supplementation can again be started on the advice of a physician or sport dietitian; this can help combat any deficiencies that exist in your diet.

## Water

Many people do not think of water as a nutrient. However, water makes up as much as 60 percent of your total body weight (75 percent in lean tissues like muscle), and adequate intake of water is critical for many physiological systems to function properly and efficiently. Dehydration, a loss of body water, can quickly lead to impaired performance. Research has shown that a water loss of as little as 1 percent can impair physical and mental performance in athletes. Because of the importance placed on hydration, we address this topic in greater detail later in the chapter.

## ENERGY FOR PERFORMANCE

You want to make sure you consume enough calories in the foods you eat to fuel your training and competitive performances, but not so much that you gain weight. Maintaining the proper energy balance is a fine line: Low energy intake can lead to health problems and performance decrements, while a high caloric intake can lead to weight gain, decreased performance, and other health concerns. Many athletes, swimmers included, surprisingly consume *too few* calories, which can lead to fatigue, loss of muscle mass, and health problems. Your energy needs will vary throughout the year depending on the volume and intensity of your training, and it is important to adjust your nutritional intake accordingly. Just as you periodize your training, you should also periodize your nutrition and nutrient intake. As you move from one training phase to another, you will need to adjust your caloric intake and the amounts of each of the essential nutrients to match the training load. Table 9.4 outlines how you should adjust your nutrition as you move through a competitive season. It is especially important to adjust nutrition during the taper as the energy requirements drop considerably from what is seen during the training phase. It is not uncommon for athletes to gain body weight during a taper simply because they do not adjust their caloric intake appropriately.

**PERFORMANCE TIP**

Swimmers who increase their energy intake as training intensity goes up tend to perform better in practices.

Carbohydrate and fat provide most of the energy to the body. Carbohydrate is broken down into sugar, and while some sugar stays in the bloodstream, most gets stored in the muscles and the liver in the form of glycogen. Carbohydrate and glycogen actually only make up a small percentage of the body's total energy stores, and believe it or not, most of the body's useable energy is stored as fat. Some of the body's available energy is stored as protein. However, protein is broken down in large amounts only in extreme situations such as starvation and provides a negligible amount of energy during training or competition.

Although both carbohydrate and fat provide energy to fuel your swimming performance, they are used by the body at different times. Exercise intensity plays a major role in determining whether you will burn fat or use muscle glycogen as your primary energy source. As a general rule, the

## Table 9.4 Nutritional Periodization

| Training phase | Carbohydrate (g/lb BW) | Protein (g/lb BW) | Fat (g/lb BW) |
|---|---|---|---|
| Preliminary phase | 1.4 to 2.3 | 0.6 to 0.9 | 0.35 to 0.45 |
| Training phase | 2.3 to 5.5 | 0.55 to 0.77 | 0.35 to 0.45 |
| Competition phase | 3.2 to 5.9 | 0.73 to 0.90 | 0.35 to 0.70 |
| Championship phase | 3.2 to 8.6 | 0.64 to 0.77 | 0.36 to 0.90 |
| Active rest phase | 1.4 to 2.3 | 0.6 to 0.9 | 0.35 to 0.45 |

Adapted from B. Seebohar, 2004, *Nutrition periodization for endurance athletes: Taking traditional sports nutrition to the next level* (Boulder, CO: Bull Publishing).

higher the swimming intensity, the more the body relies on carbohydrate and glycogen stores to fuel performance. At lower intensities, fat is broken down and used as the primary fuel source. The body never relies entirely on one fuel source. Glycogen is used in low-intensity exercise, and fat is burned during high-intensity exercise. If there is a limiting factor in swimming performance, it is the amount of glycogen available in the body. The body rarely exhausts its fat stores; if fatigue occurs, it is usually the result of glycogen depletion.

# UNDERSTANDING THE GLYCEMIC INDEX

Carbohydrate provides the quickest energy source, and it makes sense for swimmers to look to carbohydrate as the best, and quickest, way to fuel the body before, during, and after a practice or competition. But not all forms of carbohydrate are created equal. Traditionally, types of carbohydrate have been categorized according to the glycemic index (GI), a measure of how quickly the carbohydrate is broken down into sugar and enters the bloodstream. High-GI carbohydrate is broken down quickly and enters the bloodstream almost immediately, whereas low-GI carbohydrate enters the body more slowly but provides energy for a longer period. All types of carbohydrate are important for swimmers, but certain ones are better at certain times. In the remainder of the chapter we suggest the best times to consume low-GI and high-GI foods to fuel the body. Table 9.5 shows ranges of GI and foods that fall into those categories.

## Table 9.5  Glycemic Index (GI) Values for Foods

|  | GI range | Examples |
|---|---|---|
| Low GI | 55 or less | Most fruits (apples, bananas, oranges, grapes, grapefruit), many vegetables (peas, carrots, beans, sweet potatoes), pasta, fruit juices, fruit smoothies, bran cereal, low-fat ice cream, nonfat milk and chocolate milk, low-fat yogurt, chicken nuggets, popcorn |
| Medium GI | 56-69 | Shredded wheat, pineapple, wheat bread, table sugar (sucrose), pizza, many sport and energy bars (Powerbar), oatmeal, many cookies and candy bars, corn, bran muffins, soft drinks (nondiet), honey |
| High GI | 70 or more | Corn flakes, bagels, baked potato, white bread, English muffins, white rice, crackers, pretzels, sport drinks (Gatorade), Cheerios, most sweetened cereals, many cereal bars, jelly beans, pancakes, toaster pastries |

# REPLACING FLUIDS TO AVOID DEHYDRATION

Fluid replacement is just as important in swimming as it is in any other athletic activity. You may not think you sweat a great deal when you swim because the water quickly dissipates any excess heat your body generates, but in reality you do sweat, losing fluids and electrolytes in the process. In fact, swimmers lose approximately 4 ounces (120 ml) of fluid through sweat for each 1,000 meters of training at a moderate intensity. As training intensity increases, the sweat loss can increase to as much as 5.5 ounces (160 ml) for every 1,000 meters. Over the course of a 5,000-meter workout, you could expect to lose 19 to 27 ounces (560 to 800 ml) of sweat, which is nearly 2 pounds (1 kg) of water weight. It would be nice to think that we could burn off 1 to 2 pounds of fat during a workout, but unfortunately all of the lost weight is due to fluid loss. All of this fluid should be replaced before the next workout. While this makes sense, athletes (including swimmers) typically will replace only 30 to 70 percent of the fluid lost during a training session when left to their own devices.

The best way to avoid dehydration is to take a three-stage approach:

1. Make sure you are properly hydrated before getting into the pool.
2. Replace fluid as you lose it, drinking small amounts of water or a sport drink throughout practice. It is a good idea to have a water bottle with you every time you practice and an even better idea to *use it*. Start drinking small amounts early in the practice and drink regularly between sets to stay hydrated. Most swimmers should be able to drink 5 to 10 ounces (150 to 300 ml) of fluid every 15 to 20 minutes comfortably.
3. Aggressively drink fluids immediately after practice to replace any remaining fluid deficits.

It's important to note that first thing in the morning, most people are already dehydrated. So if you have morning practices, it is especially important to develop a specific prepractice, during-practice, and postpractice fluid-replacement strategy.

### PERFORMANCE TIP

For most people, 1 ounce of fluid equals one gulp of fluid. So, drinking 5 to 10 ounces of fluid equates to drinking 5 to 10 gulps.

## Estimating Fluid-Replacement Needs

How do you know if you are replacing all the fluid you lost? While you could get a costly test done at the hospital, there are several less expensive ways to tell if you are staying properly hydrated. One of the easiest ways is to note the color of your urine. If you are well hydrated, your urine should be almost clear or pale yellow. The darker the urine, the more dehydrated you are. When using this method to assess hydration, keep in mind that some supplements or vitamins, B vitamins in particular, may cause urine to become darker and that urine will be naturally darker first thing in the morning.

Another way to determine how much fluid you should replace is to weigh yourself when you are dry before and after a practice. Any weight loss is due to lost water weight and should be replaced—actually, you want to replace 150 percent of the fluid lost, taking into account fluid that will be lost in urine and sweat. A general rule is that you should drink 24 ounces (approximately 24 gulps) of water or a sport drink for every pound (about 0.5 kg) of weight lost during practice.

## Choosing Between Water and Sport Drinks

Swimmers often ask if they should drink water or sport drinks to replace lost fluid. You need three things when you swim: fluids to prevent dehydration, electrolytes (sodium in particular) to maintain a healthy fluid balance in the body, and carbohydrate to provide energy. Most sport drinks contain all of these nutrients, making them a natural fit. Experts recommend a sport drink containing 6 to 8 percent carbohydrate to provide the best, and fastest, absorption by the digestive tract and a sodium content of about 110 milligrams per 8-ounce (240 ml) serving. However, you could also get the water and carbohydrate you need by drinking plain water and eating a carbohydrate-rich food. Another benefit of sport drinks is the taste. Flavored sport drinks encourage rehydration, and many swimmers will drink more than if they were offered only water.

There are two other important things to consider when choosing between water and sport drinks. Drinking too much water, without replacing electrolytes, can lead to a potentially dangerous condition called hyponatremia (which means low sodium). Endurance athletes run the risk of developing hyponatremia when all they consume is large amounts of water to rehydrate. Additionally, water does not contain any calories, but sport drinks do. It is not uncommon for someone to think he is doing a great thing by drinking sport drinks all day to stave off dehydration, only to find he puts on weight over time. Sport drinks definitely have their place and purpose, but it is important to know when to use them and not to abuse them.

> **PERFORMANCE TIP**
>
> A fluid loss of 2.5 percent of a swimmer's body weight can reduce the capacity to perform high-intensity exercise by as much as 45 percent.

## GETTING READY FOR PRACTICE

Whenever possible, you should eat a meal composed mainly of low- to moderate-GI carbohydrate (0.5 to 1.8 grams of carbohydrate for each pound of body weight, or 75 to 270 grams for a 150-pound athlete) one to four hours before practice. The goal of this meal is to top off energy and fluid stores in the body. Keep protein and fat intake to a minimum in any prepractice or precompetition meal because these nutrients tend to slow digestion. Many practices and competitions occur in the morning, and it is unrealistic to eat four hours before you swim. In this case, you should still try to consume a smaller, carbohydrate-containing snack in the hour or two before you swim. This snack should still be made up of low- to moderate-GI carbohydrate. Be sure to stay on top of your fluid and carbohydrate replacement, ideally by drinking a sport drink, throughout the practice. Here are some additional recommendations related to prepractice nutrition:

- Commercially prepared liquid meal supplements or smoothies can be useful, particularly if you do not tolerate solid foods well before physical activity. These should match the carbohydrate and calorie requirements listed previously.

- At the same time you consume the prepractice meal, you should also drink 12 to 20 ounces (about 360 to 600 ml) of water or a sport drink to top off fluid stores and an additional 8 to 12 ounces every 15 minutes until practice begins.

- Allow more digestion time before intense activity (if you know it will be a killer workout or before a competition) than for moderate-intensity swimming.

## PREPARING PRESWIM SNACKS

With a little planning, you should find it pretty easy to put together high-carbohydrate snacks that you can eat in the hour or two before you swim. Here are some examples of snacks:

- 0.75 cup (46 g) raisin bran with 8 ounces (240 ml) of nonfat milk and a banana = 67 grams carbohydrate (345 total calories)

- 1 packet oatmeal, 8 ounces orange juice, and an apple = 62 grams carbohydrate (350 total calories)

- 1 small bagel, an orange, and 2 Fig Newtons = 68 grams carbohydrate (290 total calories)

- 1 low-fat yogurt with fruit, 1 blueberry muffin (2 oz, or 57 g) = 79 grams carbohydrate (387 total calories)

- 1 cup (140 g) cooked spaghetti, 0.5 cup (120 ml) tomato sauce, 8 ounces sport drink = 64 grams carbohydrate (345 total calories)

- 0.5 cup raisins (83 g), 8 ounces low-fat chocolate milk = 85 grams carbohydrate (405 total calories)

# FUELING THE BODY DURING PRACTICE

Your nutritional goal during practice should be to offset the glycogen, fluid, and electrolyte losses experienced while you swim rather than wait to replenish everything at the end of the workout. The following suggestions can serve as a guide:

- Try to consume 30 to 90 grams of carbohydrate per hour during each hour of exercise. If you can take in 60 grams of carbohydrate (roughly 240 calories) each hour of training (the middle of the range), you should be able to stay on top of your energy needs.
- Drink 5 to 10 ounces (150 to 300 ml) of fluid every 15 to 20 minutes during practice.

Sport drinks provide a convenient option for meeting your in-practice nutritional needs since they can be easily carried onto the pool deck and provide all three of the nutrients lost when swimming. Additionally, many swimmers do not tolerate solid foods well during practice, which makes sport drinks a logical and practical choice. However, if you can tolerate solid food while you swim, you can also eat carbohydrate-rich foods (such as salted pretzels) and water to meet your in-practice nutritional needs. Here are several options for snacks that will meet your fluid, carbohydrate, and electrolyte needs.

- 32 to 48 ounces (960 to 1440 ml) sport drink = 50 to 75 grams carbohydrate
- 2 ounces (57 g) pretzels and 20 to 32 ounces water = 45 to 55 grams carbohydrate
- 16 ounces (480 ml) sport drink, low-fat fruit yogurt, and 16 ounces water = 75 grams carbohydrate
- 1 medium banana, 16 ounces sport drink, 16 ounces water = 50 grams carbohydrate

Again, it is not so important where these nutrients come from (whether from foods or sport drinks); it's more important that you choose the carbohydrate and fluid sources that your body tolerates best. Whatever way you choose to fuel your body, use your training times to develop a nutrition and hydration strategy that works for you—*do not* wait to experiment with new nutritional schemes at a competition. The most important meet of the year is not the time you want to find out that sport drinks cause you gastrointestinal distress. Test things out in practice first to find a combination of food, water, and sport drinks that works best for you.

# EATING FOR RECOVERY

The top two priorities for a swimmer after a strenuous workout or a race should be to cool down properly and refuel the body by replenishing depleted muscle glycogen, rehydrating, and restoring normal electrolyte levels. The faster you can get food and water into the body, the more quickly you will start the recovery process and be able to race or train at peak levels again. Because many swimmers train daily, or twice a day in many college and high school programs, a focus on recovery is important. Here are some basic guidelines on optimally fueling your body for recovery:

- You should consume 0.5 to 0.7 gram of carbohydrate per pound of body weight immediately after a training session. This equates roughly to 50 to 100 grams, or 200 to 400 calories of carbohydrate, for most swimmers.

- Consume 6 to 20 grams of protein as part of the postworkout meal.

- Eat this food within 30 to 60 minutes after practice has ended. However, faster is better, and you should strive to consume this meal within the first 15 minutes after practice. If you wait too long to refuel, it could take up to twice as long to replenish the lost glycogen. If you are doing double workouts, this likely will negatively affect your performance in that second workout.

- Consider bringing your own food with you to eat when practice is over. Most clubs do not have a snack bar, but if they do, ask yourself if you really want to refuel with what they have for purchase.

- Perhaps most important, over the next 24 hours, eat 3 to 5 grams of carbohydrate per pound of body weight to completely restore the energy that was depleted in a practice. You should eat 0.3 to 0.5 gram per pound of body weight every 2 hours, and avoid trying to replace everything at once.

## WORKING MUSCLES ARE SPONGES

After a training session, muscle is just like a damp sponge that has had all of the glycogen squeezed from it. If you quickly place a sponge in water, it will soak up the water until the sponge is full. In the same way, a muscle will soak up glucose to rebuild glycogen stores. However, if a sponge is allowed to dry out, it becomes less efficient at soaking up water when the water does become available. The sponge will still eventually soak up the water—it just happens more slowly. The same is true with muscle. The more quickly you get the carbohydrate into the body, the faster the recovery will occur. An hour is better than 2 hours, and 10 minutes is better than an hour. The key is to get the carbohydrate in as quickly as possible.

## RACE-DAY NUTRITION

On competition days, your premeet nutrition should model the recommendations laid out for preparing for practice.

- Follow the same guidelines described for your prepractice nutrition. Eat a low-fat, high-carbohydrate meal several hours before your precompetition warm-up. Try to consume 2 to 2.5 grams of carbohydrate for every pound of body weight.

- After warm-up and between races, consume sport drinks or foods containing carbohydrate, sodium, and electrolytes. Avoid foods that are high in fat and protein because these will slow digestion.
- Continue to drink fluids regularly throughout the day to avoid dehydration. Use a combination of sport drinks and water.
- Do not choose a competition as the place to experiment with new foods or beverages. Stick with what you know works for you. Many athletes have been undone by gastrointestinal problems because they tried something new at their competition.
- Bring your own food and don't rely on what is offered at the meet snack bar or even the local restaurants.

### PERFORMANCE TIP

When athletes participating in an exercise to exhaustion test consumed low-GI foods as part of their precompetition meal, they performed 20 percent longer compared with those who ate a meal consisting of high-GI foods.

In a trials–finals format, after the morning session, eat a meal that is high in carbohydrate with some protein. Also drink fluids that contain some sodium. This will aid in refueling and help you with your recovery for the evening session. A high-GI meal will quicken the recovery process. Eat additional carbohydrate-rich snacks at regular intervals leading up to the finals. Also, recognize that your energy expenditure will likely be lower on competition days than during training. Adjust your caloric intake appropriately so you do not gain weight that could impair performance.

While you may think that race-day nutrition is a small thing, know that the best swimmers in the world do not take it for granted. Michael Klim, for example, an Australian swimmer and former world-record holder, placed a great deal of importance on race-day nutrition and has been quoted as saying, "I like to get replenishment in the first half hour after my race with high-carbohydrate drinks and foods, especially when I have a busy program with more than one race each night. I have to fit in swim-downs, massage, drug tests, the next race, coaches, the media. It can be frantic. I have my own supplies organized—a sport drink, bananas, or something sweet." You can take a couple of things from this comment. First, recognize that the best athletes in the world do not leave anything to chance. Race day nutrition is a priority and is not something that gets ignored until after everything else is done. Along the same lines, these athletes bring their own foods to the competition—they do not count on the snack bar having what they need to refuel and recover.

# CARBOHYDRATE LOADING

Carbohydrate loading is a technique used by endurance athletes to store higher-than-normal levels of glycogen in the muscles. Carbohydrate loading has the potential of postponing fatigue, and research has shown this practice can extend the ability to maintain moderate-intensity exercise by as much as 20 percent. Here is a commonly used carbohydrate-loading plan in the week leading up to the competition:

1. Take a three- to four-day depletion phase in which you consume lower-than-normal amounts of carbohydrate (roughly 40 to 50 percent of the daily caloric intake) while you maintain your training volume.
2. Follow this with a three- to five-day loading phase in which you back off your training intensity while consuming large amounts of carbohydrate—3.2 to 5.5 grams per pound of body weight, representing roughly 70 to 80 percent of the total caloric intake on these days.
3. Studies on well-trained athletes have shown they increase glycogen stores after three or four days of high-carbohydrate consumption when this corresponds with a taper, even though they do not go through the low-carbohydrate phase.

Theoretically, carbohydrate loading should benefit athletes who compete only in events that are long enough to bring about glycogen depletion (longer-distance races, open-water swimming, or triathlons), and it is questionable whether this practice benefits sprinters and middle-distance swimmers, especially if they have already been eating healthful, carbohydrate-rich meals.

> **PERFORMANCE TIP**
>
> Carbohydrate loading can result in body weight gains of up to 4 pounds (just under 2 kg). This is due mainly to water retention associated with the increased glycogen stored in the muscles.

Many swimmers have a tendency to go overboard with this practice, and it is not uncommon to see a detrimental weight gain during the taper because of the excess carbohydrate consumed. On the advice of some sport nutritionists, carbohydrate loading is being phased out and the newer approach of nutritional periodization is coming to the forefront as the best way to ensure that swimmers are properly fueled year-round for their training cycles.

# NUTRITIONAL SUPPLEMENTS

By definition, a nutritional supplement is *anything* put into the body other than what is consumed through a normal diet, including multivitamins and sport drinks. To many athletes, the words *nutritional supplements* conjure up images of steroids, human growth hormone, hypodermic needles, pills, or any one of the products you can purchase at the nutritional store in the mall. No matter how you define it, the numbers and types of nutritional supplements touted as enhancing performance seem to increase exponentially every year. But are these supplements safe? Do they work? These are important questions, and before putting any supplement into your body, you should research the product and find out as much as you can regarding its safety, legality of use in sport, and efficacy.

One important thing to keep in mind is that the supplement industry is largely unregulated. That means the supplement manufacturers are not held to the same standards as the U.S. Food and Drug Administration (FDA) places on companies that produce foods and beverages. So risks can be involved in taking supplements. First, many of the manufacturers' claims about how the supplements will improve performance or health are not supported by research or the FDA; most supplements will carry some type of disclaimer on their label stating that. Additionally, what's inside the bottle is not always what's on the label. This is especially important to swimmers who could be tested for performance-enhancing drugs.

In 2003, the International Olympic Committee tested over 600 supplements that they took off the shelf from supplement stores throughout the world. They found that 15 percent contained substances that were not listed on the label and would have resulted in a positive drug test had a swimmer taken them and been tested. Over 18 percent of the supplements tested from the United States were found to contain banned substances not listed on the label. The bottom line is that you are responsible for what you put in your body, and it is often worthwhile to do some research on your own to find out what is really known about a supplement. Don't just believe what is written on the label. Scour the Internet for information, particularly on risks and benefits. The Australian Institute for Sport (AIS) has developed a comprehensive Web site on nutritional supplements that can serve as a first step in your research.

Several of the supplements that are thought to be safe and have some performance-enhancing effects are creatine, caffeine, and sodium bicarbonate or sodium citrate. Potential risks and benefits are outlined in the next section. Remember that, as an athlete subject to drug testing, these are supplements that could be contaminated with other substances, and you take these at your own risk. Additionally, only *adults* should use supplements; the use of any of these substances, although legal in many cases, is discouraged for minors.

**Creatine**   Creatine is one component of creatine phosphate, the most immediate source of energy in your muscles. While the research is divided on whether creatine loading affects performance, several studies have shown a benefit in repeated, high-intensity efforts. It does not appear that creatine loading provides much or any benefit for single races or endurance efforts—so its benefits more likely are relevant for practices rather than competitions. Creatine loading protocols typically recommend taking 20 to 30 grams per day, broken into six or seven doses throughout the day, for five days. Then 2 to 5 grams should be taken per day for maintenance. Other research also suggests the same gains can be made by taking the maintenance dose for 30 days. Note that creatine is a supplement, and if you take it, you do so at your own risk. It is also necessary to drink extra fluids when taking creatine.

**Caffeine**   Caffeine may have a performance-enhancing effect on endurance swimming races since it acts as a stimulant to the central nervous system. Research done in sports other than swimming suggests an intake of 1.4 to 4.1 milligrams per pound of body weight can affect performance, although the appropriate time to ingest the caffeine has not been nailed down specifically. Therefore, if you choose to take caffeine, you will have to find a prerace strategy that works best for you (typically 60 to 90 minutes prerace or training). Note that caffeine is a stimulant, and high doses can cause tremors and anxiety and affect quality of sleep. This can have a significant effect on swimmers who need sleep to recover between the preliminary and final heats.

**Sodium Bicarbonate or Sodium Citrate Loading**   Research suggests that the use of sodium bicarbonate (baking soda) or sodium citrate (both considered to be supplements) may improve buffering capacity and allow the body to tolerate larger changes in pH in events lasting from one to seven minutes. Typical loading strategies suggest ingesting 300 milligrams per kilogram of body weight of sodium bicarbonate or 500 milligrams per kilogram of body weight of sodium citrate one to two hours before performance. Longer-term loading leading up to a competition (such as 500 milligrams per kilogram of body weight per day, broken into several smaller doses throughout the day, for five days) might also enhance competitive performance. Note that bicarbonate loading can cause gastrointestinal distress, and diarrhea is an unfortunate consequence in some people. Most people seem to tolerate sodium citrate better, but you should experiment with a loading protocol before your competition.

# Chapter 10

# Creating a Strength and Conditioning Program

N ow that you've read about the ways in which strength and conditioning can improve your swimming performance, let's discuss how you can structure your training during the course of a season. Several training principles underlie program design, but when it comes down to it, the most important thing is having a plan—knowing your specific goals or those of the swimmers you coach. Know what you want to do and when you want to do it. You might have the goal of peaking twice this year, and you want those peak performances to occur at the spring and summer state championship meets. You might differ quite a bit from someone on the national team who has the goal of peaking only once a year at the Pan Pacific Games or the World Championships, or even once every four years at the Olympic Games. Whether you're a member of the national team, a masters swimmer, an age-group swimmer, or a triathlete, a well-designed strength and conditioning program will help you take your performance to the next level. No matter what your aspirations are, the more you understand the science behind periodization and developing a training plan, the better you will become in the process of integrating your strength training with your swimming.

## PERIODIZATION FOR SWIMMERS

Periodization is the scientific and systematic process of designing a season by breaking it into various phases. For as long as athletic records have been kept, the best athletes in the world have recognized the benefits of periodized training, starting with the ancient Greeks as athletes prepared for the Games of the Ancient Olympiad. More recently, Eastern European nations used periodized training to maximize performance in athletes participating across a range of sports. Through the 20th and now 21st centuries, the principles underlying periodization have continued to be developed and become scientifically validated.

In most sports, the season is typically broken into four phases:

1. Preparation and training
2. Building power and sport-specific strength
3. Competition
4. Rest and recovery

Each of these phases serves a specific purpose in preparing athletes for the unique demands of training and competition. Swimming, as you know, is different from most other sports, and these differences extend to how you should plan your training. For one, since swimming is performed in the water, an environment governed by a different set of physical rules than land-based sports use, the periodized plan should be modified to include a fifth phase—a preliminary phase that allows you to become refamiliarized with the water at the start of the season. This will eventually become the first phase in a periodized plan.

When you follow the approach of breaking a season into phases and focusing your training to achieve certain goals within each phase, you maximize your chances of achieving peak performances at the most important competitions throughout the year. There are many reasons why periodization produces greater results than more traditional training methods, but one of the most important aspects is that periodization incorporates planned periods of rest and recovery.

**PERFORMANCE TIP**

Traditionally, the phases of a periodized plan have been named the preparation, precompetition, competition, and active rest phases. These phases have been renamed in this book and a fifth phase has been added to better reflect the demands of the swimming season.

## Benefits of Periodization Training

One of the greatest rewards for putting together a periodized program is that you can design your training so you will peak when you want to. While we have stressed that swimmers should be able to race fast at any time of the year, there is usually one competition, or several competitions, where you truly want to be at your best—where the physical, physiological, and mental sides of swimming all come together for you to achieve a peak performance. In high school, it might be the season-ending championships. In college, it could be the NCAAs or the conference championships. A masters swimmer might want to peak for the long-course nationals at the end of the summer. Periodization is a proven method for achieving peak performances at those most important times throughout the year.

The list of benefits of periodized training is quite long, but some aspects are of specific interest to swimmers:

- It helps you structure your training to develop all the attributes you need as a swimmer: endurance, strength, and power. The gains in these areas are often larger than what you would experience if you did not engage in a periodized training plan.
- It adds variety to your training and can increase enjoyment while also helping to prevent performance plateaus.
- It provides a structure and a logical progression to your training. You first build a base of strength and then focus on power development. This type of progressive overload is a healthy way to build strength and improve performance because you do not try to accomplish too much too soon.
- It reduces the risk of overtraining and burnout.
- It aids in injury prevention by providing opportunities for rest and recovery.

## Periodization and Rest

If you train long enough and hard enough, eventually your body will tell you that you need to take a break. For some, an illness might force them to take a break from training. For others, it might be an injury. One of the major benefits of a periodized training plan is that periods of rest are designed as part of a training schedule, providing opportunities for recovery. Periods of rest are actually scheduled into each training week, and longer periods of rest are incorporated into the training calendar at certain times throughout the year so you will not break down and will be ready to train and compete at your optimum.

It's important to take time each week to allow the body to recover from the stress you put it through the rest of the week. Most programs traditionally build one off day into the training week to allow for rest and recovery. This approach to training is supported by science. However, some coaches and athletes train every day without a break and have good results.

## TRAINING OLYMPIANS

In the season leading up to the 2004 Olympic Trials, we took a slightly different approach and implemented a three-to-one training schedule: We repeated a cycle of three training days followed by one off day. Within the three days of work, the workload varied depending on each athlete's event, but generally speaking, the pattern consisted of double practices on days 1 and 3 and a single practice on day 2. On days 1 and 3, the morning session was usually in the weight room, and the afternoon session was in the water. Training on the middle day of the three-day cycle was in the water. Needless to say, the team swam well enough at the Olympic Trials to place four athletes on the U.S. Olympic team; several others narrowly missed berths, proving that rest and recovery, coupled with appropriate training, can lead to great results.

During the year, it is beneficial to take a week or two away from competitive training to allow your body to become recharged both physically and mentally. Most coaches and athletes should consider including some cross-training during early phases of their training (see chapter 4). Cross-training can include activities such as soccer and biking to develop athleticism and general conditioning. This type of training helps in preparation for the progressively increasing workload that will come with swim training in the late training stages. This type of active rest away from the pool also helps you recover mentally.

In your program you might not train twice a day, but you might swim most days of the week. The principle of rest still applies; be sure to schedule rest into your training plan either by taking a complete day off from training or using certain workouts during the week to do some easy swimming.

### PERFORMANCE TIP

Periodization is based on the principles of progressive overload and general adaptation. These principles state that the body will respond in a positive way to increased demands placed on it (for example, muscular strength will increase if you lift progressively heavier weights) but that adequate rest must also be provided to allow the body to recover appropriately.

## Phases of a Periodized Training Plan for Swimming

The following pages discuss the five phases that should make up your periodized training plan for swimming:

1. Preliminary phase
2. Training phase

3. Competition phase

4. Championship phase

5. Active rest phase

The names of the phases reflect the goals and the timing in the training and competitive season. Let's look at each of these phases and what they focus on in a bit more detail.

**Preliminary Phase**   At the start of the season, you should schedule a period of several weeks to achieve the following goals:

- Get into the regularity of training, which includes regaining a feel for the water while also developing your warm-up and precompetition routines. This early phase of a season is also an ideal time to work on general nonswimming conditioning. In my club and collegiate programs, we spend several weeks doing dryland cross-training activities, such as ultimate Frisbee and soccer. I would rather have my athletes engaged in play activity than pure running for conditioning.

- Work on technique and build consistency and efficiency in the strokes. One of the greatest areas of improvement in swimming can come from improved technique, and establishing early-season technique without being compromised by fatigue is critical to your success during a season.

The preliminary phase serves as a time for you to refamiliarize yourself with the water after a time away from intense training. Typically, we come into the preliminary phase after a period of active rest (described later in the chapter).

**Training Phase**   The focus of the training phase is on developing a base level of fitness and muscular endurance—what we have previously called foundational strength and conditioning. Swimmers typically put in their highest volume of work in this phase, both in the pool and during their strength and conditioning workouts. Here are some specific guidelines that we emphasize during this phase:

- To truly build a solid strength and fitness base, dedicate at least six weeks to the training phase. An even longer block of time (eight weeks or more) can be better.

- Use moderate resistance and high repetitions in strength training to build cardiorespiratory fitness and muscular endurance.

- In the water, do something hard and fast almost every day. As long as you use good technique and the proper stroke mechanics (even while fatigued), you can maintain fast swimming throughout the season, which will lead to tremendous benefits in the championship phase of the season.

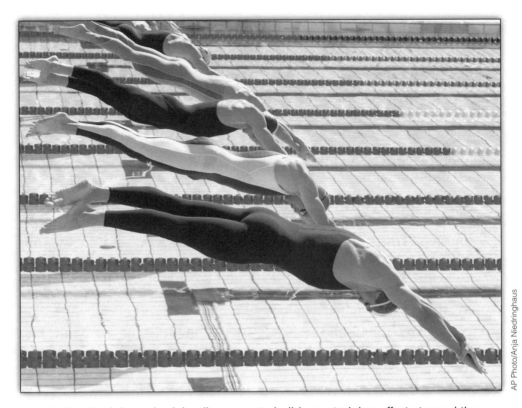

A periodized training schedule allows you to build your training efforts toward the competitions at which you want to peak.

- The work put in during this phase serves as the foundation from which you will develop power and swimming-specific strength. Your peak performances will also be determined in large part by the work done in this phase.
- If you give this phase the emphasis it deserves, it might mean training through some meets and not resting much early in the competitive schedule. The long-term benefit of putting in an extended period of solid training outweighs any potential short-term gains you might get from resting for an early-season competition.

**Competition Phase** The competition phase is the main part of the competitive season that leads up to the season-ending championship meet. In college and high school, the competition phase would be the dual-meet season. In age-group and masters swimming, this is the nonchampionship competitive season. Here are some specific points that we focus on in the competition phase:

- Build on the work put in during the training phase by making the training more specific to certain events and strokes. Emphasize swimming fast every day and building race-specific speed and mechanics (such as stroke rates and cycle counts).

- Strength training and conditioning work should become more swimming specific and shift from building muscular endurance to developing strength and power. We do this at USC by increasing training intensity while decreasing volume and incorporating more power-based exercises into training.

- Although there should still be an aerobic component to the training, the focus should be more on training with an intensity and a work-to-rest ratio that reflect the demands of the race.

- The competition phase should last four to six weeks so you can build the power and strength to swim your fastest.

**Championship Phase**   The championship phase encompasses the weeks leading up to and including the championship meet where swimmers hope to achieve their peak performances.

- The focus of the championship phase is recovery and energy replenishment (see information in the section titled Tapering for Swimmers) as well as fine-tuning your swimming so everything comes together at the main meet.

- Here again, training should be as swimming specific as possible— swimming at race paces and with race-appropriate stroke rates.

- Research indicates you can maintain a peak for only about three weeks. After that, you will have performance decrements, and you will need to go back to training levels achieved in the training phase or the competition phase in order to peak again.

## PEAKING FOR MAJOR COMPETITIONS SPACED CLOSE TOGETHER

It is possible to schedule two championship phases relatively close together on the calendar and to do well in both without having to go through every phase of the periodized plan again. The key is allowing adequate time for some hard training between the two. Take the Olympic Trials and the Olympics as an example. Because of the way they are typically scheduled, swimmers are able to peak for the Olympic Trials and then go back into the pool to do some hard training again and set their bodies up to peak again for the Olympic Games.

**Active Rest Phase**   This is a period at the end of the competitive season when you should take a mental and physical break from intense training.

- This is not supposed to be a time of physical inactivity. You should cross-train and engage in some aerobic exercise (see chapter 4) to maintain your level of fitness.

- Get into the water every couple of days to maintain your feel for the water. However, don't swim a workout. Keep things fun and play in the water. One or two weeks without swimming will not result in significant detraining.

Within each of these phases are cycles as well. For example, even if you are in the competition phase of your training, a cycle that focuses on the development of power and swimming-specific skills, you should still have days that focus on endurance. Or, if you are in the training phase, you should still have some training days that focus on developing power. The themes that were established previously represent the major focus for each phase. Cycling periods of work and rest and manipulating intensity, frequency, and variation of exercises will keep you fresh and help you achieve peak performances.

If you want to peak twice in a given year, you should go through each of these phases two times. If you try to peak more than twice in a calendar year, there is a chance you will limit what you can accomplish because you will not have enough time to put in the necessary work in each phase. Chapter 11 presents several examples of structuring a season to meet your competitive goals.

### PERFORMANCE TIP

Many articles on periodization use the words *macrocycle*, *mesocycle*, and *microcycle*. A macrocycle typically represents one full season—one time through each phase of the periodized plan. A mesocycle is a phase of your training plan (such as the training phase or the competition phase), and a microcycle is typically a one- to two-week period within the phase in which you emphasize the development of a specific skill or attribute. For example, within an eight-week training phase—the mesocycle where the major emphasis is on muscular endurance—you might have several one-week microcycles in which you focus more heavily on power development.

## TAPERING FOR SWIMMERS

The swimming season usually culminates in a taper period (a period of reduced training volume) leading up to a major competition. The purpose of the taper is to reduce the physical, mental, and emotional stress that is placed on the body so it can fully recover by the time the major competition rolls around. Tapering is built into the culture of swimming, and some tapering is necessary for swimmers to fine-tune their technique and race strategy. However, many coaches and athletes actually place too much importance on tapering and think that a good taper can make up for a year's worth of poor training or lack of structure in the seasonal training plan. Swimmers often lament, "I just missed my taper," after a bad season-ending performance, blaming everything on the taper when really the poor performances were the result of poor training.

Placing too much emphasis on the taper goes against our general training philosophy. The theory behind a taper is that you have placed such high levels of stress on your body that you now need to provide an extended period for recovery. In a properly designed training plan, structured rest should already be built into the training, and as such, you should never have extreme levels of fatigue. You should be prepared to swim fast at any time throughout the season. The taper should provide that little bit extra to allow you to achieve your best race performances.

## General Guidelines for Tapering

To assist you as you plan your taper, consider the following points taken from the research on tapering:

- The taper can bring about a 25 percent increase in swimming power, resulting in as much as a 5 percent improvement in swimming speed. (Swimmers often shave after a taper, so this increase in speed reflects a combination of tapering and shaving.)
- A typical taper should last from one to three weeks.
- The length of the taper will depend on several factors, including your training history. Someone who does a great deal of high-intensity training (such as a sprinter) will typically need a longer taper than swimmers who have less high-intensity work in their training (such as distance swimmers). The intense nature of sprinting actually places greater stresses on the body, and it takes slightly longer for the body to recover.
- During the taper, reduce the volume of swimming you do, not swimming intensity. This allows you to maintain your efficiency and power. Reduce the training volume as much as 90 percent over the course of the taper. Maintaining intensity is critical for achieving maximum results.
- A progressive taper, in which the volume of training decreases gradually, reaps greater rewards than a sudden decrease in distance.
- Once a taper starts, don't expect to gain any additional physiological conditioning. All of the improvements come from allowing your body to catch up to the training you've put in.
- Females typically require a shorter time in their tapering than males.
- Older swimmers may need more tapering time than younger swimmers.
- You also need to think about nutrition. Since you are swimming less, you will have to adjust your food intake during a taper to balance the energy you expend.

- Remember that the feel does not determine your performance. Too many athletes think the taper phase will result in a good feel. That may or may not be the result of tapering. Regardless of the feel, your body has been prepared through systematic training and will give the desired result, but it might not *feel* great. Think of the body as a car engine during a taper. Take a couple of sparkplugs out of the engine—it will feel very rough, but it will go the speed you desire.

# BUILDING YOUR PERIODIZED TRAINING PLAN

Start developing your periodized training program by identifying your major competitions during the year and then filling in around them rather than starting with the beginning of the season and planning forward from there. Following are a series of steps you can take as you put together your program. Chapter 11 also presents sample training programs that you can follow if you want to peak two times during the year, with a third smaller peak, as well as a blank seasonal planning tool you can use to help you put together your schedule.

1. Identify the most important swimming competitions, as well as any taper time leading up to them, as your championship phases.

2. Lay out your competition phases for the season. Plan at least three weeks for each; that is when you transition from building general strength to swimming-specific strength and power.

3. Schedule your active rest phases. After each major championship phase, block out one to two weeks that you will use to cross-train and take a break from swimming. Many times, planning a rest gets left until the end or gets left out of scheduling entirely. But it is one of the most important components of your training and should be scheduled appropriately.

4. Plan out the remaining phases, considering the next three points simultaneously:

   - Schedule a six- to eight-week training phase at the start of the season that you will use to build your strength and conditioning base. This phase can last even longer if you have that luxury, but remember, you want to leave at least four weeks to do your swimming-specific training during the competition phase. If you break the year into several seasons, the initial training phase should last six to eight weeks (such as at the start of the short-course season in September), but subsequent training phases need to be only four to six weeks (such as at the start of the summer long-course season).

   - Schedule an appropriate preliminary phase after each active rest phase. You should use this one to two weeks to build general conditioning back into your swimming.

- Your first time planning, you might find that everything does not fit. If this is the case, don't be discouraged. Go back and see where you can change things. Maybe you need to train hard through a competition. Reassess your priorities and realize it is what happens at the end of the road that is most important.
- Become even more detailed in your planning and outline your goals for each week of training throughout the year, including specific exercises, sets and repetitions, and loads. Chapter 11 covers this in greater detail.

# Year-Round Sample Programs

Having a knowledge of the *theory* behind strength and conditioning is great, but the rubber really meets the road when it comes to putting it all together and actually developing a training plan. Let's recap what we have accomplished up to this point.

- We've discussed the demands of swimming and the reasons why strength and conditioning is important for swimmers.
- We've presented dozens of exercises that build a foundation of strength in the core and throughout the body and develop stroke-specific strength and power.
- We've discussed the energy continuum and the importance of training to race.
- We've looked at the five phases of a periodized training plan and how to set up a training season.

In this chapter, we want to help you pull everything together and develop a training plan that is right for you. We present examples of structuring the season into the five phases, provide general examples of designing a training session, and then offer sample strength and conditioning workouts for five training scenarios:

1. Age-group swimmers aged 14 and under (taking into account the special considerations when working with these swimmers)
2. Competitive age-group swimmers over 14 years of age
3. Collegiate swimmers
4. Masters swimmers and triathletes
5. Fitness swimmers whose main goal is to maintain fitness (they might not have any desire to compete)

In each case, the goal is to show how strength and conditioning can, and should, complement in-water training to enhance swimming performance. We've made the programs appropriate to as many swimmers as possible and have done some things you will not find in any other strength and conditioning book for swimming:

- Most of the exercises were chosen because they can be performed on deck or at home with a minimal amount of special equipment.
- The workouts have been designed to take approximately 30 to 45 minutes to complete, unless otherwise noted.
- The exercise routines do not include specific warm-up or stretching exercises. Within each exercise program is a period to be devoted to these activities, but it is up to you to choose the appropriate exercises to include in your plan.
- The plans are designed for average swimmers. We recognize that you can change anything (sets, reps, number of exercises, emphasis) to match your own needs and physical capabilities. We simply want to give you an idea of how to put a strength and conditioning program together and then turn you loose to come up with your own plan and make any modifications you need.
- Included are a number of assumptions about the training environment (such as number of practices per week, hours of training per day) and the competitive or training goals. That way, if the goals do not match what you hope to accomplish or the available resources and equipment, you can modify your training plan accordingly.
- The programs are intended to guide you in your training. You can use these workouts over and over, but you will see greater improvements and enjoy the process more if you mix things up and create your own workouts using those presented here as a template.

As you go through the chapter, you will see a lot of repetition. For example, similar information is presented during the active rest phase for each scenario. Keep in mind that the chapter is not meant to be read from start to finish. If you are a masters swimmer, you will go right to the section designed for masters swimmers and triathletes, skipping over the information for competitive age-group swimmers. Similarly, age-group swimmers will want to focus their attention on the section devoted to their unique training scenario.

# TRAINING PROGRAMS FOR YOUNG AGE-GROUP SWIMMERS

Designing a strength and conditioning program for young swimmers carries with it some unique demands. When we use the words *young swimmers*, we are referring to swimmers who have not yet gone through puberty. In general, this is for boys aged 14 and under and girls aged 12 and under.

The exercise routines provided in this chapter are applicable to both boys and girls, and they are safe for swimmers as young as 8 years.

As is the case with any age-group swimmers, 14-and-under swimmers who embark on a strength and conditioning program must be well supervised and understand the importance of following specific instructions from the coach. Safety is more important than any gains that might be realized in a strength program for younger age-group swimmers. In my years with the Irvine Novaquatics, work with the novice swimmers has focused on introducing flexibility training, building some basic core stability, and preventing injury. As swimmers progress through the program and their swimming performance improves, structured and supervised sessions with low-weight medicine balls, stretch cords, and Pilates are introduced. The resistance at this stage should be light to moderate—swimmers should be able to perform 25 to 30 repetitions before fatigue sets in.

## Seasonal Training Plan for Young Age-Group Swimmers

| 1 | 2 | 3 | 4 | 5 | 6 | 7 | 8 | 9 | 10 | 11 | 12 | 13 | 14 | 15 | 16 | 17 | 18 |
|---|---|---|---|---|---|---|---|---|----|----|----|----|----|----|----|----|----|
| | September | | | | | October | | | | November | | | | December | | | |

| 19 | 20 | 21 | 22 | 23 | 24 | 25 | 26 | 27 | 28 | 29 | 30 | 31 | 32 | 33 | 34 | 35 |
|----|----|----|----|----|----|----|----|----|----|----|----|----|----|----|----|----|
| | January | | | | February | | | | March | | | | April | | | |

| 36 | 37 | 38 | 39 | 40 | 41 | 42 | 43 | 44 | 45 | 46 | 47 | 48 | 49 | 50 | 51 | 52 |
|----|----|----|----|----|----|----|----|----|----|----|----|----|----|----|----|----|
| | May | | | | June | | | | July | | | | August | | | |

Preliminary phase: ☐    Training phase: ▨    Competition phase: ▨
Championship phase: ▧    Active rest phase: ■

## Assumptions and Guidelines

This sample training program for young swimmers takes the following considerations into account:

- The primary goal of young swimmers is to develop solid technique and a strong training base that will assist in injury prevention and enhance performance later in their development.

- The swimmers have not yet gone through puberty and therefore will not be doing any power-based exercises or heavy lifting, including lifting heavy weights above their heads.

- The focus of all exercises should be on preventing injury, promoting overall athleticism, and building a foundation of muscular endurance. Resistance will be provided by body weight, light dumbbells, or low- to moderate-resistance elastic tubing.

- Before engaging in any strength training, swimmers should demonstrate the emotional maturity to stay focused through the training session and be able to follow instructions.

- The swimmers have three to five in-water training sessions each week, each lasting one to two hours.

- Strength training may be included as part of the normal training sessions, but most likely the athletes will be expected to do any dryland training at home under the supervision of an adult.

- There should be at least one complete day of rest during the week.

- The swimmers will try to peak twice a year: at a championship meet at the end of the short-course season (week 29) and again at the end of the summer long-course season (week 49). Another minor peak is included in week 16 near the end of the calendar year.

## General Strength and Conditioning

The general theme of injury prevention, athleticism, and endurance should remain fairly consistent throughout the year, regardless of the training phase. Although swimmers will gain strength, the main priority is to develop some basic skills and become familiar with exercise technique. The technique work during this developmental phase lays the foundation for more advanced training as the swimmers get older. Even though power is not the focus of the training at this age, some low-level power exercises (such as jumping rope or skipping) are included in the programs. These exercises do not involve high levels of force, and several help to build athletic skills, such as agility and balance. As swimmers progress into the competition and championship phases, they should taper their strength workouts to stay in step with their in-water workouts. It is even appropriate to stop strength training completely during those times. However, swimmers should be encouraged to continue working on flexibility—they should stretch every day if possible.

A typical workout for young swimmers can be modeled after this template:

| Time or number of exercises | Exercise | Duration |
|---|---|---|
| 5-10 minutes | Dynamic warm-up | 30 seconds per exercise |
| 2-3 exercises | Injury prevention | 1-2 × 20 reps |
| 2-3 exercises | Core stability | 2 × 20 reps or 30 seconds per exercise |
| 1-2 exercises | Foundational strength | 2 × 20 reps |
| 0-1 exercises | Low to moderate power | 2 × 15-30 seconds |
| 10-15 minutes | Static stretching | 20-30 seconds per stretch |

The following are several sample exercise routines to be used year-round:

## Sample Strength and Conditioning Workouts for Young Swimmers

| Type of exercise | Workout I | Workout II | Workout III |
|---|---|---|---|
| Warm-up | Dynamic warm-up | Dynamic warm-up | Dynamic warm-up |
| Injury prevention | Full can | Shoulder retraction with external rotation | Catch position external rotation |
| | Upper-body step-up | Shoulder blade pinch | Chest punch |
| | Standing external rotation | Ball rotation | Full can |
| Core stability | Bird dog | Leg drop | Side bridge |
| | Dying bug | Back bridge | T exercise |
| | Prone bridge | Ab crunch with rotation | Back extension |
| Foundational strength | Lunge | Monster walk | Squat |
| | Upright row | Seated row | Lunge |
| Low to moderate power | Jump rope | Skipping | Lateral line hop |
| Cool-down | Static stretching | Static stretching | Static stretching |

# TRAINING PROGRAMS FOR COMPETITIVE AGE-GROUP SWIMMERS

In a club environment, strength and conditioning and in-water training often have to be included in the same training session. Within a two-hour practice time, a swimmer might devote one hour to strength training and one hour to in-water training. This makes it especially important to have a focus for the day's training so one aspect of training does not negatively affect the other.

One of the most important considerations when putting together a strength and conditioning program for age-group swimmers (generally older than 14) is safety. Long-term development is still the goal, and in reality, strength and power will peak after a swimmer has left the age-group program and has gone on to college. Before the college experience, however, swimmers can benefit from a well-designed strength and conditioning program. The dryland program should be introductory; most of the work should focus on building endurance, using light to moderate weights and even body-weight activities (core exercises, pull-ups, lunges), doing low- to moderate-intensity power exercises with medicine balls when appropriate, and using elastic tubing to build strength. In these early stages of development, both the in-water and any dryland training programs should emphasize technique.

Here is a sample seasonal training plan for competitive age-group swimmers, which outlines how the season can be periodized into training phases.

## Seasonal Training Plan for a Competitive Age-Group Swimmer

| 1 | 2 | 3 | 4 | 5 | 6 | 7 | 8 | 9 | 10 | 11 | 12 | 13 | 14 | 15 | 16 | 17 | 18 |
|---|---|---|---|---|---|---|---|---|----|----|----|----|----|----|----|----|----|
| September | | | | | October | | | | November | | | | December | | | | |

| 19 | 20 | 21 | 22 | 23 | 24 | 25 | 26 | 27 | 28 | 29 | 30 | 31 | 32 | 33 | 34 | 35 |
|----|----|----|----|----|----|----|----|----|----|----|----|----|----|----|----|----|
| January | | | | February | | | | March | | | | | April | | | |

| 36 | 37 | 38 | 39 | 40 | 41 | 42 | 43 | 44 | 45 | 46 | 47 | 48 | 49 | 50 | 51 | 52 |
|----|----|----|----|----|----|----|----|----|----|----|----|----|----|----|----|----|
| May | | | | June | | | | | July | | | | August | | | |

Preliminary phase: ☐   Training phase: ☐   Competition phase: ☐
Championship phase: ■   Active rest phase: ■

## Assumptions and Guidelines

The seasonal plan takes the following considerations into account:

- The focus for competitive age-group swimmers should be on long-term development. Yet, the swimmers still want to achieve competitive success, peaking twice during the year—at the end of the winter-to-spring short-course season (weeks 30 to 31) and again at the end of the summer long-course season (weeks 48 to 49). Included here is one additional minor peak toward the end of the calendar year (week 16).

- These swimmers are able to train once a day for 1.5 to 3 hours in the afternoon, and they have one full day off from training during the week.

- Swimmers will do strength and conditioning for up to an hour three times per week as a part of these scheduled workouts.

- Injury prevention and performance enhancement share equal levels of importance with this group of swimmers.

- Swimmers in this program have gone through puberty and are able to engage in low- to moderate-intensity power training.

- There is a period of active rest after each championship phase. In week 17, this active rest phase may be shortened to allow the swimmers to get into holiday training.

- While in the training phase, the swimmers can still compete; however, the focus of the training is still on building general strength.

- The taper should be incorporated into the final weeks of the competition phase.

## Strength and Conditioning in the Preliminary Phase

In the preliminary phase, competitive age-group swimmers will likely want to regain a feel for the water while also easing into the new strength and conditioning program. As such, the exercises presented in this phase focus on building endurance and core stability and preventing injury. Most of these exercises can be performed as a group at the start or end of a practice. Training should occur two or three times a week, and the resistance should be such that the swimmers are starting to feel fatigued at the end of 20 to 25 repetitions.

| Time or number of exercises | Exercise | Duration |
|---|---|---|
| 10 minutes | Dynamic warm-up | 30 seconds per exercise |
| 2-3 exercises | Injury prevention | 2 × 20 reps |
| 2-3 exercises | Core stability | 2 × 20 reps or 30 seconds per exercise |
| 2-3 exercises | Foundational strength | 2 × 20 reps |
| 15-20 minutes | Static stretching | 20-30 seconds per stretch |

Several sample exercise routines for the preliminary phase are shown here:

## Preliminary Phase Workouts for Competitive Age-Group Swimmers

| Type of exercise | Workout I | Workout II | Workout III |
|---|---|---|---|
| Warm-up | Dynamic warm-up | Dynamic warm-up | Dynamic warm-up |
| Injury prevention | Full can | Standing external rotation | Catch position external rotation |
| | Chest punch | Upper-body step-up | Ball rotation |
| | Shoulder retraction with external rotation | Y exercise | Full can |
| Core stability | Leg drop | Dying bug | Back bridge |
| | Prone bridge | Prone bridge | Ab crunch with rotation |
| | Bird dog | Side bridge | Side bridge |
| Foundational strength | Lunge | Step-up | Squat |
| | Seated row | Ankle dorsiflexion | Calf raise |
| | Grip strengthening | Wrist flexion and extension | Core chest press |
| Cool-down | Static stretching | Static stretching | Static stretching |

## Strength and Conditioning in the Training Phase

Since complete teams tend to work at the same time in age-group programs, it is often appropriate to set up strength and conditioning circuits—a series of exercise stations that the swimmers rotate through—rather than have multiple sites for a given exercise. The following are some general guidelines for setting up a strength training circuit:

- Unless otherwise noted, swimmers should spend 30 seconds on and 30 seconds off, rotating stations after the 30-second work interval is completed.
- Swimmers should go through the entire circuit two times.
- The circuit can be set up so there are as many stations as there are swimmers. For the purpose of this book, it is assumed there are 15 athletes in the group.
- Resistance will be provided by body weight or moderate-resistance elastic tubing.
- Swimmers should perform a dynamic warm-up before each training session, and they should do static stretching at the end of the strength training or after swimming practice if the athletes get into the pool after the strength training.
- Swimmers should also engage in in-water strength and power training by doing such things as swimming against resistance and vertical kicking.

The general structure of the circuit should be as follows:

| Time or number of exercises | Exercise | Duration |
|---|---|---|
| 10 minutes | Dynamic warm-up | 30 seconds per exercise |
| 4 exercises | Injury prevention | 30 seconds per exercise |
| 3 exercises | Core stability | 30 seconds per exercise |
| 4 exercises | Foundational strength | 30 seconds per exercise |
| 3 exercises | Stroke-specific strength | 30 seconds per exercise |
| 1 exercise | Low to moderate power | 30 seconds per exercise |
| 10 minutes | Static stretching | 20-30 seconds per stretch |

Two examples of a strength training circuit for the training phase are presented here:

## Training Phase Workouts for Competitive Age-Group Swimmers

| Type of exercise | Workout I | Workout II |
|---|---|---|
| Warm-up | Dynamic warm-up | Dynamic warm-up |
| Injury prevention | Full can | Catch position external rotation |
| | Chest punch | Upper-body step-up |
| | Standing external rotation | Ball rotation |
| | Shoulder blade pinch | Shoulder retraction with external rotation |
| Core stability | Prone bridge | Bird dog |
| | Dying bug | Leg drop |
| | Side bridge | Back bridge |
| Foundational strength | Lunge | Squat |
| | Calf raise | Ankle dorsiflexion |
| | Seated row | Lat pull-down |
| | Triceps extension | Monster walk |
| Stroke-specific strength | Medicine ball leg lift | Straight-arm row |
| | Back extension with rotation | Walking lunge with rotation |
| | High-to-low chop | Russian twist |
| Low to moderate power | Lateral line hop | Jump rope |
| Cool-down | Static stretching | Static stretching |

## Strength and Conditioning in the Competition Phase

Continue to use a moderate-resistance strength training circuit during the competition phase of the season, performing each exercise for 30 seconds before switching. The main focus of the training is still on developing foundational strength, although some additional swimming-specific exercises and moderate-intensity power exercises are included. Since most age-group swimmers have not specialized in a given stroke, exercises for all four strokes are included as part of the workout plans. Be sure to continue your in-water strength and power development with vertical kicking and swimming against resistance.

## Competition Phase Workouts for Competitive Age-Group Swimmers

| Type of exercise | Circuit I | Circuit II |
|---|---|---|
| Warm-up | Dynamic warm-up | Dynamic warm-up |
| Injury prevention | Ball rotation | Catch position external rotation |
| | Chest punch | Shoulder blade pinch |
| | Catch position external rotation | Upper-body step-up |
| Core stability | Ab crunch with rotation | Side bridge |
| | Knees to chest | Prone bridge |
| | Bird dog | Dying bug |
| Foundational strength | Core chest press | Seated row |
| | Lunge | Squat |
| Stroke-specific strength | Walking lunge with rotation | Kicking with ankle weights |
| | Russian twist | Back extension with rotation |
| | Medicine ball V crunch | Medicine ball V crunch |
| | Straight-arm row | Sumo squat |
| | Alternate-arm Superman | High-to-low chop |
| Low to moderate power | Jump rope | 90-degree jump turn |
| Cool-down | Static stretching | Static stretching |

## Strength and Conditioning in the Championship Phase

During the championship phase, the dryland training should decline at the same rate as, or faster than, the work being done in the pool. There is still a benefit in doing some injury prevention and core work during this phase along with flexibility training, but strength and power training should be limited. Swimmers would benefit by following a program that contains 6 to 10 injury-prevention and core stability exercises using body weight and low- to moderate-resistance elastic tubing to provide the training load.

| Time or number of exercises | Exercise | Duration |
|---|---|---|
| 10 minutes | Dynamic warm-up | 30 seconds per exercise |
| 3-4 exercises | Injury prevention | 30 seconds per exercise |
| 3-4 exercises | Core stability | 30 seconds per exercise |
| 10 minutes | Static stretching | 20-30 seconds per stretch |

## Championship Phase Workouts for Competitive Age-Group Swimmers

| Type of exercise | Workout I | Workout II | Workout III |
|---|---|---|---|
| Warm-up | Dynamic warm-up | Dynamic warm-up | Dynamic warm-up |
| Injury prevention | Full can | Standing external rotation | Catch position external rotation |
| | Chest punch | Upper-body step-up | Ball rotation |
| | Shoulder retraction with external rotation | Y exercise | Full can |
| | Standing external rotation | Seated row | Shoulder blade pinch |
| Core stability | Prone bridge | Prone bridge | Back bridge |
| | Bird dog | Side bridge | T exercise |
| | Dying bug | Upper-body step-up | Leg drop |
| | Knees to chest | Ab crunch with rotation | Alternate-arm Superman |
| Cool-down | Static stretching | Static stretching | Static stretching |

## Strength and Conditioning in the Active Rest Phase

Many swimmers will have to do their strength training on their own during the active rest phase since this phase usually corresponds with a period of no practice or vacation. The focus of this phase should be on recovery; consequently, the strength and conditioning exercises should center on injury prevention and building core stability. It is necessary to strength train only one or two times per week using moderate resistance (fatiguing after 20 to 25 repetitions) to maintain strength. Be sure to cross-train to maintain cardiorespiratory fitness. Strength workouts should follow the general format provided here:

| Time or number of exercises | Exercise | Duration |
|---|---|---|
| 10 minutes | Dynamic warm-up | 30 seconds per exercise |
| 2-3 exercises | Injury prevention | 2 × 20 reps |
| 2-3 exercises | Core stability | 2 × 20 reps or 30 seconds per exercise |
| 10 minutes | Static stretching | 20-30 seconds per stretch |

Several sample active rest phase workouts are included here:

## Active Rest Phase Workouts for Competitive Age-Group Swimmers

| Type of exercise | Workout I | Workout II | Workout III |
|---|---|---|---|
| Warm-up | Dynamic warm-up | Dynamic warm-up | Dynamic warm-up |
| Injury prevention | Shoulder blade pinch | Full can | Standing external rotation |
| | Upper-body step-up | Upper-body step-up | Chest punch |
| Core stability | Side bridge | Leg drop | Ab crunch with rotation |
| | T exercise | Dying bug | Bird dog |
| | Back extension | Leg drop | Prone bridge |
| Cool-down | Static stretching | Static stretching | Static stretching |

# TRAINING PROGRAMS FOR COLLEGIATE SWIMMERS

Collegiate swimmers have some flexibility in their training, which will allow them to do varied things with their strength and conditioning. For example, many collegiate programs have the luxury of scheduling two training sessions a day, allowing for more freedom in structuring dedicated strength and conditioning sessions throughout the week. Recognize that most collegiate strength and conditioning programs are supervised by professionally certified strength coaches rather than by the swimming coaches. However, it is important that the strength coaches meet with the swimming staff to coordinate a strategy for the strength and conditioning component of training and establish a seasonal plan that focuses on

## Seasonal Training Plan for Collegiate Swimmers

| 1 | 2 | 3 | 4 | 5 | 6 | 7 | 8 | 9 | 10 | 11 | 12 | 13 | 14 | 15 | 16 | 17 | 18 |
|---|---|---|---|---|---|---|---|---|---|---|---|---|---|---|---|---|---|
| September | | | | | October | | | | November | | | | December | | | | |

| 19 | 20 | 21 | 22 | 23 | 24 | 25 | 26 | 27 | 28 | 29 | 30 | 31 | 32 | 33 | 34 | 35 |
|---|---|---|---|---|---|---|---|---|---|---|---|---|---|---|---|---|
| January | | | | February | | | | March | | | | | April | | | |

| 36 | 37 | 38 | 39 | 40 | 41 | 42 | 43 | 44 | 45 | 46 | 47 | 48 | 49 | 50 | 51 | 52 |
|---|---|---|---|---|---|---|---|---|---|---|---|---|---|---|---|---|
| May | | | | June | | | | | July | | | | August | | | |

Preliminary phase: ☐    Training phase: ☐    Competition phase: ▨
Championship phase: ▨    Active rest phase: ■

peaking during the championship season. The program at USC emphasizes development of core stability as well as general strength. It also emphasizes power development and overall athleticism, which is accomplished in part through work in the weight room, but also through such activities as Pilates, yoga, kickboxing, and stationary cycling.

## Assumptions and Guidelines

The guidelines set forth are modeled after the strength and conditioning program at USC and are applicable to other collegiate programs:

- The goal is for the swimmers to achieve competitive success, peaking at the conference championships or NCAAs (weeks 26 to 28) and again at the end of the summer long-course season (such as USA Swimming nationals, weeks 48 to 49). A smaller peak is included in week 16 because many teams have a meet at the end of the calendar year before holiday training begins. Included is the assumption that most collegiate swimmers will continue to train over the summer when school is not in session.
- Swimmers have 1.5-hour training sessions in the morning three times per week, 2.5- to 3-hour training sessions every afternoon, and a 2-hour practice once each weekend.
- Strength and conditioning or dryland workouts are conducted in the mornings and swimming workouts are in the afternoon.
- After each strength and conditioning session, schedule some in-water time to promote the transfer from the strength workout to the pool. Be sure to include some in-water strength training.
- There is at least one full day of rest during the week and preferably another half day of rest scheduled for the middle of the week.
- Coach-supervised training is limited by NCAA regulations to 20 hours per week.
- Collegiate swimmers, having built a strength and conditioning base from many years of training and because of their physical maturity, can focus a greater part of their season on developing swimming-specific strength during the competition phases.
- Injury prevention and performance enhancement share equal levels of importance with this group of swimmers. For injury prevention, swimmers will perform a high number of repetitions using a resistance that will induce fatigue after 20 to 25 repetitions or 30 seconds, depending on the exercise. Resistance and intensity should increase for power-based exercises.
- The program ideas are for a generic collegiate swimmer with no specific distance orientation or stroke preference assigned. As such, recognize that these programs can, and should, be modified to meet the needs of a specific swimmer. Sprinters, for example, should modify their

programs to include additional strength and power exercises found in chapter 6, particularly as the competitive and championship seasons approach, whereas true distance swimmers will want to maintain more of a muscular endurance focus while still including some power exercises in their routines.

## Strength and Conditioning in the Preliminary Phase

At the start of the collegiate season, we like to take a period of two weeks to prepare the body for hard training. We take considerable time to build core stability during this preliminary phase. We also familiarize the swimmers with basic injury-prevention exercises while starting to build a mix of upper-body and lower-body foundational strength. Here is a template for strength and conditioning during this phase:

| Time and number of exercises | Exercise | Duration |
|---|---|---|
| 10 minutes | Dynamic warm-up | 30 seconds per exercise |
| 4-5 exercises | Injury prevention | 2 × 15-20 reps |
| 4-5 exercises | Core stability | 2 × 20 reps or 30 seconds per exercise |
| 6-10 exercises | Foundational strength | 2 × 15-20 reps |
| 10 minutes | Static stretching | 20-30 seconds per stretch |

Included in this section, as well as throughout the entire discussion of strength training for collegiate swimmers, are more exercises than you will see for other groups. The reason for this is twofold: These athletes have the time to dedicate to higher volumes of strength training, and the swimmers are physically mature and at the peak of their strength potential. Therefore, we focus more on developing this aspect of their conditioning.

If time is a constraint, the routines can be modified and shortened as necessary. The weight (dumbbells, free weights, elastic tubing) should be heavy enough to induce fatigue at the end of each set. If swimmers are able to perform the exercise easily, the weight should be increased.

## Preliminary Phase Workouts for Collegiate Swimmers

| Type of exercise | Workout I | Workout II | Workout III |
| --- | --- | --- | --- |
| Warm-up | Dynamic warm-up | Dynamic warm-up | Dynamic warm-up |
| Injury prevention | Full can | Standing external rotation | Catch position external rotation |
| | Chest punch | Upper-body step-up | Ball rotation |
| | Shoulder retraction with external rotation | Y exercise | Full can |
| | Standing external rotation | Seated row | Shoulder blade pinch |
| Core stability | Prone bridge | Prone bridge | Back bridge |
| | Bird dog | Side bridge | T exercise |
| | Dying bug | Upper-body step-up | Leg drop |
| | Knees to chest | Ab crunch with rotation | Alternate-arm Superman |
| Foundational strength | Lunge | Lunge | Squat |
| | Squat | Calf raise | Step-up |
| | Monster walk | Seated hamstring curl | Single-leg deadlift |
| | Pull-up | Lat pull-down | Pull-up |
| | Seated row | Core chest press | Core chest press |
| | Lat pull-down | Upright row | Triceps extension |
| | Grip strengthening | Wrist flexion and extension | Wrist flexion and extension |
| Cool-down | Static stretching | Static stretching | Static stretching |

## Strength and Conditioning in the Training Phase

In the training phase, we start to ramp up the volume of strength training and introduce some stroke-specific exercises to the program. Two sample workouts are presented here. While they may seem rather long, they can be broken into four smaller training sessions. The goal in this phase is to build muscular endurance and foundational strength, so the number of repetitions for each exercise is quite high. The level of resistance is low to moderate to allow for high repetitions. Several low- to moderate-power exercises are also included in this phase. Most of these use light- to moderate-weight medicine balls, and the actions are quick and powerful. With all exercises, as strength increases, so should the resistance being used.

| Time or number of exercises | Exercise | Duration |
|---|---|---|
| 10 minutes | Dynamic warm-up | 30 seconds per exercise |
| 3-4 exercises | Injury prevention | 2 × 15-20 reps |
| 3-4 exercises | Core stability | 2 × 20 reps |
| 8-10 exercises | Foundational strength | 3 × 12-15 reps |
| 4 exercises | Stroke-specific strength | 3 × 10-12 reps |
| 3 exercises | Low to moderate power | 3 × 10-12 reps |
| 10 minutes | Static stretching | 20-30 seconds per stretch |

## Training Phase Workouts for Collegiate Swimmers

| Type of exercise | Workout I | Workout II |
|---|---|---|
| Warm-up | Dynamic warm-up | Dynamic warm-up |
| Injury prevention | Full can | Catch position external rotation |
| | Chest punch | Upper-body step-up |
| | Standing external rotation | Ball rotation |
| Core stability | Prone bridge | Bird dog |
| | Dying bug | Leg drop |
| | Knees to chest | Back bridge |
| Foundational strength | Lunge | Squat |
| | Calf raise | Monster walk |
| | Lat pull-down | Pull-up |
| | Triceps extension | Monster walk |
| | Reverse fly | Standing internal rotation |
| | Posterior chain exercise | Upright row |
| | Core chest press | Lat pull-down |
| | Grip strengthening | Wrist flexion and extension |
| Stroke-specific strength | Medicine ball leg lift | Straight-arm row |
| | Back extension with rotation | Walking lunge with rotation |
| | Medicine ball handoff | Good morning |
| | High-to-low chop | Russian twist |
| Low to moderate power | Lateral line hop | Jump rope |
| | Shoulder pullover | Seated medicine ball twist |
| | Explosive wall chest pass | Figure-eight medicine ball pass and throw |
| Cool-down | Static stretching | Static stretching |

After the strength training session, swimmers should spend 30 to 45 minutes in the pool, performing in-water strengthening and power exercises such as swimming with parachutes. The goal is to carry the strength and power developed in the dryland workout over to the water.

## Strength and Conditioning in the Competition Phase

As swimmers move into the competition phase of the season, the focus of the training shifts to developing greater power, and the workouts subsequently include several moderate- to high-power exercises in the training plan; these use moderate-weight medicine balls or loads that represent 30 to 60 percent of what a swimmer could lift one time, depending on the exercise. Additionally, athletes perform more in-water swimming-specific drills, such as vertical kicking and swimming against resistance (see chapter 6). The intensity of this training phase should be high, which is the reason the number of sets and repetitions have decreased compared to the training phase. Swimmers need to emphasize quality in each exercise.

| Time or number of exercises | Exercise | Duration |
| --- | --- | --- |
| 10 minutes | Dynamic warm-up | 30 seconds per exercise |
| 3 exercises | Injury prevention | 2 × 20 reps |
| 3 exercises | Core stability | 2 × 20 reps |
| 4 exercises | Foundational strength | 2 × 10 reps |
| 6 exercises | Stroke-specific strength | 3 × 8 reps |
| 4 exercises | Moderate to high power | 3 × 5-8 reps |
| 10 minutes | Static stretching | 20-30 seconds per stretch |

In reviewing the following strength training workouts, keep in mind that these programs were put together with no specific stroke in mind. Therefore, they represent an overall training plan that can be modified to suit an athlete's specific needs.

Instead of performing all of these exercises in one training session, you can break them into smaller groups and conduct strength training sessions more frequently throughout the week. Again, our collegiate swimmers also augment the dryland exercises with in-water training that focuses on power development and core stability—such as vertical kicking, swimming against resistance, and in-water core stability exercises. We do this in short training sessions immediately after dryland training.

## Competition Phase Workouts for Collegiate Swimmers

| Type of exercise | Workout I | Workout II |
|---|---|---|
| Warm-up | Dynamic warm-up | Dynamic warm-up |
| Injury prevention | Ball rotation | Catch position external rotation |
| | Chest punch | Shoulder blade pinch |
| | Full can | Upper-body step-up |
| Core stability | Ab crunch with rotation | Side bridge |
| | Knees to chest | Leg drop |
| | Bird dog | Dying bug |
| Foundational strength | Lunge | Squat |
| | Core chest press | Monster walk |
| | Triceps extension | Seated row |
| | Wrist flexion and extension | Reverse fly |
| Stroke-specific strength | Walking lunge with rotation | Kicking with ankle weights |
| | Russian twist | Back extension with rotation |
| | Medicine ball V crunch | Medicine ball V crunch |
| | Straight-arm row | Sumo squat |
| | Alternate-arm Superman | High-to-low chop |
| | High-to-low chop | Good morning |
| Moderate to high power | Medicine ball squat jump | Medicine ball squat with chest throw |
| | Figure-eight medicine ball pass and throw | Streamline jump |
| | Overhead medicine ball throw | Plyometric sit-up |
| | Power drop | Explosive wall chest pass |
| Cool-down | Static stretching | Static stretching |

# Strength and Conditioning in the Championship Phase

In the championship phase, collegiate swimmers should continue engaging in some type of strength training up until the competition starts, although the volume and intensity should taper off as quickly, if not more quickly, than their work in the pool. The intensity of this training is low compared to the competition phase and focuses on injury prevention and improving core stability. Therefore, the resistance should be relatively low. However, we will still include a small number of power-based exercises to help maintain neuromuscular efficiency and explosiveness. Here are sample exercise routines for the championship phase:

| Time or number of exercises | Exercise | Duration |
|---|---|---|
| 10 minutes | Dynamic warm-up | 30 seconds per exercise |
| 2 exercises | Injury prevention | 1 ×15 reps |
| 3 exercises | Core stability | 1 × 15 reps |
| 2 exercises | Foundational strength | 1 ×15 reps |
| 3 exercises | Stroke-specific strength | 1 × 6-10 reps |
| 2 exercises | Moderate power | 1 × 6-10 reps |
| 10 minutes | Static stretching | 20-30 seconds per stretch |

Note that the number of sets and repetitions decreased from those used in the competition phase. Swimmers should use moderate to low resistance for the foundational strength exercises. For the stroke-specific and power exercises, they should use moderate resistance and a high level of intensity.

## Championship Phase Workouts for Collegiate Swimmers

| Type of exercise | Workout I | Workout II | Workout III |
|---|---|---|---|
| Warm-up | Dynamic warm-up | Dynamic warm-up | Dynamic warm-up |
| Injury prevention | Full can | Standing external rotation | Catch position external rotation |
| | Chest punch | Upper-body step-up | Ball rotation |
| Core stability | Prone bridge | Prone bridge | Back bridge |
| | Bird dog | Side bridge | Knees to chest |
| | Dying bug | Upper-body step-up | Leg drop |
| Foundational strength | Lunge | Lunge | Squat |
| | Seated row | Bent-over lateral raise | Lat pull-down |
| Stroke-specific strength | High-to-low chop | Russian twist | Medicine ball V crunch |
| | Medicine ball handoff | Hip flexion and extension | Straight-arm row |
| | Back extension with rotation | Bent-over lateral raise | Good morning |
| Moderate power | Explosive wall chest pass | Jump rope | Bounding |
| | Streamline jump | Plyometric sit-up | Explosive rotational throw |
| Cool-down | Static stretching | Static stretching | Static stretching |

## Strength and Conditioning in the Active Rest Phase

During the active rest phase, we encourage all swimmers to cross-train and maintain a basic level of strength. The strength and conditioning sessions should be shorter than they were during the earlier phases of the season, but they should still contain some aspects of injury prevention, core stability, foundational strength, and swimming-specific exercises—performing a high number of repetitions against a moderate level of resistance. The following is a template; you can choose the exercises to plug into the program.

| Time and number of exercises | Exercise | Duration |
|---|---|---|
| 10 minutes | Dynamic warm-up | 30 seconds per exercise |
| 2 exercises | Injury prevention | 2 × 20 reps |
| 2 exercises | Core stability | 2 × 20 reps or 30 seconds per exercise |
| 2 exercises | Foundational strength | 2 × 20 reps |
| 2 exercises | Stroke-specific strength | 2 × 20 reps |
| 2 exercises | Power | 3 × 8 reps |
| 10 minutes | Static stretching | 20-30 seconds per stretch |

# TRAINING PROGRAMS FOR MASTERS SWIMMERS AND TRIATHLETES

Programs for masters swimmers and triathletes are grouped together since these athletes often have similar training and competitive goals and because they often train together. While both groups of athletes typically compete and want to do well in those competitions, an equally compelling goal is often to maintain fitness. The goals of a strength and conditioning program for masters swimmers and triathletes focus on building full-body foundational strength and preventing injury. There are also shorter periods of training throughout the year in which the emphasis is on developing power and stroke-specific strength. With that said, athletes in this group should be able to safely engage in power exercises if the necessary strength base has been established, and the workouts can be tweaked to meet individual needs. Keep in mind that it takes longer for the body to recover as it ages. As the championship phases approach, strength and conditioning should cease or be dialed back to focus only on injury prevention, core stability, and flexibility.

# Seasonal Training Plan for Masters Swimmers and Triathletes

| 1 | 2 | 3 | 4 | 5 | 6 | 7 | 8 | 9 | 10 | 11 | 12 | 13 | 14 | 15 | 16 | 17 | 18 |
|---|---|---|---|---|---|---|---|---|----|----|----|----|----|----|----|----|----|
| September | | | | | October | | | | November | | | | December | | | | |

| 19 | 20 | 21 | 22 | 23 | 24 | 25 | 26 | 27 | 28 | 29 | 30 | 31 | 32 | 33 | 34 | 35 |
|----|----|----|----|----|----|----|----|----|----|----|----|----|----|----|----|----|
| January | | | | February | | | | March | | | | | April | | | |

| 36 | 37 | 38 | 39 | 40 | 41 | 42 | 43 | 44 | 45 | 46 | 47 | 48 | 49 | 50 | 51 | 52 |
|----|----|----|----|----|----|----|----|----|----|----|----|----|----|----|----|----|
| May | | | | June | | | | | July | | | | August | | | |

Preliminary phase: ☐   Training phase: ▨   Competition phase: ▨
Championship phase: ■   Active rest phase: ■

## Assumptions and Guidelines

This strength and conditioning program for masters swimmers and triathletes takes the following considerations into account:

- The primary goal of masters swimmers and triathletes is to achieve competitive success; a secondary goal is to maintain fitness.
- Swimmers have three to five in-water training sessions each week, each lasting 1.5 to 2 hours.
- These athletes will have 30 to 60 minutes at least two other days of the week to engage in strength training or cross-training.
- There is at least one full day of rest during the week.
- Swimmers will try to peak twice a year (such as masters short-course nationals, weeks 37 and 38, and the long-course nationals, weeks 49 and 50, or in triathlon competitions). A third minor peak is included near the end of the calendar year to break up the long training phase.

## Strength and Conditioning in the Preliminary Phase

The goal during the preliminary phase is to get back into the swing of things after a time away. The workouts focus on injury prevention, flexibility, and core stability. Athletes should choose a resistance that will allow them to complete the desired number of sets and repetitions or time so that the muscles are fatigued at the end of each set. When the set becomes easy to complete, it is time to increase the load. Also included are several foundational strength exercises. In short, strength workouts in the preliminary phase should follow the general format presented here and should be performed at least twice a week:

| Time or number of exercises | Exercise | Duration |
|---|---|---|
| 10 minutes | Dynamic warm-up | 30 seconds per exercise |
| 2-3 exercises | Injury prevention | 2 × 20 reps |
| 2-3 exercises | Core stability | 2 × 20 reps or 30 seconds per exercise |
| 2-3 exercises | Foundational strength | 1-2 × 20 reps |
| 15-20 minutes | Static stretching | 20-30 seconds per stretch |

Several sample exercise routines for the preliminary phase are included here:

## Preliminary Phase Workouts for Masters Swimmers and Triathletes

| Type of exercise | Workout I | Workout II | Workout III |
|---|---|---|---|
| Warm-up | Dynamic warm-up | Dynamic warm-up | Dynamic warm-up |
| Injury prevention | Full can | Standing external rotation | Catch position external rotation |
| | Chest punch | Upper-body step-up | Ball rotation |
| | Shoulder retraction with external rotation | Y exercise | Full can |
| Core stability | Leg drop | Dying bug | Back bridge |
| | Knees to chest | Prone bridge | Ab crunch with rotation |
| | Bird dog | Side bridge | T exercise |
| Foundational strength | Lunge | Step-up | Squat |
| | Seated row | Ankle dorsiflexion | Seated hamstring curl |
| | Grip strengthening | Wrist flexion and extension | Core chest press |
| Cool-down | Static stretching | Static stretching | Static stretching |

## Strength and Conditioning in the Training Phase

During the training phase, the focus is on building foundational strength. Some power and swimming-specific strengthening exercises should be integrated into the plan. The repetitions are high and the resistance moderate for many of the exercises. A template is presented here:

| Time or number of exercises | Exercise | Duration |
|---|---|---|
| 10 minutes | Dynamic warm-up | 30 seconds per exercise |
| 2 exercises | Injury prevention | 2 × 20 reps |
| 2-3 exercises | Core stability | 2 × 20 reps or 30 seconds per exercise |
| 2-3 exercises | Foundational strength | 2 × 20 reps |
| 1-2 exercises | Stroke-specific strength | 3 × 8 reps or 30 seconds per exercise |
| 1 exercise | Low to moderate power | 2 × 15-30 seconds |
| 10 minutes | Static stretching | 20-30 seconds per stretch |

The following are sample training phase workouts. The programs are designed for freestyle swimmers, and the swimming-specific exercises in the program were chosen for this reason. However, other swimming-specific exercises from chapter 3 that are appropriate for other strokes can be substituted.

## Training Phase Workouts for Masters Swimmers and Triathletes

| Type of exercise | Workout I | Workout II | Workout III |
|---|---|---|---|
| Warm-up | Dynamic warm-up | Dynamic warm-up | Dynamic warm-up |
| Injury prevention | Full can | Catch position external rotation | Shoulder retraction with external rotation |
|  | Chest punch | Upper-body step-up | Ball rotation |
| Core stability | Dying bug | Bird dog | Prone bridge |
|  | Side bridge | Back bridge | Knees to chest |
| Foundational strength | Lunge | Single-leg deadlift | Seated hamstring curl |
|  | Upright row | Seated row | Pull-up and lat pull-down |
|  | Grip strengthening | Triceps extension | Reverse fly |
| Stroke-specific strength | Vertical kicking | Walking lunge with rotation | Russian twist |
|  | High-to-low chop | Freestyle sculling | Straight-arm row |
| Low to moderate power | Seated medicine ball twist | Streamline jump | Plyometric sit-up |
| Cool-down | Static stretching | Static stretching | Static stretching |

## Strength and Conditioning in the Competition Phase

During the short competition phases, the training shifts slightly to focus more on stroke-specific strengthening and power development while still maintaining the injury prevention and core stability training started earlier in the season. The loads should allow swimmers to perform the desired number of sets and repetitions while maintaining proper form. The power exercises involve the use of light- to moderate-weight medicine balls and should be performed in a quick and explosive manner. The training sessions include the following components.

| Time or number of exercises | Exercise | Duration |
|---|---|---|
| 10 minutes | Dynamic warm-up | 30 seconds per exercise |
| 2 exercises | Injury prevention | 2 × 20 reps |
| 2 exercises | Core stability | 2 × 20 reps or 30 seconds per exercise |
| 1-2 exercises | Foundational strength | 2 × 20 reps |
| 3-4 exercises | Stroke-specific strength | 3 × 8 reps or 30 seconds per exercise |
| 2 exercises | Moderate to high power | 2 × 15-30 seconds |
| 10 minutes | Static stretching | 20-30 seconds per stretch |

The following are sample competition phase workouts. As in the training phase, the programs are for freestyle swimmers, but other swimming-specific exercises that are appropriate for other strokes can be substituted.

## Competition Phase Workouts for Masters Swimmers and Triathletes

| Type of exercise | Workout I | Workout II | Workout III |
|---|---|---|---|
| Warm-up | Dynamic warm-up | Dynamic warm-up | Dynamic warm-up |
| Injury prevention | Ball rotation | Catch position external rotation | Y exercise |
| | Chest punch | Upper-body step-up | Full can |
| Core stability | Dying bug | Back extension | Ab crunch with rotation |
| | Leg drop | Side bridge | Knees to chest |

| Type of exercise | Workout I | Workout II | Workout III |
|---|---|---|---|
| Foundational strength | Squat | Calf raise | Pull-up and lat pull-down |
| | Core chest press | Posterior chain exercise | Standing internal rotation |
| Stroke-specific strength | Walking lunge with rotation | High-to-low chop | Vertical kicking |
| | Vertical kicking | Kicking with ankle weights | Alternate-arm Superman |
| | High-to-low chop | Freestyle sculling | Back extension with rotation |
| Moderate to high power | Medicine ball squat jump | 90-degree jump turn | Lateral line hop |
| | Seated medicine ball twist | Shoulder pullover | Plyometric sit-up |
| Cool-down | Static stretching | Static stretching | Static stretching |

## Strength and Conditioning in the Championship Phase

At the beginning of the championship phase, strength training should decrease considerably and even be eliminated from the training program altogether. Any exercises during this phase should be low- to moderate-resistance exercises for the core and injury prevention as well as static stretching. However, that should make up the bulk of your training. Here are guidelines for strength workouts:

| Time or number of exercises | Exercise | Duration |
|---|---|---|
| 10 minutes | Dynamic warm-up | 30 seconds per exercise |
| 2-3 exercises | Injury prevention | 2 × 20 reps |
| 2-3 exercises | Core stability | 2 × 20 reps or 30 seconds per exercise |
| 10 minutes | Static stretching | 20-30 seconds per stretch |

Additionally, here are several sample championship phase workouts:

## Championship Phase Workouts for Masters Swimmers and Triathletes

| Type of exercise | Workout I | Workout II | Workout III |
|---|---|---|---|
| Warm-up | Dynamic warm-up | Dynamic warm-up | Dynamic warm-up |
| Injury prevention | Shoulder blade pinch | Full can | Standing external rotation |
| | Upper-body step-up | Upper-body step-up | Chest punch |
| Core stability | Side bridge | Leg drop | Ab crunch with rotation |
| | T exercise | Dying bug | Bird dog |
| | Back extension | Leg drop | Prone bridge |
| Cool-down | Static stretching | Static stretching | Static stretching |

## Strength and Conditioning in the Active Rest Phase

The focus during the active rest phase should be on rest and recovery. The strength and conditioning during this time should focus almost entirely on injury prevention and building core stability and should be done in conjunction with cross-training. During this phase, it is necessary to strength train only one or two times per week. The workout guidelines for the championship phase apply during the active rest.

# TRAINING PROGRAMS FOR FITNESS SWIMMERS

True fitness swimmers swim with the goal of maintaining fitness and might have no desire to race in meets. The strength and conditioning program should complement this goal, focusing on building foundational strength, preventing injury, and maintaining fitness. The following is the seasonal plan; specific guidelines for preliminary, training, and active rest phases are provided in greater detail in the paragraphs that follow.

## Seasonal Training Plan for Fitness Swimmers

| 1 | 2 | 3 | 4 | 5 | 6 | 7 | 8 | 9 | 10 | 11 | 12 | 13 | 14 | 15 | 16 | 17 | 18 |
|---|---|---|---|---|---|---|---|---|---|---|---|---|---|---|---|---|---|
| | September | | | | | October | | | | November | | | | December | | | |

| 19 | 20 | 21 | 22 | 23 | 24 | 25 | 26 | 27 | 28 | 29 | 30 | 31 | 32 | 33 | 34 | 35 |
|---|---|---|---|---|---|---|---|---|---|---|---|---|---|---|---|---|
| | January | | | February | | | | March | | | | April | | | |

| 36 | 37 | 38 | 39 | 40 | 41 | 42 | 43 | 44 | 45 | 46 | 47 | 48 | 49 | 50 | 51 | 52 |
|---|---|---|---|---|---|---|---|---|---|---|---|---|---|---|---|---|
| | May | | | June | | | | July | | | | August | | | |

Preliminary phase: ☐   Training phase: ☐   Active rest phase: ■

## Assumptions and Guidelines

The seasonal plan and exercise routines for fitness swimmers take the following assumptions and guidelines into account:

- The primary goal for these swimmers is fitness, but there may be a secondary goal of competition.
- Fitness swimmers have three to five in-pool training sessions each week, lasting one to two hours.
- These swimmers have the ability to engage in two one-hour strength training sessions outside of their in-water training.
- Resistance should be moderate, allowing some fatigue upon completion of the desired number of sets and repetitions.
- There is at least one full day of rest during the week.

## Strength and Conditioning in the Preliminary Phase

The goal of the preliminary phase is to regain a feel for the water at the start of the season or after a period of active rest. The workouts should focus on injury prevention, flexibility, and core stability. Several foundational strength exercises are included in the training plan. In short, strength workouts in the preliminary phase should follow the general format presented here and should be performed at least twice a week:

| Time and number of exercises | Exercise | Duration |
| --- | --- | --- |
| 10 minutes | Dynamic warm-up | 30 seconds per exercise |
| 2-3 exercises | Injury prevention | 2 ×20 reps |
| 2-3 exercises | Core stability | 2 × 20 reps or 30 seconds per exercise |
| 2-3 exercises | Foundational strength | 2 × 20 reps |
| 15-20 minutes | Static stretching | 20-30 seconds per stretch |

Several sample exercise routines for the preliminary phase are presented here:

## Preliminary Phase Workouts for Fitness Swimmers

| Type of exercise | Workout I | Workout II | Workout III |
|---|---|---|---|
| Warm-up | Dynamic warm-up | Dynamic warm-up | Dynamic warm-up |
| Injury prevention | Full can | Standing external rotation | Catch position external rotation |
| | Chest punch | Upper-body step-up | Ball rotation |
| | Shoulder retraction with external rotation | Y exercise | Full can |
| Core stability | Leg drop | Dying bug | Back bridge |
| | Knees to chest | Prone bridge | Ab crunch with rotation |
| | Bird dog | Side bridge | T exercise |
| Foundational strength | Lunge | Step-up | Squat |
| | Seated row | Ankle dorsiflexion | Seated hamstring curl |
| | Grip strengthening | Wrist flexion and extension | Core chest press |
| Cool-down | Static stretching | Static stretching | Static stretching |

## Strength and Conditioning in the Training Phase

The following is a template for a strength workout during the training phase. Several foundational strength and low-power exercises are added. At least two workouts per week are recommended during this phase:

| Time or number of exercises | Exercise | Duration |
|---|---|---|
| 10 minutes | Dynamic warm-up | 30 seconds per exercise |
| 3-4 exercises | Injury prevention | 2 × 20 reps |
| 2-3 exercises | Core stability | 2 × 20 reps or 30 seconds per exercise |
| 3-4 exercises | Foundational strength | 2 × 20 reps |
| 0-2 exercises | Low to moderate power | 2 × 15-30 seconds |
| 10 minutes | Static stretching | 20-30 seconds per stretch |

Several sample training phase workouts are presented here:

## Training Phase Workouts for Fitness Swimmers

| Type of exercise | Workout I | Workout II | Workout III |
|---|---|---|---|
| Warm-up | Dynamic warm-up | Dynamic warm-up | Dynamic warm-up |
| Injury prevention | Full can | Standing external rotation | Catch position external rotation |
| | Chest punch | Upper-body step-up | Ball rotation |
| | Shoulder retraction with external rotation | Y exercise | Full can |
| Core stability | Prone bridge | Bird dog | Back bridge |
| | Back extension | Leg drop | Ab crunch with rotation |
| Foundational strength | Star drill | Squat | Knees to chest |
| | Pull-up and lat pull-down | Monster walk | Step-up |
| | Upright row | Seated row | Lunge |
| | Grip strengthening | Triceps extension | Reverse fly |
| Low to moderate power | Lateral line hop | Explosive wall chest pass | Jump rope |
| Cool-down | Static stretching | Static stretching | Static stretching |

## Strength and Conditioning in the Active Rest Phase

The focus should be on recovery during the active rest phase. The strength and conditioning exercises should center on preventing injury and developing core stability. It is necessary to strength train only one or two times per week to maintain strength and combine strength training with some cross-training. Strength workouts should follow this general format:

| Time and number of exercises | Exercise | Duration |
|---|---|---|
| 10 minutes | Dynamic warm-up | 30 seconds per exercise |
| 2-3 exercises | Injury prevention | 2 × 20 reps |
| 2-3 exercises | Core stability | 2 × 20 reps or 30 seconds per exercise |
| 10 minutes | Static stretching | 20-30 seconds per stretch |

Several sample active rest phase workouts are presented here:

## Active Rest Phase Workouts for Fitness Swimmers

| Type of exercise | Workout I | Workout II | Workout III |
|---|---|---|---|
| Warm-up | Dynamic warm-up | Dynamic warm-up | Dynamic warm-up |
| Injury prevention | Shoulder blade pinch | Full can | Standing external rotation |
| | Upper-body step-up | Upper-body step-up | Chest punch |
| Core stability | Side bridge | Leg drop | Ab crunch with rotation |
| | T exercise | Dying bug | Bird dog |
| | Back extension | Leg drop | Prone bridge |
| Cool-down | Static stretching | Static stretching | Static stretching |

# Race Data of Elite Swimmers

I t is interesting to see how the best in the world swim their races. This appendix presents race data, including average velocities, stroke rates, and distance-per-stroke cycles recorded during the 2000 U.S. Olympic Trials and the 2000 Sydney Olympic Games. As you compare your race variables to those of these elite athletes, keep in mind that there is some variability in the data and that no two swimmers approach a race in the same way. These are averages for the entire race and do not take into account how variables change during the course of a race (see appendix B for this information). Additionally, just because someone swims a race a certain way does not mean you need to swim it the same way. These tables are meant as a tool for comparison. Your best strategy is to compare yourself to yourself—measure your stroke rates and compute your distance-per-stroke cycle and track them. Then you can more accurately assess how you are improving over time.

Note: In the text we discuss swimming velocity and that it equals SR × DPS. In the tables presented in this appendix, we provide the average *race velocity,* which is slightly different (race velocity = race distance divided by race time). To compute the average swimming velocity, plug the data from the tables into the following equation:

$$\text{Swimming velocity} = \frac{\text{SR} \times \text{DPS}}{60}$$

The average swimming velocity will be lower than the race velocity since it does not include the start and turns—areas where the velocity is typically higher than when swimming.

# Table 1　Race Analysis Data for Freestyle Events

## 50-meter freestyle

| | Men | | | Women | | |
|---|---|---|---|---|---|---|
| | SR (cycl/min) | DPS (m/cycl) | Velocity (m/sec) | SR (cycl/min) | DPS (m/cycl) | Velocity (m/sec) |
| Olympics top 8 | 58.46 | 2.18 | 2.25 | 61.70 | 1.84 | 2.00 |
| U.S. Olympic Trials top 8 | 60.91 | 2.13 | 2.25 | 60.50 | 1.87 | 1.96 |
| U.S. Olympic Trials 9-16 | 60.35 | 2.05 | 2.18 | 60.59 | 1.83 | 1.93 |
| Other elite U.S. swimmers | 60.33 | 1.99 | 2.12 | 58.58 | 1.81 | 1.86 |

## 100-meter freestyle

| | Men | | | Women | | |
|---|---|---|---|---|---|---|
| | SR | DPS | Velocity | SR | DPS | Velocity |
| Olympics top 8 | 51.44 | 2.29 | 2.04 | 52.48 | 1.99 | 1.83 |
| U.S. Olympic Trials top 8 | 52.60 | 2.28 | 2.03 | 50.99 | 2.08 | 1.81 |
| U.S. Olympic Trials 9-16 | 52.02 | 2.26 | 2.00 | 52.28 | 1.99 | 1.78 |
| Other elite U.S. swimmers | 51.59 | 2.20 | 1.95 | 50.62 | 1.98 | 1.74 |

## 200-meter freestyle

| | Men | | | Women | | |
|---|---|---|---|---|---|---|
| | SR | DPS | Velocity | SR | DPS | Velocity |
| Olympics top 8 | 46.51 | 2.34 | 1.86 | 48.35 | 2.03 | 1.68 |
| U.S. Olympic Trials top 8 | 46.41 | 2.37 | 1.84 | 46.67 | 2.10 | 1.65 |
| U.S. Olympic Trials 9-16 | 44.75 | 2.39 | 1.80 | 48.14 | 2.03 | 1.63 |
| Other elite U.S. swimmers | 43.83 | 2.38 | 1.77 | 45.61 | 2.08 | 1.60 |

## 400-meter freestyle

| | Men | | | Women | | |
|---|---|---|---|---|---|---|
| | SR | DPS | Velocity | SR | DPS | Velocity |
| Olympics top 8 | 41.90 | 2.45 | 1.77 | 43.23 | 2.40 | 1.60 |
| U.S. Olympic Trials top 8 | 43.23 | 2.36 | 1.71 | 47.96 | 1.94 | 1.57 |
| Other elite U.S. swimmers | 46.38 | 2.12 | 1.67 | 44.85 | 2.00 | 1.51 |

## Men's 1,500- and women's 800-meter freestyle

| | Men | | | Women | | |
|---|---|---|---|---|---|---|
| | SR | DPS | Velocity | SR | DPS | Velocity |
| Olympics top 8 | 41.04 | 2.37 | 1.66 | 47.28 | 1.95 | 1.58 |
| U.S. Olympic Trials top 8 | 41.83 | 2.28 | 1.62 | 48.27 | 1.90 | 1.55 |
| Other elite U.S. swimmers | 42.92 | 2.14 | 1.55 | 43.92 | 2.00 | 1.48 |

Adapted from reports arising from the Pfizer-funded IOC Medical Commission Grant to Complete Competition Analysis in Swimming at the 2000 Sydney Olympic Games.

# Table 2    Race Analysis Data for Butterfly Events

## 100-meter butterfly

| | Men | | | Women | | |
|---|---|---|---|---|---|---|
| | SR (cycl/min) | DPS (m/cycl) | Velocity (m/sec) | SR (cycl/min) | DPS (m/cycl) | Velocity (m/sec) |
| Olympics top 8 | 56.49 | 1.92 | 1.90 | 56.90 | 1.74 | 1.71 |
| U.S. Olympic Trials top 8 | 57.11 | 1.90 | 1.88 | 57.56 | 1.70 | 1.69 |
| U.S. Olympic Trials 9-16 | 55.10 | 1.91 | 1.84 | 55.87 | 1.72 | 1.65 |
| Other elite U.S. swimmers | 52.47 | 1.94 | 1.80 | 55.64 | 1.70 | 1.63 |

## 200-meter butterfly

| | Men | | | Women | | |
|---|---|---|---|---|---|---|
| | SR | DPS | Velocity | SR | DPS | Velocity |
| Olympics top 8 | 49.68 | 2.01 | 1.71 | 52.13 | 1.75 | 1.56 |
| U.S. Olympic Trials top 8 | 50.62 | 1.99 | 1.69 | 52.07 | 1.72 | 1.51 |
| U.S. Olympic Trials 9-16 | 49.56 | 1.99 | 1.66 | 49.33 | 1.77 | 1.48 |
| Other elite U.S. swimmers | 49.11 | 1.94 | 1.63 | 51.27 | 1.66 | 1.45 |

Adapted from reports arising from the Pfizer-funded IOC Medical Commission Grant to Complete Competition Analysis in Swimming at the 2000 Sydney Olympic Games.


# Table 3    Race Analysis Data for Backstroke Events

## 100-meter backstroke

| | Men | | | Women | | |
|---|---|---|---|---|---|---|
| | SR (cycl/min) | DPS (m/cycl) | Velocity (m/sec) | SR (cycl/min) | DPS (m/cycl) | Velocity (m/sec) |
| Olympics top 8 | 48.64 | 2.14 | 1.83 | 48.78 | 1.94 | 1.63 |
| U.S. Olympic Trials top 8 | 49.15 | 2.18 | 1.81 | 47.82 | 1.98 | 1.61 |
| U.S. Olympic Trials 9-16 | 47.90 | 2.17 | 1.78 | 47.08 | 1.96 | 1.57 |
| Other elite U.S. swimmers | 44.56 | 2.29 | 1.74 | 45.62 | 1.96 | 1.53 |

## 200-meter backstroke

| | Men | | | Women | | |
|---|---|---|---|---|---|---|
| | SR | DPS | Velocity | SR | DPS | Velocity |
| Olympics top 8 | 42.29 | 2.30 | 1.69 | 41.96 | 2.10 | 1.52 |
| U.S. Olympic Trials top 8 | 42.71 | 2.35 | 1.67 | 42.51 | 2.07 | 1.48 |
| U.S. Olympic Trials 9-16 | 40.94 | 2.37 | 1.63 | 40.65 | 2.13 | 1.45 |
| Other elite U.S. swimmers | 40.04 | 2.34 | 1.57 | 38.09 | 2.18 | 1.41 |

Adapted from reports arising from the Pfizer-funded IOC Medical Commission Grant to Complete Competition Analysis in Swimming at the 2000 Sydney Olympic Games.

# Table 4   Race Analysis Data for Breaststroke Events

## 100-meter breaststroke

| | Men | | | Women | | |
|---|---|---|---|---|---|---|
| | SR (cycl/min) | DPS (m/cycl) | Velocity (m/sec) | SR (cycl/min) | DPS (m/cycl) | Velocity (m/sec) |
| Olympics top 8 | 50.81 | 1.84 | 1.63 | 51.89 | 1.65 | 1.47 |
| U.S. Olympic Trials top 8 | 53.10 | 1.77 | 1.62 | 50.99 | 1.67 | 1.46 |
| U.S. Olympic Trials 9-16 | 51.37 | 1.76 | 1.59 | 50.24 | 1.65 | 1.41 |
| Other elite U.S. swimmers | 50.85 | 1.74 | 1.56 | 48.81 | 1.60 | 1.37 |

## 200-meter breaststroke

| | Men | | | Women | | |
|---|---|---|---|---|---|---|
| | SR | DPS | Velocity | SR | DPS | Velocity |
| Olympics top 8 | 37.93 | 2.32 | 1.51 | 41.06 | 1.97 | 1.37 |
| U.S. Olympic Trials top 8 | 41.24 | 2.12 | 1.48 | 40.07 | 1.98 | 1.35 |
| U.S. Olympic Trials 9-16 | 40.81 | 2.08 | 1.45 | 41.51 | 1.89 | 1.31 |
| Other elite U.S. swimmers | 40.10 | 2.03 | 1.41 | 40.93 | 1.83 | 1.27 |

Adapted from reports arising from the Pfizer-funded IOC Medical Commission Grant to Complete Competition Analysis in Swimming at the 2000 Sydney Olympic Games.

# Changes in Elite Swimmers' Race Data During a Race

What happens during the course of the race and how does technique change? Appendix A presents average values for race velocity, stroke rate (SR), and distance per stroke (DPS) that were computed over the entire race distance. The two following tables show how these variables change during the course of a race. The data is from the 2000 U.S. Olympic Swimming Trials, and races are broken down into 50-meter increments. SR, DPS, and average velocity are computed for each 50-meter segment. Now you can see how the race strategy differs and plays out for the finalists, semifinalists, and other Olympic Trials participants.

As in appendix A, these tables present the average race velocity (distance divided by time) and not swimming velocity. Actual swimming velocity can be computed by multiplying SR and DPS (see the introduction to appendix A).

# Table 1  Men's Race Analysis Data From the 2000 U.S. Olympic Trials

**Men's 50 freestyle**

| | 50 | | |
|---|---|---|---|
| | SR (cycl/min) | DPS (m/cycl) | Velocity (m/sec) |
| Finalists (1-8) | 60.91 | 2.13 | 2.25 |
| Semifinalists (9-16) | 60.35 | 2.05 | 2.18 |
| Olympic Trials participants | 60.33 | 1.99 | 2.12 |

**Men's 100 freestyle**

| | 50 | | | 100 | | |
|---|---|---|---|---|---|---|
| | SR | DPS | Velocity | SR | DPS | Velocity |
| Finalists (1-8) | 54.71 | 2.36 | 2.15 | 50.48 | 2.20 | 1.91 |
| Semifinalists (9-16) | 52.51 | 2.35 | 2.09 | 51.53 | 2.17 | 1.90 |
| Olympic Trials participants | 52.71 | 2.29 | 2.04 | 50.46 | 2.11 | 1.85 |

**Men's 200 freestyle**

| | 50 | | | 100 | | | 150 | | | 200 | | |
|---|---|---|---|---|---|---|---|---|---|---|---|---|
| | SR | DPS | Velocity | SR | DPS | Velocity | SR | DPS | Velocity | SR | DPS | Velocity |
| Finalists (1-8) | 48.04 | 2.49 | 1.98 | 45.05 | 2.43 | 1.82 | 45.93 | 2.34 | 1.80 | 46.63 | 2.20 | 1.77 |
| Semifinalists (9-16) | 45.09 | 2.55 | 1.92 | 43.18 | 2.47 | 1.78 | 44.74 | 2.34 | 1.75 | 45.98 | 2.21 | 1.76 |
| Olympic Trials participants | 44.74 | 2.50 | 1.92 | 42.98 | 2.45 | 1.76 | 43.55 | 2.35 | 1.71 | 44.05 | 2.22 | 1.69 |

**Men's 400 freestyle**

| | 100 | | | 200 | | | 300 | | | 400 | | |
|---|---|---|---|---|---|---|---|---|---|---|---|---|
| | SR | DPS | Velocity | SR | DPS | Velocity | SR | DPS | Velocity | SR | DPS | Velocity |
| Finalists (1-8) | 42.44 | 2.44 | 1.72 | 42.75 | 2.38 | 1.70 | 43.31 | 2.35 | 1.69 | 44.41 | 2.25 | 1.72 |
| Olympic Trials participants | 45.99 | 2.18 | 1.69 | 46.28 | 2.14 | 1.65 | 46.30 | 2.10 | 1.63 | 46.94 | 2.07 | 1.69 |

**Men's 1500 freestyle**

| | 400 | | | 800 | | | 1200 | | | 1500 | | |
|---|---|---|---|---|---|---|---|---|---|---|---|---|
| | SR | DPS | Velocity | SR | DPS | Velocity | SR | DPS | Velocity | SR | DPS | Velocity |
| Finalists (1-8) | 41.05 | 2.34 | 1.61 | 41.69 | 2.33 | 1.63 | 41.96 | 2.27 | 1.60 | 42.63 | 2.18 | 1.62 |
| Olympic Trials participants | 42.35 | 2.19 | 1.56 | 42.50 | 2.15 | 1.54 | 42.60 | 2.12 | 1.52 | 44.21 | 2.08 | 1.59 |

**Men's 100 backstroke**

| | 50 | | | 100 | | |
|---|---|---|---|---|---|---|
| | SR | DPS | Velocity | SR | DPS | Velocity |
| Finalists (1-8) | 50.70 | 2.22 | 1.87 | 47.60 | 2.14 | 1.75 |
| Semifinalists (9-16) | 49.39 | 2.23 | 1.84 | 46.40 | 2.11 | 1.71 |
| Olympic Trials participants | 45.78 | 2.35 | 1.79 | 43.33 | 2.22 | 1.68 |

**Men's 200 backstroke**

| | 50 | | | 100 | | | 150 | | | 200 | | |
|---|---|---|---|---|---|---|---|---|---|---|---|---|
| | SR | DPS | Velocity | SR | DPS | Velocity | SR | DPS | Velocity | SR | DPS | Velocity |
| Finalists (1-8) | 44.76 | 2.41 | 1.78 | 41.78 | 2.44 | 1.67 | 42.16 | 2.35 | 1.62 | 42.14 | 2.20 | 1.59 |

| | 50 | | | 100 | | | 150 | | | 200 | | |
|---|---|---|---|---|---|---|---|---|---|---|---|---|
| | SR | DPS | Velocity | SR | DPS | Velocity | SR | DPS | Velocity | SR | DPS | Velocity |
| Semifinalists (9-16) | 42.70 | 2.42 | 1.73 | 39.88 | 2.45 | 1.62 | 40.43 | 2.36 | 1.58 | 40.76 | 2.23 | 1.57 |
| Olympic Trials participants | 41.87 | 2.40 | 1.69 | 39.46 | 2.41 | 1.56 | 39.40 | 2.34 | 1.52 | 39.40 | 2.20 | 1.51 |

**Men's 100 breaststroke**

| | 50 | | | 100 | | |
|---|---|---|---|---|---|---|
| | SR | DPS | Velocity | SR | DPS | Velocity |
| Finalists (1-8) | 53.04 | 1.85 | 1.74 | 53.15 | 1.69 | 1.50 |
| Semifinalists (9-16) | 50.76 | 1.84 | 1.69 | 51.98 | 1.68 | 1.48 |
| Olympic Trials participants | 50.41 | 1.80 | 1.66 | 51.29 | 1.67 | 1.45 |

**Men's 200 breaststroke**

| | 50 | | | 100 | | | 150 | | | 200 | | |
|---|---|---|---|---|---|---|---|---|---|---|---|---|
| | SR | DPS | Velocity | SR | DPS | Velocity | SR | DPS | Velocity | SR | DPS | Velocity |
| Finalists (1-8) | 39.90 | 2.27 | 1.64 | 38.19 | 2.28 | 1.46 | 40.84 | 2.11 | 1.44 | 46.03 | 1.81 | 1.39 |
| Semifinalists (9-16) | 40.75 | 2.19 | 1.61 | 38.31 | 2.23 | 1.43 | 40.66 | 2.05 | 1.40 | 43.53 | 1.84 | 1.36 |
| Olympic Trials participants | 39.82 | 2.11 | 1.56 | 38.34 | 2.17 | 1.39 | 39.29 | 2.02 | 1.35 | 42.96 | 1.82 | 1.33 |

**Men's 100 butterfly**

| | 50 | | | 100 | | |
|---|---|---|---|---|---|---|
| | SR | DPS | Velocity | SR | DPS | Velocity |
| Finalists (1-8) | 57.64 | 1.98 | 2.01 | 56.58 | 1.81 | 1.74 |
| Semifinalists (9-16) | 55.51 | 1.99 | 1.97 | 54.68 | 1.82 | 1.71 |
| Olympic Trials participants | 52.94 | 2.02 | 1.94 | 51.99 | 1.86 | 1.66 |

**Men's 200 butterfly**

| | 50 | | | 100 | | | 150 | | | 200 | | |
|---|---|---|---|---|---|---|---|---|---|---|---|---|
| | SR | DPS | Velocity | SR | DPS | Velocity | SR | DPS | Velocity | SR | DPS | Velocity |
| Finalists (1-8) | 52.05 | 2.07 | 1.87 | 49.58 | 2.03 | 1.67 | 50.00 | 1.96 | 1.62 | 50.90 | 1.89 | 1.58 |
| Semifinalists (9-16) | 50.49 | 2.09 | 1.86 | 48.91 | 2.02 | 1.63 | 49.11 | 1.97 | 1.59 | 49.74 | 1.88 | 1.55 |
| Olympic Trials participants | 50.22 | 2.03 | 1.84 | 48.87 | 1.98 | 1.62 | 48.82 | 1.91 | 1.56 | 48.53 | 1.82 | 1.49 |

**Men's 200 IM**

| | 50 | | | 100 | | | 150 | | | 200 | | |
|---|---|---|---|---|---|---|---|---|---|---|---|---|
| | SR | DPS | Velocity | SR | DPS | Velocity | SR | DPS | Velocity | SR | DPS | Velocity |
| Finalists (1-8) | 53.38 | 1.99 | 1.89 | 42.45 | 2.26 | 1.60 | 44.60 | 1.85 | 1.40 | 48.59 | 2.05 | 1.67 |
| Semifinalists (9-16) | 54.41 | 1.87 | 1.84 | 40.88 | 2.28 | 1.55 | 41.09 | 1.90 | 1.34 | 47.48 | 2.11 | 1.67 |
| Olympic Trials participants | 53.37 | 1.91 | 1.83 | 39.52 | 2.23 | 1.50 | 42.48 | 1.84 | 1.35 | 45.07 | 2.15 | 1.63 |

**Men's 400 IM**

| | 100 | | | 200 | | | 300 | | | 400 | | |
|---|---|---|---|---|---|---|---|---|---|---|---|---|
| | SR | DPS | Velocity | SR | DPS | Velocity | SR | DPS | Velocity | SR | DPS | Velocity |
| Finalists (1-8) | 48.65 | 1.97 | 1.60 | 39.13 | 2.27 | 1.54 | 41.16 | 1.88 | 1.32 | 44.81 | 2.17 | 1.67 |
| Olympic Trials participants | 50.72 | 1.85 | 1.55 | 36.08 | 2.33 | 1.45 | 41.57 | 1.75 | 1.24 | 43.90 | 2.12 | 1.61 |

Reprinted from S. Tuffey, G. Sokolovas, and S. Riewald, 2001, "Sport Science Olympic Trials Project: Characterizing our most successful swimmers," *Coaches Quarterly* 7(2): 1-9. Courtesy of USA Swimming.

# Table 2 Women's Race Analysis Data From the 2000 U.S. Olympic Trials

### Women's 50 freestyle

| | 50 | | |
| | SR (cycl/min) | DPS (m/cycl) | Velocity (m/sec) |
|---|---|---|---|
| Finalists (1-8) | 60.50 | 1.87 | 1.96 |
| Semifinalists (9-16) | 60.59 | 1.83 | 1.93 |
| Olympic Trials participants | 58.58 | 1.81 | 1.86 |

### Women's 100 freestyle

| | 50 | | | 100 | | |
| | SR | DPS | Velocity | SR | DPS | Velocity |
|---|---|---|---|---|---|---|
| Finalists (1-8) | 52.19 | 2.15 | 1.89 | 49.79 | 2.01 | 1.72 |
| Semifinalists (9-16) | 53.60 | 2.04 | 1.86 | 50.96 | 1.94 | 1.70 |
| Olympic Trials participants | 51.58 | 2.03 | 1.81 | 49.65 | 1.93 | 1.67 |

### Women's 200 freestyle

| | 50 | | | 100 | | | 150 | | | 200 | | |
| | SR | DPS | Velocity | SR | DPS | Velocity | SR | DPS | Velocity | SR | DPS | Velocity |
|---|---|---|---|---|---|---|---|---|---|---|---|---|
| Finalists (1-8) | 49.48 | 2.16 | 1.78 | 46.10 | 2.14 | 1.65 | 45.40 | 2.11 | 1.60 | 45.70 | 2.00 | 1.58 |
| Semifinalists (9-16) | 48.63 | 2.13 | 1.73 | 47.70 | 2.09 | 1.63 | 47.85 | 1.99 | 1.59 | 48.36 | 1.89 | 1.57 |
| Olympic Trials participants | 47.26 | 2.16 | 1.72 | 45.76 | 2.10 | 1.60 | 44.98 | 2.05 | 1.54 | 44.42 | 2.00 | 1.53 |

### Women's 400 freestyle

| | 100 | | | 200 | | | 300 | | | 400 | | |
| | SR | DPS | Velocity | SR | DPS | Velocity | SR | DPS | Velocity | SR | DPS | Velocity |
|---|---|---|---|---|---|---|---|---|---|---|---|---|
| Finalists (1-8) | 48.39 | 1.95 | 1.59 | 48.15 | 1.92 | 1.55 | 47.63 | 1.94 | 1.55 | 47.68 | 1.95 | 1.60 |
| Olympic Trials participants | 45.43 | 2.03 | 1.55 | 44.63 | 2.01 | 1.50 | 44.37 | 1.99 | 1.48 | 44.95 | 1.97 | 1.52 |

### Women's 800 freestyle

| | 200 | | | 400 | | | 600 | | | 800 | | |
| | SR | DPS | Velocity | SR | DPS | Velocity | SR | DPS | Velocity | SR | DPS | Velocity |
|---|---|---|---|---|---|---|---|---|---|---|---|---|
| Finalists (1-8) | 47.71 | 1.92 | 1.55 | 48.11 | 1.90 | 1.54 | 48.66 | 1.87 | 1.53 | 48.59 | 1.90 | 1.57 |
| Olympic Trials participants | 43.91 | 2.01 | 1.49 | 43.86 | 2.00 | 1.47 | 43.70 | 2.00 | 1.46 | 44.21 | 1.98 | 1.49 |

### Women's 100 backstroke

| | 50 | | | 100 | | |
| | SR | DPS | Velocity | SR | DPS | Velocity |
|---|---|---|---|---|---|---|
| Finalists (1-8) | 49.19 | 2.06 | 1.66 | 46.44 | 1.90 | 1.55 |
| Semifinalists (9-16) | 48.24 | 2.01 | 1.61 | 45.91 | 1.91 | 1.52 |
| Olympic Trials participants | 46.94 | 2.01 | 1.57 | 44.29 | 1.91 | 1.48 |

### Women's 200 backstroke

| | 50 | | | 100 | | | 150 | | | 200 | | |
| | SR | DPS | Velocity | SR | DPS | Velocity | SR | DPS | Velocity | SR | DPS | Velocity |
|---|---|---|---|---|---|---|---|---|---|---|---|---|
| Finalists (1-8) | 44.64 | 2.17 | 1.57 | 41.61 | 2.11 | 1.48 | 41.49 | 2.07 | 1.45 | 42.30 | 1.94 | 1.43 |
| Semifinalists (9-16) | 42.89 | 2.17 | 1.53 | 39.41 | 2.18 | 1.44 | 39.70 | 2.13 | 1.42 | 40.58 | 2.02 | 1.42 |
| Olympic Trials participants | 40.75 | 2.24 | 1.51 | 36.90 | 2.20 | 1.41 | 37.26 | 2.18 | 1.36 | 37.43 | 2.09 | 1.35 |

**Women's 100 breaststroke**

| | 50 | | | 100 | | |
|---|---|---|---|---|---|---|
| | SR | DPS | Velocity | SR | DPS | Velocity |
| Finalists (1-8) | 50.54 | 1.76 | 1.55 | 51.44 | 1.58 | 1.36 |
| Semifinalists (9-16) | 49.63 | 1.71 | 1.50 | 50.86 | 1.58 | 1.32 |
| Olympic Trials participants | 49.98 | 1.63 | 1.46 | 47.65 | 1.57 | 1.27 |

**Women's 200 breaststroke**

| | 50 | | | 100 | | | 150 | | | 200 | | |
|---|---|---|---|---|---|---|---|---|---|---|---|---|
| | SR | DPS | Velocity | SR | DPS | Velocity | SR | DPS | Velocity | SR | DPS | Velocity |
| Finalists (1-8) | 39.38 | 2.11 | 1.47 | 38.28 | 2.09 | 1.34 | 39.39 | 1.97 | 1.30 | 43.21 | 1.76 | 1.28 |
| Semifinalists (9-16) | 42.80 | 1.95 | 1.44 | 40.56 | 1.95 | 1.29 | 40.68 | 1.89 | 1.26 | 42.01 | 1.77 | 1.23 |
| Olympic Trials participants | 41.57 | 1.92 | 1.40 | 39.50 | 1.91 | 1.25 | 40.45 | 1.82 | 1.22 | 42.19 | 1.68 | 1.19 |

**Women's 100 butterfly**

| | 50 | | | 100 | | |
|---|---|---|---|---|---|---|
| | SR | DPS | Velocity | SR | DPS | Velocity |
| Finalists (1-8) | 58.93 | 1.75 | 1.82 | 56.18 | 1.64 | 1.56 |
| Semifinalists (9-16) | 56.63 | 1.76 | 1.75 | 55.10 | 1.68 | 1.54 |
| Olympic Trials participants | 56.75 | 1.74 | 1.74 | 54.52 | 1.65 | 1.52 |

**Women's 200 butterfly**

| | 50 | | | 100 | | | 150 | | | 200 | | |
|---|---|---|---|---|---|---|---|---|---|---|---|---|
| | SR | DPS | Velocity | SR | DPS | Velocity | SR | DPS | Velocity | SR | DPS | Velocity |
| Finalists (1-8) | 54.20 | 1.78 | 1.69 | 51.74 | 1.75 | 1.51 | 51.46 | 1.69 | 1.45 | 50.89 | 1.64 | 1.40 |
| Semifinalists (9-16) | 51.08 | 1.82 | 1.65 | 49.08 | 1.81 | 1.47 | 48.25 | 1.76 | 1.42 | 48.91 | 1.69 | 1.39 |
| Olympic Trials participants | 52.96 | 1.75 | 1.62 | 50.60 | 1.68 | 1.44 | 51.01 | 1.61 | 1.39 | 50.52 | 1.59 | 1.36 |

**Women's 200 IM**

| | 50 | | | 100 | | | 150 | | | 200 | | |
|---|---|---|---|---|---|---|---|---|---|---|---|---|
| | SR | DPS | Velocity | SR | DPS | Velocity | SR | DPS | Velocity | SR | DPS | Velocity |
| Finalists (1-8) | 55.90 | 1.73 | 1.70 | 40.41 | 2.10 | 1.42 | 44.41 | 1.70 | 1.27 | 47.81 | 1.94 | 1.55 |
| Semifinalists (9-16) | 54.39 | 1.76 | 1.68 | 39.52 | 2.09 | 1.40 | 39.41 | 1.86 | 1.24 | 45.24 | 2.02 | 1.53 |
| Olympic Trials participants | 55.27 | 1.68 | 1.65 | 41.09 | 1.99 | 1.38 | 42.09 | 1.67 | 1.20 | 46.73 | 1.93 | 1.50 |

**Women's 400 IM**

| | 100 | | | 200 | | | 300 | | | 400 | | |
|---|---|---|---|---|---|---|---|---|---|---|---|---|
| | SR | DPS | Velocity | SR | DPS | Velocity | SR | DPS | Velocity | SR | DPS | Velocity |
| Finalists (1-8) | 53.20 | 1.64 | 1.46 | 38.54 | 2.05 | 1.37 | 42.19 | 1.73 | 1.20 | 46.10 | 1.92 | 1.52 |
| Olympic Trials participants | 50.52 | 1.67 | 1.41 | 35.79 | 2.10 | 1.31 | 39.16 | 1.73 | 1.13 | 43.55 | 1.98 | 1.49 |

Reprinted from S. Tuffey, G. Sokolovas, and S. Riewald, 2001, "Sport Science Olympic Trials Project: Characterizing our most successful swimmers," *Coaches Quarterly* 7(2): 1-9. Courtesy of USA Swimming.

# Index

*Note:* The italicized *f* and *t* following page numbers refer to figures and tables, respectively.

# About the Authors

**Dave Salo** has been one of the nation's top swimming coaches for more than 15 years and currently is the head coach of the USC men's and women's swimming teams. Before joining the Trojan swim program, Salo served as head coach of Irvine Novaquatics, where he trained Olympic medalists Lenny Krayzelburg, Aaron Peirsol, Amanda Beard, and Jason Lezak. Over his career, he has continued to serve at the national level, accepting coaching assignments for the United States at the 2005 World Championships and the 2001 Goodwill Games. Salo earned his MS and PhD in exercise physiology from USC and currently resides in Los Angeles.

**Scott Riewald** is a performance technologist for the U.S. Olympic Committee, where he focuses on biomechanics and technology for endurance sports. Previously, he was USA Swimming's biomechanics director at the U.S. Olympic Training Center in Colorado Springs, where he worked with many of the nation's top swimmers. During his tenure, he lectured throughout the United Sates on the use of science to improve performance of individual swimmers and entire teams. He also worked as the biomechanics director for the United States Tennis Association in Key Biscayne, Florida.

Riewald is a certified strength and conditioning specialist (CSCS) and a certified personal trainer, and he earned his MS and PhD in biomedical engineering at Northwestern University. As an undergraduate, he was a competitive swimmer at Boston University, where he still holds several school and conference records. In his spare time, he enjoys mountain biking, photography, and spending time with his family.